THE UNBUILT BENCH

THE UNBUILT BENCH

EXPERIMENTAL PSYCHOLOGY ON THE VERGE OF SCIENCE

DAVID PETERSON

Columbia University Press   *New York*

Columbia University Press
Publishers Since 1893
New York   Chichester, West Sussex

Library of Congress Cataloging-in-Publication Data
Names: Peterson, David (Professor of sociology), author.
Title: The unbuilt bench : experimental psychology on the
verge of science / David Peterson.
Description: New York : Columbia University Press, [2025] |
Includes bibliographical references and index.
Identifiers: LCCN 2024032490 | ISBN 9780231217316 (hardback) |
ISBN 9780231217323 (trade paperback) | ISBN 9780231561679 (ebook)
Subjects: LCSH: Psychology—Research. | Psychology, Experimental.
Classification: LCC BF76.5 .P38 2025 | DDC 150.72/4—dc23/eng/20241125

Cover design: Julia Kushnirsky
Cover image: iStock

GPSR Authorized Representative: Easy Access System Europe,
Mustamäe tee 50, 10621 Tallinn, Estonia, gpsr.requests@easproject.com

CONTENTS

FOREWORD

Psychological expertise is ubiquitous in Western societies. From schools to prisons, hospitals to city halls, psychologists categorize, enumerate, diagnose, and plan. They are perhaps *the* professional group most associated with the practices that Foucault called "technologies of the self." These are the domains of expertise that emerge between subjectivity and liberal governance, encouraging or coercing self-regulation. Under the psychologist's gaze, behavior, thought, and emotion become scientific topics which are objectified and returned to individuals as scientific facts meant to explain their experience and provide expectations to be met.[1]

Nikolas Rose has described the seeming omnipresence of psychological expertise in both public and private spheres:

> Psychological experts, psychological vocabularies, psychological evaluations, and psychological techniques have made themselves indispensable in the workplace and the marketplace, in the electoral process and the business of politics, in family life and sexuality, in pedagogy and child rearing, in the apparatus of law and punishment and in the medico-welfare complex. Further, it is increasingly to psychologists that the citizens of such societies look when they seek to comprehend and surmount the problems that beset the human condition—despair, loss, tragedy, conflict—living their lives according to a psychological ethic.[2]

Psychological expertise is one of the great and powerful arms of liberal governance because of its ability to bridge the emotional and spiritual needs of the individual with the designs of institutions, thus hastening the dissolution of that boundary. It is the technique by which the depths of human subjectivity are made visible and tractable to meet the operational necessities of increasingly large and interconnected organizations and systems.

Yet despite its integration into all aspects of modern life, psychology has always been dogged by status anxiety. Although psychological experts inhabit many domains, they are the uncontested authority in few. And, unlike many scientific fields, psychological research has yielded relatively few technologies that are considered unambiguous successes. There are no accomplishments in the field of psychological science that one could compare to rocketry or the polio vaccine.

Rather than a history of technological success, the field has thrived on the basis of its promise. The promise of experimental psychology is not a concrete technology, method, or theory. It is not a scientific product. It is, instead, an idea which recurs in different guises throughout the landscape of modern life—the idea that human thought and behavior can and, thus, should be studied using the same experimental methods that have brought technological progress to the natural sciences. The promise of experimental psychology is fueled by the dream that human thought and behavior can be predicted and controlled to the degree they can yield behavioral technologies. After all, the production of technology is one of the central reasons modern science holds a high status. Like other forms of technoscience, however, the development of behavioral technology rests on the premise that causal relationships discovered or created in artificial laboratory environments can eventually be exported into tother contexts. Thus, the promise of experimental psychology ultimately rests on the premise of successful lab science.

Yet the staggering variety of psychological theories, tools, and methods invites another interpretation—a promise unfulfilled. Ironically, the feature of psychological science that commentators sometimes cite as its greatest strength—its diversity—has just as often been treated as evidence of its backwardness and lack of discipline. Anxiety over fragmentation has persisted throughout the history of psychology. How can psychology, as Rose argues, effectively "tie together diverse sites, problems, and concerns" when it seems unable to hold itself together?[3]

Rather than a powerful arm of modern social control, critics ridicule psychology as a weak and rambling discipline, unable to cohere around a set of theories or methods because none offer a foundation solid enough to unite a fractious field. Famously, physicist Richard Feynman dismissed psychology as a "cargo cult."[4] During World War II, the Allies used islands in the Pacific as staging bases. Islanders witnessed the ongoing arrival of goods via the air strips. After the soldiers left, they built their own air strips, believing these bamboo recreations would attract planes. To Feynman, psychologists were engaged in the same futile mimicry. Psychologists run labs, conduct experiments, and write scientific articles but are missing something essential.

Although Feynman's critique remains one of the more pointed attacks on the scientific status of psychology, it gives voice to a skepticism which psychology has never been able to fully shake. Recent discussions about a "replication crisis" in the field have resulted in a barrage of negative stories in the press and have motivated a series of mass replication efforts to evaluate the trustworthiness of the published literature. This is not the behavior of a field confident in its authority.

Yet critics of psychological science often stop short of saying what a successful psychology would look like. Comparisons to physics are unlikely to be flattering for any field, and if empirical studies of scientific cultures have shown us anything, it is that there is no univocal model of scientific practice. What if progress in psychology simply looks different?

Such a conclusion would be harmonious with the last four decades of research in the social studies of science which has repeatedly demonstrated how experimental communities "curl up upon themselves" to create their own cultures of practice and evaluation.[5] This tradition provides a needed antidote to blithe arguments about the "unity of science."[6] Yet they render the question about progress in psychology unanswerable. If there are no universal features of science, then each field can only be judged by its own internal standards.

However, judgments about the relative merits of different scientific fields are unavoidable. Policymakers must decide from which experts they will solicit advice. Funding agencies must decide where to invest research dollars. Students must decide which field to enter. Seemingly endless criticisms of psychology in the popular media are based, implicitly or not, on the idea that it is somehow failing to do what other experimental sciences have achieved.

Rather than drive straight at unwieldy questions about psychology's cultural role or its status as a science, in this book I address the more tangible question of whether psychology is engaged in a different sort of epistemic activity than other experimental sciences.

In the following chapters, I focus on the material evolutions in research practice and technology at the site of data collection, an ongoing process that I call "bench-building." Rather than contributing facts or extending existing theory, bench-building provides new experimental possibilities by either gaining greater control over an experimental object or refining perception of it in a way that makes the object more visible for categorization and measurement. Technological advancements generate excitement because they stimulate and give shape to questions. They extend the horizon of what can be achieved and, thus, remake the cutting edge of the field.

The central theoretical argument of this book is that all great technoscience innovations are concatenations of these small feats of bench-building whereby researchers are able to sharpen their perception or improve their ability to intervene in systems. Like the historical trajectory that can be traced from the discovery of fire to smelting to steel to rocketry, every technological innovation can be decomposed into more modest innovations in technique or technology that provided the basis for future advances. Much of laboratory life is dedicated to these seemingly mundane acts of bench-building that extend a researcher's power.

The central empirical argument in book is that while bench-building is the central activity in many scientific laboratories, it plays a diminished role in psychology labs. Using molecular biology as a contrast case, I show that biologists are overwhelmingly concerned with buying or building new technologies and developing new techniques. This was a minor concern for psychologists who had limited ability to refine their research practices. Psychological fields are rarely organized around the evolution of technologically dynamic "experimental systems."[7] Paradoxically, the dynamism which continually transforms their field plays a key role in integrating and fostering consensus in molecular biology. The struggle to maintain their positions at the frontier of possibility plays a significant role disciplining biology. Lacking this, psychologists develop alternative systems for the integration of their fields and the evaluation of progress.

Bench-building is just one dimension of scientific progress, yet attending to bench-building raises profound ethical, moral, and political questions. Despite all the handwringing about psychology's legitimacy, few have actually answered a basic question: What would a successful experimental psychology look like? That is, what would it look like if experimental psychology were able to continually develop evermore powerful, exacting, and diverse forms of manipulation and prediction?

Technoscience is power. Although all scientific invention has social ramifications, nothing could transform social life more profoundly and directly than a technologically advanced psychological science. Such an outcome is both the dream of utopian social engineers and the nightmare of dystopian novels. Would it be compatible with democracy as we know it? What would be the necessary societal conditions for such a science? These are big questions of progress, technology, authority, and legitimacy. Yet to begin addressing any of these areas, we must begin by better understanding what psychologists are actually doing when they engage in experimental science.

THE UNBUILT BENCH

1

THE PROMISE OF
EXPERIMENTAL PSYCHOLOGY

This is no science, it is only the hope of a science.

William James, *Psychology: Briefer Course*

n the aftermath of the 9/11 terrorist attacks, the U.S. government began a complete overhaul of the security infrastructure in airports. Among the programs developed was a training regimen for select members of the Transportation Security Administration (TSA) which was designed to use insights from psychology to better detect terrorists before they had a chance to board airplanes. The "Screening Passengers by Observational Techniques" (SPOT) program was designed to provide another line of defense in the war on terror. Using research on facial expressions, emotions, and nonverbal behavior, the SPOT program trained agents to assign points to a variety of potentially suspicious behaviors including "excessive throat clearing," "gazing down," and "exaggerated yawning." Additional points could be accumulated during a more involved screening if they were carrying "unusual items" like almanacs. Conversely, points could be deducted for facts about the passenger that made him or her seem less likely to be a terrorist, including age. Women received a one-point deduction after the age of fifty-five, men after the age of sixty-five.[1]

However, when the program came to light publicly, it quickly became the target of intense criticism focusing on the legitimacy of the research informing it and its nearly $1 billion price tag. When the Government Accountability Office investigated, they could not find a single case where SPOT resulted in the arrest of someone planning terrorist activity and suggested Congress redirect funding to more scientifically grounded methods.[2] One of the main problems was that researchers could not even agree on what a controlled test of the program would look like. Typically, testers would have confederates posing as terrorists attempt to pass through screening undetected, a method one psychologist who helped develop the program called "totally bogus" since the actors were unlikely to be able to emulate the extreme emotions would-be terrorists would likely be feeling.[3]

In addition to controversy regarding its scientific credibility, critics have argued that the SPOT program provided a quasi-scientific rationale for the abuse of civil liberties. In one interview, a former TSA agent who received the behavioral detection training noted that the SPOT techniques provided legal cover to law enforcement rather than a useful checklist.[4] In response, the American Civil Liberty Union (ACLU) filed a complaint alleging that the SPOT program resulted in racial profiling.[5] In light of the controversy, the TSA has redirected $20 million into research on an automated system of behavioral detection designed by another pair of psychologists.[6] Rather than rely on human judgment, these researchers have been working on technology designed to test psychophysiological reactions thought to be associated with deception including changes in cardiac rate and skin conductance.[7] However, critics have pointed out that any technology designed to unmask terrorists using stress-detection is going to face unavoidable and, possibly, insurmountable challenges in an environment that is as inherently stressful as modern air travel.[8]

The saga surrounding the TSA's behavioral detection program is indicative of the complex status of psychological science in modern life. There is clearly a desire for psychological expertise. When nineteen men, armed with weapons available at any hardware store, can murder thousands and ground to a halt nearly all activity in the largest economy on Earth, there is strong motivation to create systems that can detect and prevent such attacks. Psychologists—a community of experts tasked with understanding, predicting, and controlling human behavior—were recruited to help shape the response. However, the outcome of this program was, at best, ambiguous. At worst, psychology was accused of providing a scientific imprimatur to agencies engaging in racial profiling.[9]

Again and again, psychology has found itself in an uncomfortable position. Its expertise is desperately wanted, yet it is often unable to provide the types of technological solutions that other sciences have produced. Meanwhile the technologies it has produced—things like intelligence tests and personality classifications—remain persistent objects of debate.[10]

This book is about psychological science, or, rather, the perpetual hope for a psychological science, the perpetual hope that psychologists can answer age-old questions about human nature, provide succor for existential angst, and produce tools to create a better world through human engineering. If physicists can trace the origins of the universe back to a single point, surely psychologists can find the roots of cognition. If biologists can discover the blueprints of life, surely psychologists can find the fundamental elements of personality.

Yet major scientific discoveries begin as mundane technical victories in laboratories. So, psychology's struggle to fulfill these hopes begins and ends in the psychology laboratory. Thus, this is a book about the genesis of psychology's scientific credibility—its ability to produce robust findings that can eventually be exported as pieces of technology. Most ambitiously, this book is about the nature of scientific progress when the research object is as protean as the human mind and the discipline is as unruly as modern experimental psychology.

THE UNENDING "CRISIS IN PSYCHOLOGY"

The social sciences surfaced in modernity's turbulent wake. Although not as well-researched as the growth of democratic nation-states or the emergence of global capitalism, neither can be understood without social science. The growth of democracy was simultaneously the birth of mass society, a powerful but fickle social aggregate which presented new challenges to the stability and integration of society. Societies that were previously arranged on traditional, feudal, or racial lines increasingly looked for rational ways to organize their schools, businesses, governments, and militaries. At the same time, the existential vacuum that resulted from the weakening of traditional systems of meaning opened a space for a new class of experts to help provide "objective" answers to the problems of modern life. Attempts to control, organize, aid, mollify, and understand the masses led directly to the birth of the social sciences.

However, while social scientific fields like anthropology and sociology maintained a level of epistemic diversity that left them in the intellectually rambunctious hinterland between the humanities and natural sciences, the field of psychology marginalized its critical voices and focused instead on the practical work of creating an experimental science of human behavior, thought, and emotion. As a result of this approach—alternatively positivist and pragmatic—psychological experts are now ubiquitous.

The American Psychological Association has come to define its domain in the broadest possible terms:

> Psychology is the study of mind and behavior. The discipline embraces all aspects of the human experience—from the functions of the brain to the actions of nations, from child development to care for the aged. In every conceivable setting from scientific research centers to mental healthcare services, "the understanding of behavior" is the enterprise of psychologists.[11]

The very diversity of its influence creates an analytic problem. One of the challenges in studying psychology is that it has achieved a paradoxical level of success. On one hand, psychologists are pervasive. They advertise to us, conduct our performance reviews, help design our cities and stores, write our children's standardized tests, and advise us on our marriages. They are every place where those in positions of authority over other people wish to make their decisions "evidence based." As such, the promise of experimental psychology represents one outcome of the West's almost religious belief in the unerring progress of the sciences, a faith one commentator has dubbed "the high modernist ideology."[12]

Claiming dominion over everything from "the functions of the brain to the actions of nation states" seems like an incredible act of intellectual hubris. The proliferation of theories makes the psy-disciplines amenable to a dizzying variety of uses. As Nikolas Rose explains, "psychologization does not imply that a single model of the person was imposed or adopted in a totalitarian manner, indeed psychology's celebrated 'nonparadigmatic' character ensures a kind of perpetual contestation over the characteristics of personhood." Rather than a limitation, the diversity of theories and methods "is a key to the wide-ranging power of psychology, for it enables the discipline to tie together diverse sites, problems, and concerns."[13] Instead of a symbol of failure, the lack of a stable core is the source of psychology's growth.

Yet, contrary to Rose's assertion, psychology's nonparadigmatic character is disparaged more than its celebrated. From the earliest days of psychology, this lack of a coherent core has been viewed as an embarrassment.[14] For instance, H. L Mencken used a 1927 review of a new introduction to psychology to express his frustration with the (then) current status of the field: "The so-called science of psychology is now in chaos, with no sign that order is soon to be restored. It is hard to find two of its professors who agree [. . .] It's hard for the layman to keep his head in this whirl. Not even anthropology offers a larger assortment of conflicting theories . . ."[15] This skepticism was

hardly unique. Just three years prior, the humorist Stephen Leacock diagnosed the United States with an "outbreak of psychology,"
complaining that "there is not only a psychology in the academic
or college sense, but also a Psychology of Business, a Psychology of
Education, a Psychology of Salesmanship, a Psychology of Religion, a
Psychology of Boxing, a Psychology of Investment, and a Psychology
of Playing the Banjo."[16]

Ongoing anxieties—given voice by Mencken, Leacock, and hun-
dreds of other reviews, critiques, and commentaries throughout the
last century—suggest the field is composed of little more than a mot-
ley bricolage of concepts, theories, and approaches with no connect-
ing thread. Although these anxieties have taken different forms, they
are united by the fear that psychology trails behind other sciences.

It is unsurprising, then, that the history of psychology is a history of explicit and self-conscious attempts to unify around whatever
that generation conceived of as ideal scientific practice. The rise and
influence of behaviorism on American psychology in the middle of
last century was largely due to its promise to eliminate all "mental-
istic" and "introspectionist" concepts. In the place of such subjective
constructs, behaviorists offered a science based on purely "objective"
phenomena. This is explained succinctly in John B. Watson's early
behaviorist manifesto: "Psychology as the behaviorist views it is a
purely objective experimental branch of natural science. Its theoretical goal is the prediction and control of behavior."[17] Through behaviorism, and its consolidation around observable behaviors as its unit
of analysis, psychology seemed to find what the philosopher Charles
Taylor has called "brute data."[18] These are data which are immediately
evident, intersubjectively univocal, and, thus, require no complex process of interpretation: the type of evidence that could be the bedrock
to support a flourishing science.

Behaviorist innovations were significant for a field attempting to
distance itself from its philosophical roots and discipline a fractious
field. White rats provided a simplified model of human behavior,

and mazes provided a standardized task.[19] With this, the slow, sober work of aggregative science could begin in earnest. The basic premise of behaviorist research of the time—that insights gleaned from rat experiments would eventually aggregate and lead to important knowledge about humans—was not accepted by all. Some felt the self-imposed restrictions too constraining and tried to make the rigid stimulus-response "meta-language"[20] more accommodating to the study of complex behavior. For instance, the Columbia psychologist Robert S. Woodsworth introduced a modified S-R (stimulus-response) schema known as the S-O-R formula where the O stood for processes internal to the organism. This freed researchers from having to fully detail the chains of S-R links which were believed to underlie complex behavior and thus allowed psychologists to study behavior in humans without feeling like poor scientists.

These "intervening variables" became increasingly significant in psychology.[21] Gradually, the language of stimulus and response shifted to a more flexible language of independent and dependent "variables." This change was especially embraced by the "softer" areas of psychology like personality and social psychology.

The variable metalanguage provided an "escape from their Tower of Babel"[22] since it resulted in a unity of process that could organize a field that lacked a unity of theory. However, the wholesale adoption of statistical terminology by psychology was, itself, a theory-laden act. Psychological categories, even rather imprecise ones like personality characteristics, came to be viewed as distinct "entities" that represented natural kinds. Thus, the human mind was increasingly conceived of as a complex system of interacting variables which could be manipulated independently. Although the physical existence of these variables could not be confirmed, such questions became irrelevant in a research logic founded on statistical correlation.

Developing a logic of research based upon correlation provided psychology with a flexible way to approach the many diverse questions regarding mind and behavior. Yet it produced another important benefit. Psychology has always faced the problem of demarcating its domain from folk knowledge. After all, the marketplace for theories of human behavior is crowded with sellers. Public intellectuals, religious leaders, self-help gurus, and outright charlatans have always hawked their own theories of human thought, emotion, and behavior. The insecure status of psychology among the sciences motivated the field to more aggressively adopt statistical techniques in an attempt to become more quantitative and, therefore, more scientific.[23] Psychology could claim to be a science because it gathered evidence in laboratories and analyzed it using the unassailable mathematics of statistics.

Thus, lacking the promise of theoretical unity, psychologists came to unify around methodology in a way that is unusual in many sciences. "Methods" play a role in every science. The process by which an assay is analyzed or the way that astronomical observations are recorded may be codified to ensure quality and standardization. "Method*ology*," on the other hand, is concerned with a the more encompassing issue of the general *logic of methods*. What are the activities that are essential to scientific development? For psychologists, the answer was a reconstruction of what was believed to happen in more respected sciences, especially regarding experimentation and quantification. Historians have noted the "zeal for methods" embraced by post-World War II social science, going so far as to label psychology's orientation "methodolotry."[24]

Psychologists have adopted the methods of what they viewed to be more successful sciences. Yet, ironically, the very focus on scientific methodology was entirely alien to those more established fields. For instance, philosopher of science Karl Popper lamented that "students who work in one or another of the social sciences are greatly concerned with problems of method; and much of their discussion of these problems is conducted with an eye upon the methods of the more flourishing sciences, especially physics."[25] Fifty years later, the historian Steven Shapin expressed a nearly identical sentiment, arguing that, although natural scientists rarely take general methodology courses, "many psychologists or sociologists will have experienced almost total immersion in such material—modeled on what is taken to be formal natural scientific method."[26]

The fact that psychology was united around a shared understanding of methodology rather than common theoretical entities or the production of technological goods has hardly unified the field in a meaningful way. Rather, it has resulted in a field wherein a thin patina of agreement glosses over profound disagreements. One commentator has noted that the canonical "histories" of psychology have increasingly become histories of specific theories in areas like perception or cognition: "As such, it calls into question the extent to which the research programs that travel today under the name of psychology are unified by anything more than a common physical object (the individual human) studied in a controlled physical environment (the laboratory)."[27] Similarly, the psychologist Howard Gardner acknowledges that progress has been made along specific trajectories of psychological research but asks, "have these advances added up to a unified discipline whose components interrelate with one another? Are they worth to be called a science in the same sense that biology, chemistry, and physics—or, for that matter, economics or demography— merit that label?"[28] His answer was no.

Psychology's Latest Crisis

Recently, psychology has entered a new period of self-doubt that has spilled across the pages of professional journals, popular news outlets, and social media. These debates were sparked by a series of unrelated events that brought negative attention to the field. These included a series of data-fraud investigations that ensnared well-regarded psychologists at Harvard University, the University of Michigan, the University of Amsterdam, and others. In the most notorious case, the

Dutch psychologist Diederick Stapel was found to have fabricated or manipulated data in at least fifty-five articles. Another significant episode was the publication of "Feeling the Future" in the *Journal of Personality and Social Psychology* by Cornell psychologist Daryl Bem. In the article, Bem, a researcher with many well-regarded contributions to psychological science, presented evidence meant to demonstrate the existence of precognition (the prediction of the future using paranormal means). The fact that an article harkening back to the dark days when psychologists were associated with the study of psychic powers could make it through peer review at the top journal in social psychology struck some psychologists as evidence that the peer review and publication systems were broken.[29]

A group of psychologists who have long promoted greater rigor in the field have used the opportunity brought by these embarrassments to draw attention to what they perceive to be a field pervaded by sloppy methods and low standards, advocating for new regulations meant to improve psychology and prevent the problems presented above.[30] This includes pressuring journals to incentivize transparency and replications over flashy, new findings. One product of this was a large-scale, multinational attempt to replicate one hundred recent psychological studies to gauge the quality of research in the field.[31] Finding a disappointing replication rate, around one third, the team behind the effort concluded that psychology had much room for improvement. This project was hailed by *Science* as one of the top scientific breakthroughs of 2015 and received major media interest.[32]

Although certain aspects of the recent debates are novel developments—e.g., the integration with the emergent Open Science movement and focus on large-scale replication efforts—there are echoes of long familiar criticisms. More importantly, the current debate once again raises the possibility that much of the published literature in psychology might not rise to the level of "real" science. Despite *looking* like science, it may represent little more than, borrowing a metaphor from one of my interviewees, sandcastles that will disappear and be forgotten when the tide rolls in. Paul Meehl, a great methodological gadfly of psychology, argued that many psychological theories "tend neither to be refuted nor corroborated, but instead merely fade away as people lose interest." He lamented one of the theories that was considered foundational during his training "did not get killed or resurrected or transformed or solidified; it just kind of dried up and blew away, and we no longer wanted to talk about it or do experimental research on it."[33] For critics, this type of internal change is more characteristic of shifting fads in fashion than the sure march of science.

Of course, the hopeful reformers of psychology do not paint such a gloomy picture. Although often bitingly critical of current practice, their message is ultimately optimistic. But the brilliant future they project, just the most recent iteration of the evergreen promise of experimental psychology, only finds its hopeful glow in contrast to a grim present. The appeal of their campaign rests on the premise that after more than a century, *they* will be the ones to finally move psychology into the age of scientific maturity.[34]

William Wundt is recognized as establishing the first experimental psychological laboratory in Leipzig in 1879. An early student of Wundt's, James Cattell, advocated for the expansion of the field, noting that, "whenever experiment has been introduced into science, a rapid and almost sudden advance has followed."[35] In the 140 years since the experimental method was introduced to psychology, this has not happened. Psychologists continue to debate the merits of their science and point fingers. Yet despite all the talk about method, there has been a surprising lack of attention given to what psychologists are actually doing—with their bodies, with their machines, with their words—when they experiment.

THE LABORATORY BENCH: AT THE ORIGIN OF SCIENTIFIC AUTHORITY

Modern psychology is a tangle of contradictions. It is ubiquitous but fragmented, enormous but divided against itself. It is simultaneously the hardest of the soft sciences and the softest of the hard sciences. It straddles the fraught borders between mind and brain, individual and collective, thought and action. What unites the field is the sense that the human mind and behavior can best be understood through experimental science. Thus, in order to understand the promise of experimental psychology, we must go to where all experimental sciences find their authority—the laboratory.[36] The laboratory—and, more precisely, the laboratory bench where experiments take place—is said to be key to the epistemic authority of science more broadly. Rather than rely on tradition or sanctified authorities, the laboratory provides a forum in which any person can see and judge the truth for themself.[37]

If this were truly the case, all scientific controversies would be easily resolved. Yet there are many areas in which controversies linger like wounds and require that scientists live in an ongoing state of "suspended certainty," unable to effectively counter critiques.[38] Coining the term "misbehaving science" to describe fields in which "scientific norms and standards are ambiguous, underdeveloped, or inappropriate to the situation," the sociologist Aaron Panofsky shows how the pattern of persistent conflict in the field of behavior genetics has produced a fragmented field with ongoing ambiguity regarding its scientific authority.[39] For him, the cause of misbehaving science in behavior genetics is a result of the field's engagement with political controversies, especially in regard to debates over the relationship between race and IQ. In addition to more narrowly focused technical arguments, behavior genetics is torn by murky philosophical questions about freedom, determinism, and inequality.

Psychology is clearly a misbehaving science. It is a fragmented field with few unambiguously settled controversies and has faced persistent challenges to its authority. Psychologists have not been shy about wading into muddy waters that lead to charges of engaging in ideology rather than "science" (for instance, in justifying torture during interrogations or theorizing the origins of homosexuality[40]), yet questions about the coherence and authority of psychology do not stem from this. The scandals that have motivated the current crisis in psychology do not concern the research of politically explosive topics. Rather, they revolve around the quality of the concepts, the rigor of the methods, and the effectiveness of the field's self-correction mechanisms. These are fundamental questions of scientific practice. As such, they beg the question: are experimental psychologists *doing* something different than their natural science counterparts? Is Feynman's critique that psychologists are self-deludedly pursuing "cargo cult science" fair? Or are they engaging in the same type of rigorous practice but getting different results because of the unavoidably variable nature of their research object or the complexity of the concepts? Without seeing inside the lab walls, we cannot answer this question.

To the detriment of the social studies of science, comparison has been an underutilized tool.[41] This is surprising because a pathbreaking work of comparative laboratory ethnography, Karen Knorr Cetina's *Epistemic Cultures*, found significant differences between the practices of molecular biologists and particle physicists.[42] Whereas molecular biologists were building theory in an open-ended process in which the experimenter's body was tightly coupled with the research objects and technologies, physicists operated in a closed system of highly elaborated, formal theories, and they interacted with their research objects only through the medium of massive technical apparatuses. Despite this compelling study, there has been little attempt to systematically explore differences between epistemic cultures.

In an earlier piece, Knorr Cetina provides one clue as to how to potentially thematize epistemic cultures.[43] In an article summarizing the state of laboratory ethnographies, she describes what make labs unique places. She argues labs are characterized by their ability to overcome the limitations of natural objects in three ways: First, they are not limited to dealing with objects as they appear in nature. Labs change and simplify objects. Second, they are not limited to studying objects where they are in nature. Labs extract objects from their natural settings. Third, they are not limited by when processes naturally occur. Labs start or stop, speed up or slow down, naturally occurring processes.

Thus, if labs are defined by their ability to transform, transplant, and manipulate objects, any systematic differences in these abilities would produce divergent outcomes. Attention to anthropological details is a common feature of the "practice turn" in science and technology studies.[44] However, where previous studies have narrowly circumscribed their objects of study to develop rich accounts, the need to properly conceptualize experimental practice psychology demands a more sweeping strategy. Rather than a single case study, it requires studying multiple sites.

Over a four-year period, I observed ten psychology labs focusing on cognitive neuroscience as well as developmental, social, cognitive, and cultural psychology. In addition, to better understand how the scientific study of humans differs from the scientific study of natural sciences, I spent a year observing one of the more well-studied epistemic communities within the social studies of science—molecular biologists. I also participated in a social psychological journal club for a year and conducted 52 interviews with researchers, post docs, and graduate students.

This sort of large-scale, comparative methodology is unusual in an area of study heavily influenced by anthropological norms of data collection. In most lab ethnographies, the researcher will spend their entire time in a single lab, diving deep into its culture. This book takes a different approach. The focus of this work is comparative. Specifically, I compare data collection and analysis practices across developmental psychology, social psychology, and molecular biology to show that psychologists are doing something different in their routine, day-to-day research tasks than natural scientists. Although they have the same abstract goal to discover and produce robust, repeatable empirical relationships, and although they follow the same abstract process of hypothesis-experimentation-analysis-conclusion, the concrete practices that give life to these abstractions diverge significantly.

Mundane Acts of Scientific Progress

My focus on the "bench" (i.e., the sometimes literal, sometimes meta-phorical site of data production) is meant to highlight one signifi-cant, but undertheorized, aspect of scientific progress—the ongoing process of accumulating commonplace technical accomplishments in order to create the conditions for more robust and significant tech-nological products. I label this practice "bench-building" to draw attention to the fact that much experimental work is concerned with altering the very possibilities of data collection.

In the previous decades, scholars of science have turned their atten-tion to the material ecologies of laboratory work alternatively labeled "instrumentalities," "experimental systems," "instrumentaria," and "ensembles of research technologies."[45] Yet these systems of machines are not merely the medium for laboratory research, "black boxes" that take in nature and spit out data. The material culture—including both research technologies and skilled bodies—is an important object of experimental attention and a source of dynamism and change in most labs.[46]

In line with scholars who argue that experimental science is best understood through its material interventions rather than its facts or theories,[47] my focus in this book is on the manipulative capacities of laboratories. Rather than just intervene on objects of interest, I argue that interventions are often focused on the material cultural of the lab. That is, much of the work that happens *at* the bench is ultimately concerned *with* the bench. Interventions focus not just on "objects" external to the machinery of the laboratory, but also on altering the relationship between the researcher, experimental system, and object. This recursive process produces a cybernetic evolution that alters the possibilities of data collection.

The following chapters illustrate that psychology labs largely lack an emphasis on bench-building. While the elaboration of techniques and the integration of new technologies were the central activities in molecular biology, they were peripheral concerns in psychology. While the most visible aspects of a science are often its facts and theories, it is its technologies and techniques that discipline it, standardize practices, and allow products to leave the lab.[48]

Chapter Two will be devoted to detailing the theoretical features of bench-building. The type of minor, technical developments that characterize bench-building are typically left out of theories of scientific progress. Authors have tended to focus on conceptual advances and transformative theories and technologies: e.g., the theory of relativity, the invention of cellular radio, the theory of natural selection, and the discovery of the double-helix structure of DNA. In the narrative histories of science, the plot points are often stunning developments which redirect the course of human history. Compared to these triumphs, a lab using a new fluorescent dye to successfully identify a subclass of cells hardly seems to rate. Who cares if a researcher is able to accomplish or refine some technical task that is not even enough of an advance on which to base an article? Yet, in the day-to-day life of labs, researchers are consumed by precisely these sorts of minor, technical projects.

Trivial frustrations and low-key victories play a major role in the coming pages. One of my central arguments is that these unsung struggles at the bench play an important role in the production of technoscience. Unscrew any piece of modern technology, decompose any medicine into its elements, unpack the facts that support any significant scientific theory, and you will find dozens of strands of technoscientific development. Follow any thread back to its origins, and you will find an experimenter wrestling with equipment, struggling to improve their technique, and introducing new tools. In other words, you will find bench-building.

Theories of scientific progress are rarely pitched at this scale. Technical frustrations may appear, but as bumps along the road to significant technological or conceptual advances. Yet, whether it leads to pathbreaking science or down a fruitless alley, these commonplace struggles

are significant. They are the method by which experimenters gain purchase on their research objects, either through increasing control over
restive objects or attuning themselves to nature's subtle rhythms.

Of course, nature is indifferent to our plans. It resists or remains
just out of grasp. It speaks in a code too complex for us to perceive.
Paths that once seemed promising are foreclosed. Under these conditions, bench-building sputters and becomes an exercise in futility.
Savvy scientists then divert to activities more profitable than refining
data collection. This, I will argue, is largely what happens with experimental psychology.

Although the topic of this book is technological progress in science, bench-building alone does not capture everything that needs
to be included in a complete account of scientific progress. Scientific
progress occurs along multiple, parallel, and crisscrossing dimensions. In addition to the technical developments of bench-building,
science makes progress through the development and refinement of
theories and the expansion into new markets. In the history of science, it is common to see a herky-jerky movement where a development along one dimension will spur movement in one or both of the
others. An advancement in theory can lead to a new piece of technology which can open new markets. Or a novel piece of technology
can produce previously unattainable data which forms the backbone
of new theories. Increased investment can spur both theoretical and
technological innovation.

Although this book is primarily concerned with experimental
psychology, it cannot address difficulties in technological progress in
that field without confronting the larger question of what constitutes
scientific progress. The growth and diversification of experimental
psychology is evidence that it has had success theory- and market-
building. But the spotty record of technological accomplishment suggests that something is missing. A full theory of scientific progress
is beyond the scope of this book. Yet, like an underdeveloped limb
can tell us something vital about ontogeny, a study of an undeveloped

science can have broader meaning. By focusing on this dimension of scientific practice that is sometimes missing, sometimes just stunted in experimental psychology, it will contribute to broader discussions about what constitutes progress in science. Although the relationship between bench-, theory-, and market-building will be explored briefly in the last chapter, the goal of this book is to draw attention to the importance of bench-building both for accounts of psychology and theories of scientific progress more generally.

OUTLINE OF THE BOOK

The book has two broad arcs. The first includes chapters 2, 3, and 4 and is oriented around the concept of bench-building. Chapter 2, which contains the central theoretical arguments, introduces the idea that bench-building is the process by which researchers extend their perceptive or manipulative capacities through the development of skills or the integration of technologies. Drawing on pragmatist philosophy, I argue that bench-building is merely the controlled extension of normal, everyday problem-solving that offers a way to understand an underappreciated dimension of scientific progress without resorting to the often-criticized idea of scientific method.

Following the theoretical discussion of bench-building, there are two chapters dedicated to detailing what it looks like in practice. The first empirical chapter draws on one of the most heavily studied sites in science and technologies studies—the molecular biology lab. In line with previous studies of molecular biology, the frontier of experimentation I detail is a challenging environment of ambiguous and uncontrollable elements. Molecular biologists engage with the frontier to make it more amenable to observation and control. The process involves trial-and-error probing into biological systems, trying out new techniques and introducing novel technologies in order to draw out its constitutive elements. If the system reveals itself, more precise experiments of greater precision are conducted. The process unfolds as a form of cybernetic evolution in which researchers' perceptive and manipulative capacities are extended through growth of new techniques and the integration of emerging technologies.

After describing what bench-building is and how it operates in molecular biology, I look for evidence of bench-building in psychology labs. Specifically, I show that psychology laboratories are characterized by deficits in the embodied skills and technologies that drive bench-building in other fields. Experimentalists in both developmental and social psychology have few tacit skills, and the labs are characterized by relatively simple technologies. I argue that this is due to both ethical and ontological problems which constrain bench-building in the domain of psychology.

Within the first arc, the central contrast is between molecular biology and experimental psychology. The second half of the book shifts to comparisons between fields in experimental psychology to outline the different cultures psychologists have developed to structure their research and evaluate research considering the constraints on bench-building. Thus, the second half asks the question: How are fields disciplined in the relative absence of bench-building? That is, how is work organized, evaluations made, and progress conceptualized in fields with little technological advancement?

Developmental psychologists face the burden of working with objects that are both difficult to bring into the lab and difficult to work with when they come. Like trying to erect a high-rise on a swamp, it may seem like an impossible feat trying to build a science with such trying material. Yet developmental psychologists have created a thriving science by embracing a rigid theoretical orientation and adopting a permissive attitude toward experimentation and analysis. Thus, even in the face of big practical challenges, the field has crafted something that looks very much like what Kuhn referred to as "normal science."

Social psychologists, in contrast, have embraced a different strategy. If developmental psychologists have built normal science by operating within a theoretical framework, social psychologists operate in something of a perpetual scientific revolution. Rather than limit themselves empirically or theoretically, social psychologists have embraced flexibility as a way to produce research that is interesting. In this environment, which operates as a market of "interesting" ideas, the slow accumulation of facts is viewed with disdain as researchers move from one counterintuitive finding to the next.

In the current debates over replication in psychology, psychologists are increasingly rejecting the types of strategies used by developmentalists and social psychologists. The penultimate chapter details a group of reformers who are attempting to overcome the limitations of bench-building by building a more ascetic scientific culture. Based loosely on Merton's Norms of Science, these researchers are attempting to put psychology on sure footing by focusing on the aspects of the research process that can be controlled. Gaining traction in psychology, reforms meant to increase study sizes, demand open data and methods, and encourage more replications raise significant questions about what rigorous science looks like in conditions where bench-building is severely constrained.

The book concludes by confronting the challenges of progress in experimental psychology and interrogating what a technologically successful psychology would even look like. Although bench-building is a significant and previously-unappreciated aspect of scientific progress, to understand scientific progress in its full complexity, I resituate the development of new technological capacities alongside other dimensions of scientific progress—specifically, theory- and market-building. I both draw on and criticize phenomenological and constructivist accounts of the natural vs. social science distinction and offer a competing schema based upon their relationship to bench-building. "Technologically evolving science" is characterized by its ongoing withdrawal from the world of lay meaning and into an increasingly specialized and technical environment driven by bench-building. "Non-technologically evolving science," on the other hand, is primarily interested in objects of lay meaning and, thus, cannot withdraw and become technical without transforming their object of interest. Despite its struggles with bench-building, non-technologically evolving science remains a significant intellectual project. I finish by addressing the social and political implications of a technological psychology that could accurately predict or control behavior.

2

BENCH-BUILDING AS
THE MEANS AND ENDS OF
TECHNOLOGICAL PROGRESS

Three very different sites—a lab studying cognitive development in infants, a social psychology lab investigating emotions and power, and a molecular cell biology lab specializing in the development of the retina—offer a broad spectrum of laboratory practice. Differences abound. Researchers cannot treat an infant the same way they can a mouse pup. Nor can they rely on the interaction of emotional variables to display the sort of predictable regularity a biologist may come to depend on in the innerworkings of a cell. These differences ramify through the labs and affect nearly every aspect of its practice. Though the rationale for these differences is immediately understandable, they are essential for understanding the types of unique challenges that experimental psychologists face.

At this stage in the history of science and technology studies (STS)—the field dedicated to using empirical methods to study the practices, organizations, and products of science—it is a banal observation to say that scientific fields develop unique cultures. Like all forms of social organization, scientific communities evolve in unique tensions between forces both internal and external to themselves.

At one point, however, this seemed like a radical position. Classical scholars of science sought to discover some underlying theoretical unity at the basis of science, some Scientific Method that animated and legitimized all things scientific and would, thus, serve as a hidden knot tying together diverse fields.[1] A central contribution of STS has been to undermine the claim that there is a unifying Method organized by a set of objective rules that can help sort the wheat from the chaff at the experimental frontier. By attending to practices of producing science rather than the rhetorical presentation of its final products, science studies researchers found no domain of activity where a rational Scientific Method began and the irrational practice of human behavior ended. And, significant for this book, STS scholars have found the ways that fields pose questions, collecte and analyze data, and evaluate research differ across the sciences. Summarizing three decades of work in STS, Shapin states, "science is not one, indivisible, and unified, but that the sciences are many, diverse, and disunified."[2] Scientific Method itself was argued to be little more than a cultural label that scientists fought to keep for themselves and deny others.[3]

The rejection of scientific unity around Method has raised serious problems, however.[4] After all, if science is defined by its diversity, to what degree is a field like STS even a coherent entity? For present purposes, wearing this theoretical straitjacket would make the investigation of psychology labs impossible because, sharing no common essence, the comparison between fields would be meaningless. And although scholars criticize the unity of science thesis, experimentalists from a variety of fields continue to produce research that yields undeniable technological achievements. Thus, even as they are disunified by their cultures and how they produce science, they maintain a unity of ends.

This chapter presents a set of concepts meant to aid the comparison of experimental labs. By focusing on the dynamics of experimental practice, I argue that all experimental science shares a goal—the production of theoretically interesting and replicable phenomena. This is accomplished through a series of analytically distinct steps in which researchers move in between the field, the lab, and the bench. Conceptualizing experimental science as a process unified by analytically distinct phases provides a method for comparing research practices.

Differences in bench practice play an especially central role in the forthcoming account. The bench is the crucible of creation for technoscience. Technological products have their origins in the controlled production of phenomena at the bench. Without the latter, there is no former. In the second half of the chapter, I introduce "bench-building," a concept that structures the rest of the book. Bench-building represents an integration of the pragmatist theory of action with the science studies topics of tacit knowledge and technology. Benchbuilding is an experimental practice that changes the possibilities for data collection through the development of new techniques and the integration of new technologies. Cycles of transformation produce an ongoing evolution which is both destabilizing (as innovations create asymmetries in labs) and unifying (as stabilized innovations become standardized). Skill and technology are both the product and precondition for bench-building and, thus, are windows into how experimental fields confront the frontier of the possible.

FIELDS AND BENCHES

Developmental psychology, social psychology, and molecular cell biology—the three sites observed in this study—share little in the way of methods, research objects, or approaches. In one lab, researchers chase after toddling siblings and reassure embarrassed mothers of crying babies while, in another, they sit at clean steel stables and manipulate tissue smaller than a grain of rice. While one lab debates the meaning of concepts like humility, another frets over the meaning of tiny changes in electrical activity. The developmental psychology lab looks like a daycare: warm and bright. The molecular biology lab is intimidating and cold. Furniture in the former is soft and safe, while everything in the latter is hard and sterile. The social psych lab looks like an unfinished office. It is a row of empty rooms, a space without character. While these researchers are ostensibly in the professional category of "research scientist," their work is separated by gulfs that can seem unbridgeable.

Although the differences between these labs are a major theme in this project, they are not *merely* different. Underneath the surface differences, there is a common goal—the production of theoretically significant and replicable findings. Drawing on Bourdieusian field theory, it is possible to highlight some general features that characterize how all experimental sciences seek this goal.[5] Scientific fields are organized by competition between participants over resources within the context of field-specific logics, the structures of which are, themselves, objects of contention. Thus, scientific fields share similarities with other fields like the arts or sports. Yet they differ in one key respect; the logic of the field is, *at least partially*, defined by nature. This is what distinguishes experimental sciences from other knowledge-producing fields like the humanities. Because of this, as Pierre Bourdieu acknowledged, scientific fields are governed by both social *and* natural forces.[6] In experimental sciences, researchers hypothesize, plan, and carry out experiments, analyze data, and draw conclusions in a circuit that moves back and forth from the field to the bench where data is collected.

The Phases of Laboratory Work

The goal of theoretically interesting and replicable findings is pursued through a recursive movement that engages with open theoretical areas from the field; creates manageable, empirical questions; attempts to produce interesting, replicable phenomena; and then frames a narrative of what was done for the field's consumption. This occurs through a series of analytically distinguishable phases. In what follows, I discuss five: planning, data capture, coding, data cleaning and analysis, and data presentation and narrative creation (Figure 2.1). Although there are clear differences in how these phases manifest

Planning —— Data capture —— Coding —— Data cleaning and analysis —— Data presentation and narrative creation

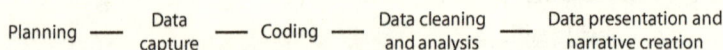

FIGURE 2.1 Phases of Laboratory Research

themselves in developmental psychology, social psychology, and cell biology, the logic is uniform.

1. *Planning.* Planning involves all aspects of experimentation that occur as preparation for data collection. This involves aspects like research design and logistics planning (e.g., gathering materials, securing technology, recruiting subjects, etc.). There is wide variation in how much planning goes into individual studies. One lab I observed spent months designing and preparing a particularly complex experiment. Quite similar to survey research in sociology, the goal was to develop the entire edifice of experimentation—consisting of questionnaires, scales, and tasks—before the main data collection began. Other labs spent far less time planning. The lab that deemphasized planning the most was the molecular neuroscience lab. There was very little discussion about rigorously designing and plotting future experiments. Instead, the lab spent most of their time focused on ongoing experiments. Thus, instead of a neatly separable "planning" phase, planning often occurred throughout the process as course corrections.

2. *Data capture.* Data capture is the phase where the goals of the researcher meet with the resistance of nature. This is decided by the specific methods used which may attempt to measure the research object *au natural* or after a planned manipulation. The capture involves recording some aspect of empirical reality. Videos of human subjects and electrical recordings of neurons represent two types of capture. The capture is essentially what is taken from the research object and determines what will be remembered and what will be

forgotten. Decisions about data capture are an ongoing negotiation between what nature will reveal, what the field expects, and what the laboratory can accomplish given its abilities and limitations.

3. *Coding.* Coding involves the projection of an analytic system onto a data capture. This translates data into a format intelligible for analysis. The importance of coding can become irrelevant when the capture itself is extremely restrictive and is, more or less, already a code. This is the case with forced-choice questions in surveys, for instance. Because the nature of these captures is already in a format beneficial for analysis, there is no need to project a scheme onto them. Coding becomes most important when the original capture is complex and open to multiple interpretations. Thus, videos produced during social psychological experiments are often not immediately meaningful in a scientific sense. There's simply too much going on. To transform the stream of video into sensible data, a scheme must be projected over the video to draw out meaningful units. Similarly, images of cells may be beautiful, but for them to be valuable in advancing an argument, there must be a way to categorize what is being seen.

4. *Data cleaning and analysis.* Data cleaning is a process meant to "improve" the data by removing cases judged to "contaminate" the experiment. This can occur for a wide variety of reasons. Human subjects can be unable or unwilling to cooperate. They might misunderstand the question or task. They might simply be extremely strange and, thus, not a good case to include when looking for "normal" variation. Alternatively, a cell traumatized during dissection might produce unusual readings. Machines might be dirty or may be incorrectly calibrated leading to systematic errors. Data analysis involves the strategies used by scientists to find patterns in their data. This involves choices about which analyses to run and how to graphically represent findings. Data cleaning and analysis are sociologically interesting because, unlike the other steps in this process, data cleaning nearly always happens in isolation and involves a level of subjective judgment that is not found in other phases.[7]

5. *Data presentation and narrative creation.* After data are cleaned and analyzed, they are prepared for presentation. Typically, this is done by condensing complex data into summary statistics and data visualizations and then crafting a narrative that presents the findings as an advance within an existing line of inquiry. Authors seek to make their contribution appear significant and unambiguous while positioning it at the cutting-edge of their field.

From Field to Bench and Back Again

The phases of experimental research should not be thought of as a strictly linear process. It is logically impossible for researchers to go from, say, planning an experiment to data cleaning without actually capturing data. And it can be ethically problematic to move from narrative creation back to coding. However, there is a good deal of back and forth between neighboring steps of the process. For instance, planning may lead to a pilot study which motivates more planning. Or questions that arise during narrative creation may stimulate more data analysis. Despite the stutter steps and reversals that occur empirically, there is a rough linearity to these phases.

Significantly, the phases are not of apiece. Instead, they require the researcher participate in work that occurs in different spheres. Research begins with questions (or, often, a shapeless "curiosity") that originate from a field's literature, moves to an empirical site where those questions can be addressed, and presents those answers in a way to influence the field. Through the medium of the lab, experimentalists move from field to bench, and back to field.

Fields. As Bourdieu has argued, for us to understand what happens in labs, it is important to understand the lab's place within a wider field. Thus, the entire sequence laid out above is only sensible in reference to the mutual antagonism and shared interests that define fields. The production of scientific knowledge is only meaningful in the context of a field in which certain questions are considered worth asking. Both planning and narrative creation are oriented toward the larger scientific field. Individual labs interpret the state of a field to decide how to position themselves, which questions to ask, how to ask them, and what constitutes an acceptable answer.

Labs. The lab mediates the field and the bench. Even when a researcher works alone, there is an idealized "generalized other" that helps shape the work. The lab functions as a lower-stakes, friendlier microcosm of the field at large. It critiques with the voice of the field but is generally more supportive and invested. It also helps researchers make sense of what is happening at the bench.

Benches. What separates lab science from other intellectual endeavors which may involve similar collective problem-solving and field-orientation, however, is the process of data capture which, in theory, constrains the interpretations researchers can make. Data capture is done at the (real or metaphorical) bench. The bench is the chiasm between the goals of the researcher and the world. Using trusted tools, scientists push into uncharted waters. From the known, they enter the unknown and the results are unpredictable. The best laid plans go awry while an accident yields a major finding.

Thus, the phases of scientific research are shaped by the particular characteristics of not only fields but also lab cultures and the contingencies of benchwork (Figure 2.2).

By sketching an outline of the phases of scientific practice above, it is possible to draw out commonalities despite the many practical differences. All experimental sciences attempt to create theoretically significant findings that are replicable. Doing this involves an ongoing exchange between fields, labs, and benches. Ultimately, however, the furnace of creation in experimental science is the bench. What is made at the bench is interpreted in the lab and sold to the field, but without bench-work, there is nothing to interpret and nothing to sell.

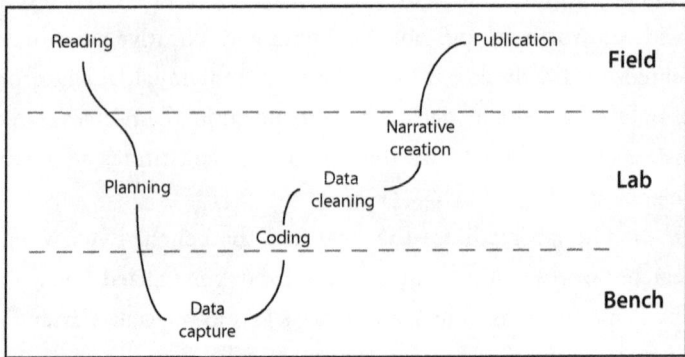

FIGURE 2.2 Field, Lab, and Benchwork

The acute anxiety over replication in psychology suggests that the field's struggles to produce reliable, useful technoscience have their source at the bench. This begs the question: what is happening—or, in the case of psychology, not happening—at the bench? Decades of laboratory ethnographies have sought to answer this question through painstaking, detailed observations. Although I will contribute to this literature through my case studies in later chapters, I begin with a general observation about bench practice. The work of achieving "interactive stabilization" between researcher, experimental technology, and research object that results in robust experimental science is a process of problem-solving.[8] Although experimental science has some unique features which will be discussed later in the chapter, its roots are the same as problem-solving in everyday life.

THE STRUCTURE OF ORDINARY PROBLEM-SOLVING

The basic logic of inquiry which I will be drawing from in the remainder of this chapter was detailed by John Dewey across a series of works designed to draw continuities between ordinary, everyday thought and the development of scientific knowledge. There are several links between Dewey, pragmatism, and more recent research in science studies.[9] I am reaching back to this early work because he grounds his investigation on an exploration of the fundamental characteristics of problem-solving. As I will argue, data capture at the bench is consumed with what appear to be mundane problems. Some achieve definite shape while others remain frustratingly formless; some are eventually overcome while others remain persistent irritants. The very commonality of problem-solving between everyday life and the scientific lab—and, significantly here, between labs—provides a useful comparative tool.

Although he named his concern with problem-solving "logic," it is completely divorced from the abstract rules for symbol manipulation that characterize the study of logic in modern philosophy. Instead, he defined logic as the inquiry *into* inquiry. Inquiry, according to Dewey, is a controlled process by which an indeterminate situation is transformed into a unified whole with discernible elements and dynamics.[10] Conceived this way, his study of "logic" was concerned with the lived experience of investigation.

Importantly, for Dewey, scientific research does not differ in essence from mundane inquiries. A woman learning how to play piano and a biologist getting trained in dissection are engaged in the same practice. A toddler figuring out the purpose of TV remote control and a social psychologist developing a theory of the effects of power on romantic relationships are both seeking to move from the unknown to the known through the medium of inquiry. Rather than be directed by Method toward Truth, inquiry is conducted via unsteady steps, wrong ideas, and foggy theories to eventually produce a situation that is "good enough" to support activity.

Dewey argues that inquiry is not a purely mental operation, but it involves material interventions into the indeterminate situation.[11] As a personal example, one day I was leaving my apartment to get to an important appointment when I found that the front door bolt would not unlock. After several attempts at turning the bolt, which would twist a few centimeters and then move no more, I stood by the door and thought about my predicament. The building was over a century old, and the locks may well have been original. They had always been finicky but had never been completely unworkable. I stood motionless by the door for a few moments working through my confusion. I decided to leave through the back door instead but, as I was gathering my things, it dawned on me suddenly that my keys were not in my pocket. I was searching the apartment for them when a dread shot through me. I knew where they were. My keys were dangling from the deadbolt lock on the other side of the door, and, for some reason, that rendered the deadbolt immobile. Because my building was secured by outer doors, I could not simply exit out the backdoor and walk around to the front to retrieve my keys. There was no way to get the keys from the other side. I would need to either stay inside until my partner returned with another set of keys, call the landlord, or figure out a way to open an old steel lock that had no intention of budging. Because I had an appointment I had to get to, I kept trying.

First, I tried to overpower the lock, figuring that the key was simply adding some additional resistance that might give with some elbow grease. The lock turned a few centimeters but then hit something and did not budge at all. When that failed, I tried shaking the door to jar the key loose. That strategy was as loud as it was fruitless. Next, I tried shaking the door while turning the deadbolt. Still, no luck. However, during the jostling, the deadbolt turned a bit farther than it had on previous attempts. This gave me an idea. I noticed that, even closed, the door had a small amount of room to move before it hit the doorjamb, and, in its resting state, its full weight was pressing against the bolt. I pushed the door outward to release the tension on the deadbolt, and it unlocked easily.

For Dewey, there is a logical continuity between what I went through to solve my problem and the processes a research scientist goes through. In all cases, scientific and lay, the process of inquiry can be understood as a series of steps. It starts with an "indeterminate situation" which is confusing, frustrating, or doubtful. This can be caused by the frustration of some goal (as in the case of my locked door) or because the goal is, as of yet, unknown. Indeterminate situations can be avoided and, in most cases, are. There are an unlimited number of things we do not know, an unlimited number of problems for which we do not have solutions. We normally do not go around looking for confusion and dissatisfaction. But when an indeterminacy arises during an action that one is invested in, it demands a response.

The next step is "the institution of a problem." After a situation has been deemed problematic, an inquiry begins, and the indeterminate situation is translated into a problem with specific contours: "A problem represents the partial transformation by inquiry of a problematic situation into a determinate situation. It is a familiar and significant saying that a problem well defined is half-solved."[12] First facing the jammed lock, I had no idea what the problem might be. It was not until I understood the problem—the key still in the lock on the other side of the door—that the contours of a solution began to present themselves.

The third step is "the determination of a problem-solution." If the situation is not utter chaos, the inquirer can begin to decipher and observe the situation's constituent elements in order to discover relationships and make predictions. By understanding the problem as a part of a system of interacting elements, different aspects can be manipulated to see their effect on the system. In my case, the key, lock, and door were all variables that came into focus as I tried various methods for getting out of my apartment. Finally, a solution is developed in which the meanings of constituent elements are joined together, and the situation becomes meaningful as a whole. Significantly, it was a failed attempt (shaking the lock) that led me to the solution.

The final step is "reasoning" which involves developing a revised understanding of the system in question. After my minor ordeal, I had a far better idea of the way my lock and door interacted. A few months later, when I made the same mistake and, again, left my keys in the lock, I immediately pushed the door toward the frame and unlocked the deadbolt. In my case, this solution solved my pressing problem but, besides that, had little systematic effect on my life. However, in other cases where the variables are interlocked with many others (as we shall see regarding scientific fields), the effects of reasoning can ramify across the system.

Two important points need to be made about the general features of problem-solving before transitioning to the more specific domain of scientific inquiry: first, inquiry is more than just an intellectual process, and second, the problem was solved and knowledge was gained without engaging with the idea of Truth.

1.   *Inquiry involves perception, manipulation, and conception.* Dewey is clear; although new concepts are developed during inquiry, the process is not purely, or even primarily, intellectual.[13] Rather, the process requires "experimental operations" that alter the material dynamics of the indeterminate situation in order to "bring into high relief conditions previously obscure, and relegate to the background other aspects that were at the outset conspicuous."[14] During the process of inquiry, the conception of the situation evolves *in response* to probes that force elements in the system to react. In stimulating them to act, behavior is revealed, and new possibilities for intervention are discovered. For example, it was not until I began shaking the lock back and forth that I noticed that the door was a bit loose and was resting on the deadbolt.

Inquiry involves a cycle of increasing perceptual acuity, the development of manipulations, and the creation of conceptual content. These three aspects cannot be separated. A new way of viewing something that doesn't yield new manipulative possibilities may be interesting but not necessarily helpful. Similarly, a novel manipulation technique that does not produce any new conceptual insights is pointless.[15]

2. *Successful inquiry is only loosely coupled with Truth.* The result of my predicament was success. Plans that were frustrated were put back on track. I managed to unbolt the door, retrieve my keys, and leave. When I faced the same problem several months later, I was able to solve it immediately. I had gained enough knowledge to achieve my desired end. Yet, beyond that, I learned little. The locking mechanism itself remains a complete mystery to me. I have no idea why the combination of the key in the lock and the pressure on the bolt led to an inability to turn the lock. I have only a vague notion that the weight of the door caused the bolt to press against some steel piece inside the lock, but I am not sure. If I, one day, were to again find my bolt stuck only to realize that my keys were in my pocket, it would force me to rethink the role the key played in keeping the lock from turning. Or, if my trick of pushing the door toward the frame to release the tension on the bolt no longer worked, I would be thrown back into an unsettled situation similar to the first (except I would now be armed with the knowledge that my first solution was somehow wrong or incomplete). For ordinary problems, there is little need to probe into these possibilities and meet them before they arise naturally.[16] There are enough problems in life, and people have little desire to manufacture more. Once a solution is found, they happily move on.

For scientists, however, the situation is different. Like their lay counterparts, researchers attempting to solve a problem are happy when a solution works. Any stable, reproducible outcome can be considered good news even when it is not entirely clear what is happening.[17] However, the culture of critique in science means that proposed solutions to problems are often tested both in-lab to adjudicate between competing explanations and by other labs looking to undermine or extend an original finding. It is important to point out, however, that in every one of the these cases, the best possible outcome is one and the same: an unsettled situation becomes understood as a system composed of components that can be independently manipulated to produce some outcome, "transforming the disordered into the orderly, the mixed-up into the distinguished or placed, the unclear and ambiguous into the defined and unequivocal, the disconnected into the systematized."[18] Because these are open systems, however, knowledge about them is never complete or final. This is why knowledge never loses its "hypothetic quality."[19] Each end point is simply another proposed solution that holds until different needs arise.

PROBLEM-SOLVING IN SCIENCE

Figuring out how to free myself from my apartment does not meet many definitions of science. Yet, for Dewey, all inquiry involves some of the same steps—an evolution of a situation from problematic to settled through a process of probing, observation, and theorization. However, there are two major differences between everyday problem-solving and science. First, we normally do not go looking for problems to solve. Getting locked in my house frustrated my plans. I solved that problem so I could get on with my life.[20] In contrast, science is characterized by the unending search for new problems. Indeterminate situations are transformed into settled situations, only to use those newly settled facts to ask even further questions. Rather than problems being impediments to one's objective, in science, the problems *are* the objective.

Second, as Dewey notes, in common sense inquiry, symbols which are used to define problems, determine their constituents, and detail solutions are bound to specific languages and ways of life. In contrast, in scientific inquiry "meanings are related to one another on the ground of their character *as* meanings, freed from direct reference to the concerns of a limited group [. . .] Consequently a new language, a new system of symbols related together on a new basis, comes into existence, and in this new language semantic coherence, as such, is the controlling consideration."[21] The preexisting systems of meanings (which we might call "theories") and the demands for coherence between them are important features of scientific problem-solving. To return to the earlier example, the knowledge acquired working on the lock had little significance in other domains of knowledge. I still know little about how locks work, and what little knowledge I do have remains localized to that specific situation.

Scientific fields, on the other hand, are organized around networks of preexisting meanings that are made explicit. The claim that "Manipulation A affects Object B along Dimension C under Conditions D" is shared publicly and put under scrutiny. If the claim can withstand criticism, it becomes a part of the constellation of meaning in the field that is maintained through training and publication. It is a fact that must be either accepted in one's own work or an obstacle that must be confronted. Claims that are incompatible with what is currently taken to be truth demand a response. They either must be integrated into a more complex web of meanings or shown to be wrong. Thus, unlike problem-solving in everyday contexts, in science, problems and their solutions emerge within a regulated, explicit system of claims.

However, when claims are scrutinized in science, it is typically not just their logical form or internal validity that is questioned. Not even the logical coherence of the claim in the context of the field's universe of accepted facts is the ultimate concern (although this is certainly _a_ concern). Rather, the ultimate value of the claim is whether the relationship it purports actually exists as a measurable phenomenon. Another way to say this is that claims made by experimental laboratories are claims that specific processes will produce specific outcomes. These processes are not mental. They occur through the machinery and technique that transform natural objects. Thus, beyond just a web of meanings, claims enter the "experimental systems" that constitute the material culture of the field.[22] For a claim to be evaluated, it demands that others be able to reproduce its claimed outcome with the technologies and techniques common to the field. Of course, the ambiguity inherent in this procedure should not be ignored. What qualifies as a successful replication can become fiercely debated.[23] Regardless, the notion of replication plays an important regulative role, and, in technologically elaborated fields, it is inarguable that the ability to reliably produce certain outcomes are the foundation for being judged capable of evaluating new and possibly contentious findings. Nitpicky debates only arise once the replication reaches a level of technical and technological competence that justifies its ability to speak to an original finding.

Extending the pragmatism outlined above yields two important insights. The *first* is that, like ordinary problem-solving, scientific inquiry operates by probing systems, noting changes, developing theories to explain these changes, and probing again. Technology is both *the means and ends* of this procedure. It is the *means* because probing involves developing techniques and introducing technologies to preexisting systems.[24] As Andrew Pickering has written, technologies expand the horizon of human intentionality and extend the possibilities for prediction and control. They are included in the research process to the extent that they further these goals. Yet the development of technology is also the *ends* of science because both the short- and long-term goal is the production of a stable relationship. An outcome is a mere phantom until it can be repeated, and a replication is a mere novelty until it can be proved to be stable enough to travel to other labs. However, once enough is known to produce an outcome with desired regularity, it can become a basis for further activity. This might be activity used by non-scientists who gain something through the newfound power or other researchers who use the manipulation to experiment further.

The *second* contribution of pragmatism to this discussion is its sensitivity to the importance of the ongoing material development of the laboratory. Scientific technology is not stable because science is based upon settling unsettled areas. Technology, when successful, only leads to further areas of inquiry. Thus, the process of scientific inquiry runs parallel with the development of new instrumentation. At a basic level, this instrumentation involves elaborated physical activity. However, what makes the evolution of this form of tacit knowledge different than the kind evinced by chefs or mechanics is that it is continually given new power through the introduction of new instruments. In fact, it is reasonable to say that in many scientific fields, there is an ongoing cybernetic evolution between the all-purpose human and newly integrated tools that extend human perception and intentionality into new horizons. I will illustrate how this works empirically in the following chapter. For now, I will sketch a theoretical outline of the process I call bench-building.

BENCH-BUILDING

As I have been using it, the "bench" is a generic term that includes all places where data is captured. The term is taken from chemistry and biology laboratories that do experiments at stainless steel workstations. However, I mean to use bench in the widest metaphorical sense. The "bench" is any site of data collection in a context conceived of as experimental. Beyond the cold metal benches of bio labs, this includes the surveys that social psychology subjects take after being presented with stimuli designed to change their feelings and the puppet stages developmental psychologists use to present stimuli to infant subjects.

The pursuit of theoretically interesting, replicable findings takes researchers through a series of analytically distinct phases that I outlined above. In this process, the bench is where data is captured. Yet the "bench" is not necessarily a static place or organization of technology, although it can be. As I will argue, this largely describes the data capture in developmental and social psychology. However, the bench can also be a site of dynamism and growth. The struggle to develop the bench and give it fresh powers to ask nature new or sharper questions is the key to understanding the production of technology in science. Bench-building is one of the central dimensions of scientific evolution.

To begin with a simple definition: *bench-building is the development and refinement of techniques and technologies that enhance perception and/ or extend the possibilities for manipulation.* There are three major pieces of this definition, and each requires elaboration.

First, bench-building involves *development and refinement.* Much of science takes place using settled technologies. This is especially true in laboratories with limited funding and, as such, are relegated to asking questions that can be answered with less expensive equipment. It is also true of laboratories in fields with largely settled technological cultures. Knowledge collected through more settled methods is incremental and should not be discounted. However, the contributions of such work are bounded by the limits of the technology. Bench-building is concerned with breaching these limits to collect data that could never have been captured before. In fields oriented toward bench-work, maintaining one's place at the cutting edge means constantly reaching new horizons of possibility and overcoming constraints.

Second, the development and refinement characteristic of bench-building occurs with the *introduction of new techniques and technologies.* The bench is the chiasm between the researcher and the research object. In order to probe nature, the researcher employs tools that improve perception or extends the ability to manipulate. On one hand, this involves improving skills. The role of embodied skill has been an ongoing concern in science studies since Michael Polanyi directed attention to the "tacit" dimension of knowledge.[25] Researchers have shown that tacit knowledge is a necessary component of successful laboratory work.[26] But the body is just one piece of an evolving, cybernetic system that is given new or more extensive powers through the integration of technologies.

Finally, the development of skills and incorporation of technology alters the conditions of research by *enhancing perception or extending the capacity for manipulation.*[27] The purpose of developing and refining new techniques and technologies is to gain new insight into or purchase on the object of study. Naturally, not just any change in the conditions of research is an improvement. Simply futzing with the system in the hopes that something new and interesting will materialize is a foolish waste of time.[28] Learning what types of changes might be profitable and which are likely to be dead ends is one of the most important aspects of scientific training. Developing a "feel" for the object studied, having a sense of its untapped possibilities and limitations, allows researchers to make intelligent substitutions and possibly develop new ways of interacting with it.

Hans-Jörg Rheinberger has argued that experimental systems are evolving technologies designed to project conceptual questions onto the physical world. However, the ongoing evolution of these systems is continually challenged by the stabilization and routinization of procedures. Yet this rarely produces rigor mortis because these technologies become the shoulders on which future experiments stand. Specifically, he argues that achieving manipulations and solving problems are typically not "dead-end streets" because these newly reliable manipulations can "become integrated as stable subroutines into other, still growing experimental systems and may help to produce unprecedented events in different contexts."[29] Mirroring Dewey's stages of inquiry, bench-building occurs as a series of phases. This process can be understood as a cycle in which mere possibilities become achieved, stabilized, and standardized before becoming the material conditions for a new set of possibilities (Figure 2.3).

Rheinberger, again, clarifies that what distinguishes a meaningful result is that it can be "reintegrated as a component of the system and can thus enlarge or change the setup."[30]

Thus, bench-building exists in an ongoing tension with the process of "black boxing," popularized by actor-network theorists.[31] Black boxing describes "the way scientific and technical work is made invisible by its own success."[32] This happens when a piece of machinery

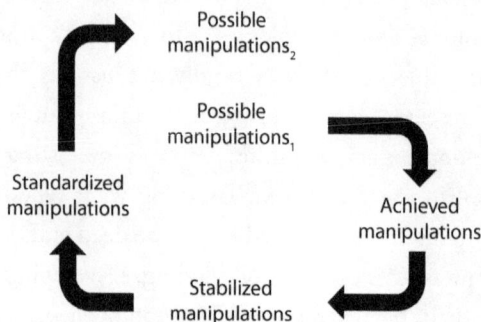

FIGURE 2.3 Bench-Building Expanding the Horizon of Possibilities

becomes so central to a research specialty that it becomes sacrosanct, questioned only by iconoclasts who would willingly risk the coherence of the field. This corresponds to the state of "standardized manipulations" which provide the shared toolkit of a field. Through bench-building, unstable or challenging processes become the object of intense attention and visibility to make them tractable. Once accomplished, they can fade into the background as new challenges enter focus.[33]

The history of science is a history of important pieces of technology that change the horizon of possibilities. For example, for much of its history, biology was largely an observational science "confined to studying life as the end product of two billion and more years of evolution."[34] The entire field was upended by the introduction of technology that allowed researchers to clone and manipulate DNA. Rather than merely observe and compare, the new technology allowed researchers to intervene proactively for the first time and, thus, transform a stable, slow-moving science into a dynamic one.

Recombinant DNA technology is a shining example of technological progress in science, and, like all such examples, attending to the success of hugely influential technologies risks blinding us to the smaller and more localized developments that were its necessary preconditions. Significant technologies do not spring whole like Athena from Zeus's head. They tend to be the amalgamation of many smaller technological developments that, while independently having value only in reference to a parochial community of scientists, can combine to produce technologies of external usefulness. For instance, recombinant DNA technology was only made possible by the integration of several lines of independent research including the discovery of the double-helix structure, the study of simple DNA in viruses, the development of DNA-cleaving enzymes, the isolation of individual cellular genes through work in bacterial genetics, and the development of techniques for the insertion and amplification of genes. Each of these were products of other technological developments. It is bench-building all the way down.

Bench-Building as Construction

In a literal sense, bench-building is a process of construction. As such, my account is in line with the traditions of social constructionism in social theory and constructivism in STS. However, these theories encompass an enormous amount of theoretical scope and diversity that can make the labels meaningless.[35] One attempt to delineate claims in this area suggest there are four common aspects of science that are often said to be constructed: (1) institutions, (2) theories and accounts, (3) laboratory artifacts, and (4) the objects of thought and representation.[36] Bench-building is a process of "construction" in regards to the third category. More specifically, however, the focus is on how the *quality* of these laboratory artifacts—how robust they are, how easily reproduced, how communicable and transferable—affects other dimensions of scientific practice (and their construction).

In the evolving conditions of laboratory experimentation, entire fields are transformed through the development of new techniques and integration of technologies. Researchers devote time and financial resources to gain new purchase on the site of data collection despite its extreme challenges. It is impossible to know which findings will move from the ambiguous frontier of science to its trusted core due to the utter unpredictability of the specific direction of evolution within fields. The gulf between frontier and core, science-in-the-making and established facts, can make the creation of facts and the invention of technologies seem deeply mysterious. The truth is that there is a lot of fumbling; Some things work; some do not. Although human plans give order to the work, intentionality is not destiny. According to an old Yiddish proverb, "Man plans, God laughs."

The unpredictability of the growth of human knowledge should be, as it was for Popper, a fundamental tenet in the philosophy of science.[37] Like all evolutionary processes, bench-building is non-directed in an ultimate sense. Bench-building occurs at the cutting edge of fields and is the process that extends horizons of possibilities in often unforeseen directions. Yet thinking about bench-building *solely* in terms of activity that occurs at the cutting edge of the field is a misrepresentation and mystification of an utterly common practice that occurs every time a researcher replicates an experiment, learns a new technique, or incorporates a new piece of technology.

As walking is the frontier of physical activity for the toddling infant, sophisticated dissection skills remain just out of reach for the novice biologist. In both cases, they will struggle to, and likely accomplish, what others before them have already accomplished. Bench-building produces novel outcomes, but it is also the ways that other labs *repro-duce* those outcomes. Thus, innovation is key to success in science, but getting to a point where one can innovate often requires doing what someone else has done, if only to tweak or extend it. During innovation, bench-building occurs through a series of trials in which failure is the normal outcome (Figure 2.4).

Possible manipulations are attempted. Most fail. However, some are achieved. Of these, only a subset can be reproduced with enough regularity to be incorporated into practice. Once manipulations

SUCCESS	Possible manipulations	→	Achieved manipulations	→	Routine manipulations	→ Technologies
FAILURE		↘ Cannot be produced		↘ Cannot be reproduced with regularity		↘ Cannot be exported

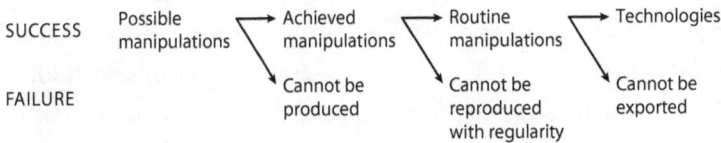

FIGURE 2.4 Settling the Frontier

become routine, they can be disseminated into similar laboratories. If the manipulations show independent value, scientists and engineers attempt to translate them into technologies that can be exported into non-laboratory environments. Some can withstand the new environments while others are not robust enough to survive outside of very specific laboratory conditions.

Because this process is so unpredictable, it may make bench-building seem mystifying. Yet the exact same steps occur in a more predictable way when researchers integrate techniques or technologies developed by other labs into their own.

Bench-Building as Integration
(Or, the Mundanity of Replication)

When researchers attempt to retrace the trail blazed by another lab, the same process occurs but with one importance difference. The uncertainty is diminished because of the presence of a definite goal. When a musician attempts to learn a complex passage, a recording of the piece can provide a clear goal, a behavioral scheme that the player can grow into. Likewise, bench-building in this case has a telos: the development of skill and integration of technology meant to produce the same outcome as another lab. When the development of skills and incorporation of new technologies are meant to reproduce manipulations previously achieved by other labs, bench-building is a form of replication focused on integration rather than verification. As I will argue, the vast amount of replication that occurred in the molecular biology lab had nothing to do with evaluating claims. Instead, its goal was the reproduction of *ends* achieved or made routine in other laboratories.

These two forms of replication follow sharply different logics. The form of replication made famous by Harry Collins focused on adversarial replications. For instance, in his case studies of famous debates in parapsychology and gravity wave physics, replication was used by adversaries to challenge findings. In this form of replication, researchers attempt to faithfully reproduce *the method of a study*, while remaining ostensibly *disinterested in its outcome*. Panofsky and I have labelled this "diagnostic replication" since its goal is often to diagnose the truth value of a claim. In contrast, we have suggested that much replication practice that occurs in labs should be considered "integrative" since it is driven by a desire to achieve *the same end* rather than evaluate a claim.[38]

The difference between diagnostic replication and integrative replication can be illustrated with an example from cooking. At a party, John eats a slice of delicious cake made by Sue, the host. John asks Sue for the recipe. John's goal is clearly not to "verify" the deliciousness of the cake but, rather, to reproduce the taste. If John follows the directions step-by-step and the cake turns out overly sweet or undercooked, it does not mean that Sue's cake was not delicious. Instead, John might assume he made a mistake or lacked Sue's skill, that she left out some necessary instruction, or that her superior baking equipment and professional oven elevated the taste. The point is that John is interested in doing what Sue did, not verifying to see Sue did what she said she did. Of course, if nothing John tried allowed him to replicate the taste, he might develop some doubts about the origins of Sue's cake and might, if he were the paranoid type, demand that Sue make her cake in front of him to verify it. However, this adversarial situation, the typical way that replication is discussed in science studies literature is the exception rather than the rule.

In fields where bench-building is common, replication occurs as a part of normal practice. Thus, the Mertonian description of replication as a functional activity that disincentivizes fraudulent or sloppy science makes sense. If John and Sue are constantly exchanging recipes, it makes little sense for Sue to pass off a store-bought cake as her own. (On the other hand, if John heavily rewards Sue for her baking but has *never* asked for a recipe, it may tempt her to deceive John, a danger in fields not characterized by bench-building.)

To extend the metaphor just one step further, because the goal is to reproduce an *outcome* rather than strictly replicate a *method*, the process is flexible. If the recipe calls for olive oil and John has none, he may substitute vegetable oil. Lacking brown sugar, he may use granulated sugar. If the recipe calls for the dough to chill in the fridge overnight, he might elect to cut this step short. If the cake comes out with the right taste, he may feel more liberty to make further changes. If it comes out badly, he may adhere more closely to Sue's recipe the next time he makes it. In contrast to the flexibility of integrative replication, alterations of method are strictly proscribed in diagnostic replication attempts because it makes their outcomes ambiguous. Failures can be attributed to the changes introduced by replicators and become potentially uninterpretable.[39]

Both innovations and integrations follow the same path of bench-building, the same focus on transforming the conditions of data collection to enhance perceptive or manipulative capacities. Equating these processes highlights the mundane nature of innovative science and reveals an important source of social cohesion in scientific communities. Randall Collins has argued that what separates the social sciences from "high consensus, rapid discovery" sciences was the existence of an exciting frontier of technology that leads researchers to abandon controversies when new technologies open up new avenues of exploration.[40] While I believe the core of this argument is correct, I believe Collins' argument obscures the fundamental dynamic at play. New technologies are not rapidly adopted because they are new.

They are adopted because they offer new perceptual and manipulative abilities. They materially alter the site of data collection.[41] The attempt to reproduce another's finding occurs not necessarily as a test of truth but as an attempt to push the possibilities of one's own lab toward the horizon already achieved by another lab. This is why Hacking identifies replication as a "philosophical pseudo-problem" because "roughly speaking, no one ever repeats an experiment. Typically, serious repetitions of an experiment are attempts to do the same thing better—to produce a more stable, less noisy version of the phenomenon."[42] This is not to say that in most fields replication never occurs in the context of explicit tests. But conceiving of replication solely and wholly in this way is to remain caught within a one-sided, intellectualist theory of scientific development and miss the role of replication in the creation and dissemination of technology.

Thus, innovation and integration become the key dynamic in the practical unity of scientific fields. Despite rapid change across the field, labs can achieve comity through an integrative process which gives them the same powers at the bench as their neighbors. As I elaborate in the next chapter, in fields characterized by ongoing bench-building, replication occurs as an organic part of maintaining one's position at the cutting edge of the field.[43]

3

BENCH-BUILDING IN MOLECULAR BIOLOGY

Mice spend roughly the first two weeks of life with their eyes closed. Yet, even during the period when the retinas are getting no external stimuli, there is a good deal of seemingly spontaneous neuronal activity in the retina. Biologists believe that this activity is involved with how retinal circuits form. Using a mixture of imaging, electrophysiology, and anatomical techniques, the lab of Dr. Sandra Harden investigated the mechanisms and functions involved with spontaneous activity of retinal circuits during development.

At the time I began my observations at the molecular biology lab of Dr. Sandra Harden, I had already spent two years in psychology labs. As I was leaving after my first day, Alicia, one of the lab members, asked me what I thought of the lab. I told her I was overwhelmed and felt like I only understood 10 percent of what was said. She laughed and told me that, even after being in the lab for several years, she only understood 40 percent. After describing this exchange in my fieldnotes, I wrote, "This is important, but I can't say why just yet." As Alicia made clear, this confusion was not unique to me as an outsider to the lab. I discovered that the struggle for comprehension was the modus operandi of the lab because, even as they wrangled with their own research projects, innovations and inventions across their field were constantly changing the ground beneath their feet.

Constructivist research has mined the confusion that characterizes the bleeding-edge science of science because it contrasts so starkly with official accounts from scientists themselves. Yet it is unclear what these theories add besides critique. If technology exists, and it is neither the ineluctable outcome of Scientific Method nor totally random gifts from the universe, then it must be undergirded by some discernible logic. And this logic must be elucidated if we are to understand differential patterns of technological development across scientific fields.

The biological sciences have been the subject of many foundational texts in science studies. In what follows, I will draw liberally on these texts to highlight areas of agreement with my ethnographic observations. Classic themes like the selection and taming of working objects, tacit knowledge, interpretive ambiguity, and the relationship between the conceptual and material aspects of laboratory practice are all central. Yet the focus of this chapter is how these disparate threads unite to produce the small technical advances and to comprise bench-building.

This depiction of Harden's lab gives bench-building flesh by showing how it occurs as a routine practice in a molecular biology laboratory. Thus a line is drawn from the unsure, unstable frontier of the scientific to the creation and stabilization of new perceptive and manipulative capacities that makes the frontier more legible. Tracing how this process occurs in molecular biology will provide a necessary contrast when trying to understand struggles in experimental psychology.

Indeterminacy at the Frontier of Science

Every six weeks or so, the Harden lab would hold a journal club where they would review a recent article in molecular biology or neuroscience. The first time I attended, I was shocked that they could spend two hours discussing a five-page article. However, this time investment became understandable as I came to see how even experienced members of the lab struggled to understand cutting-edge work from other labs. The following quotes were all transcribed during my first journal club:

"I don't get it."

"The y-axis on [graph] J is still making my head hurt."

"What the hell is this plot?"

"It's all going to depend upon density. What's density?"

"They shock them [a specific subtype of retinal cells], which I've never heard of."

"That distribution doesn't look normal to me. It's a peaked distribution but it doesn't look normal."

"I don't know enough about the colliculus. Are there really no pathways between them? No septum?"

"If they have more information, why show less information?"

What surprised me was that these weren't the confused reactions of a first-year graduate student, but they all came from Dr. Harden, a full professor and the head of the lab. This difficulty was not considered a mark against the paper which Dr. Harden called "awesome." The researchers in that article had been able to do something novel, and there was no expectation that the article would be immediately comprehensible.

Work that occurs on the frontier is, by definition, a technical and conceptual struggle. In the Harden lab, many results were presented during weekly meetings as mysteries rather than answers. Unstable but intriguing outcomes were made the object of scrutiny with the goal of simply finding some solid ground, some way to produce the outcome with acceptable regularity. I found the research frontier in both biology and psychology characterized by low levels of consensus.[1] However, molecular biologists engaged with this ambiguity to a much greater degree than psychologists.

After I had been in the lab for a few months, I asked Dr. Anderson, a postdoc who was in the Harden lab for her third year, about the pace of change in the field. She explained,

> I think that most of us feel like we understand nothing most of the time. That's why those conversations are so prolonged. I mean, when we read a paper, the papers we read are hard. There's a lot of technical detail. So, we discuss it so long because we're trying to figure out what the person's doing. Does that make sense to us? Do we believe the results? If we were to use it in our methods, what would we do differently?

Cutting-edge research develops along multiple dimensions of interest to the lab. Innovations in optics, imaging, genetics, and other fields can open new avenues to explore and new tools to integrate.

This causes a general sense of disorientation among even the veterans of the lab. Yet rather than avoid this instability, the demands of their field require they stay abreast of these changes. For instance, to ignore innovations in optics means getting left behind as other labs begin producing data at a better resolution. Thus another lab member told me, "The questions that we can ask are limited by the ways that we ask them. If we have the latest and greatest technology, we can ask more sophisticated questions."

Nearly every week, the lab meeting opened with a discussion about purchasing a new strain of mouse, dye, virus, or small piece of equipment. When I entered the lab, they had just purchased their eighth rig (a workstation with a microscope and supporting technologies) and were building their ninth when I left. This constant change created a culture of volatility. As Blake explained, "All the tools are advancing at the same time." He later told me that their field "pushes hard even if we don't know where we're going" and compared the constantly receding technological frontier to the Wild West.

Ambiguity is an unavoidable aspect of a bench-building process that is based upon technical ingenuity and the physical skills of researchers. Because cutting-edge research pushes into uncharted territories using new techniques and technologies that are not yet well explicated, they are sources of both inspiration and frustration to their audience. Decades ago, G. Nigel Gilbert and Michael Mulkay noted that methods sections in articles were often incomplete descriptions because the "feel" of doing experiments was an irreducible necessity.[2] However, only results that remained tethered to particular researchers or labs came to be seen as deeply dubious. As Theodore Porter explains, "In the early life of a new technique, when it is still on the cutting edge, personal contact will most often be crucial for its spread to other laboratories. Indeed, this may be just what 'cutting edge' means in experimental science. But experiments that succeed, again perhaps by definition, will not long remain in the domain of intricate craft skill and personal apprenticeship."[3] Although inexplicability is a defining characteristic of the research frontier, it is, like Dewey's indeterminate situation, only the initial stage in a process.

DATA THINNING

Rather than producing data which either clearly "supports" or "does not support" a particular hypothesis, much of the data gathered by cell biologists is too complex to be easily interpreted. The language of "hypothesis testing" is simply wrong. Also like Dewey's indeterminate situation, the research frontier overwhelms the researcher with its heterogeneity and unpredictability. Confronting this ambiguity means trying to understand data that afford no obvious interpretation. Thus, much research activity is dedicated to simply producing a situation in which hypotheses can be proposed to which evidence can speak.

At the frontier of science, researchers are confronted with what I will call "thick data." Inspired by Gilbert Ryle's and Clifford Geertz's discussions of "thick description,"[4] thick data are those forms of evidence that cannot be understood in isolation and demand a process of interpretation. Unlike previous alignments which would categorize "thick" evidence as inherently qualitative, thick data can be based on quantitative values. It may indicate the frequency and amplitude of neurons firing after being exposed to a virus designed to limit the release of specific neurotransmitters, for instance. The graph itself is clearly a representation of quantitative values. Yet the density of the graph may prevent the type of uncontentious interpretation that are often attributed to quantitative evidence. Thick data may be quantitative, but they require an interpretive process that blurs the line between quantitative and qualitative data analysis.

Jagged Graphs

A simple example using a 2 × 2 graph can illustrate my meaning. Data visualizations can be arranged based upon their complexity. On one side, there is the unfortunate outcome represented in Figure 3.1: a graph that is completely random. In this visual chaos, no meaning is possible.

On the other side, there is a simple relationship represented in Figure 3.2 (e.g., "a one unit increase in X leads to one unit increase

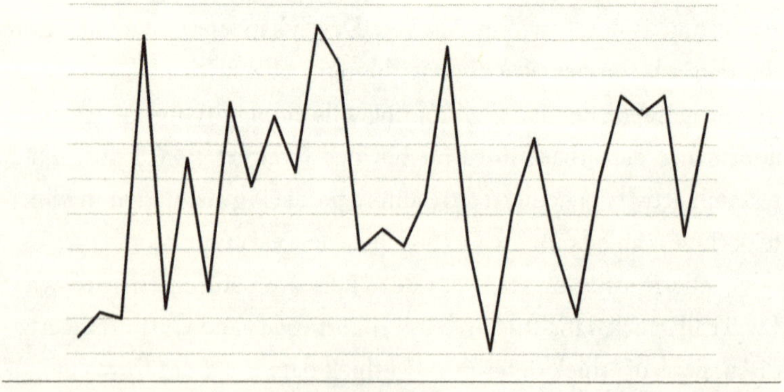

FIGURE 3.1 Randomness

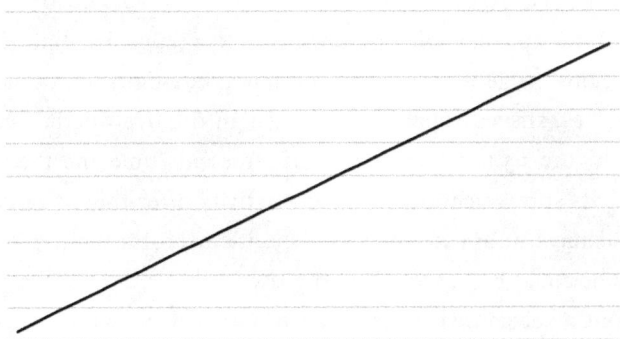

FIGURE 3.2 Perfect Correlation

in *Y*"). The relationship has immediate visual logic that is immediately graspable.

But in between simple graphs and meaningless chaos, both theoretically and temporally, there exists a gradient of complexity that is suggestive, that hints at a meaningful relationship, but resists any univocal interpretation. In the Harden lab, the majority of presented findings were of the type represented in Figure 3.3.

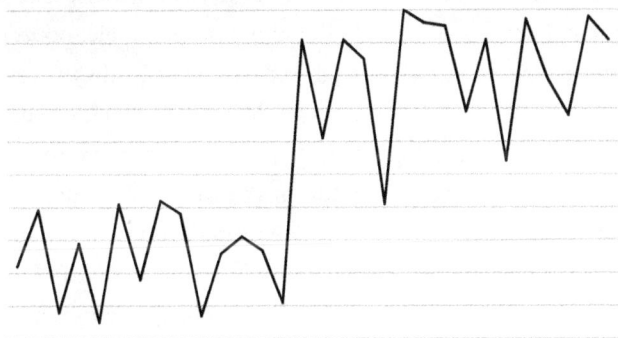

FIGURE 3.3 Jagged Graph

The jagged graph is one that is suggestive but non-definitive, offering multiple possible interpretations to a set of data but no easy conclusions. Jagged graphs raise intriguing questions but do not, by themselves, answer them. For instance, in the hypothetical example of Figure 3.3 in which the x-axis represents time and the y-axis represents some measure of cellular activity after the introduction of a chemical meant to suppress a specific neurotransmitter, several questions could be raised: Does the rise in the middle of the graph represent a substantively important change? How should we interpret the gentle decline that precipitated it? What does the volatility after the rise mean? Are any of these jags reproducible? If so, are they interesting?

Rather than baffling failures or unambiguous successes, the Harden lab presentations were typically focused on the collective interpretation of these sorts of obscure, but suggestive, findings. These were not, of course, all represented in line graphs. But whether such evidence was presented in still pictures, video clips, heat maps, histograms, scatterplots, or in tabular form, it typically confronted the lab as a question worth asking rather than an answer. It was the *beginning* of an investigation rather than its end. It was a step in a long, iterative process rather than a final product.

Naturally, there are various statistical techniques to smooth lines and discern the amount of signal in the noise, but these differ in a fundamental way from bench-building. These techniques occur in the data analysis phase of the research process. That is, they occur after data capture at the bench has occurred. When the data "are what they are," when there is little opportunity to alter or improve them, then it makes sense to concentrate effort at the data analysis phase of the research process. However, when there is opportunity to improve the quality of the data, to pull out the elements of the system and manipulate them, then the evidence represented in jagged graphs and their ilk points in one direction—back to the bench.

These data visualizations were not meant for public consumption. Nor were they produced to bludgeon competing scientists into acceptance, which is frequently how science studies scholars have thought about the role of data visualizations. Rather, in the Harden lab, they were used to evaluate manipulations and to strategize for future steps. Because of this, researchers approached the graphs in a completely different way from those that were to be published.

Qualification

One of the most striking things I encountered in Dr. Harden's lab was the way collective attention was used to interpret and attribute meaning to some blurry image or jagged graph. It was akin to what one would expect in a class on art criticism. I saw them attempt to interpret images and video clips and trace their fingers over graph lines while trying to narrate its jags. From the perspective of a strict hierarchy of science where a field's rank is equivalent to its level of formalism—e.g., its proximity to the ideal absence of ambiguity often attributed to mathematics—this seems perplexing. Yet from a pragmatist perspective, where indeterminate situations must first be *qualified* before they can be systematized and quantified, it makes perfect sense. Thick data must be thinned. Clarity, quantification, and intersubjective agreement were outcomes of a process that began in ambiguity, qualification, and subjective interpretation.

The first step in such discussions was to establish the contours of the data. During a presentation to the lab, Alicia displayed some images captured by previous members of the lab, reminding them of what they had already achieved in that area to better explain how she was going to build on it. Rather than let this review pass by without comment, Dr. Harden stopped her and spent several minutes interrogating her on the image.

Who did the imaging?

What were they using to image?

How old were the animals when these images were taken?

Alicia responded to each. The images were taken by members of the lab about five years ago. They used Oregon Green dye to image. However, when she told Dr. Harden that the images were taken on embryonic day eight, Dr. Harden pointed out that the cells in the image showed some morphological features indicating that they were older than eight days. Alicia looked through her notes and conceded that the cells were actually eighteen days old. Although this interrogation may seem nit-picky to an outsider, it served to clarify and affix the few settled facts to provide necessary context.

In another case, Ian presented some exploratory data to the lab. However, he only presented a set of summary statistics. At the end of the presentation, the first question Dr. Harden asked was about the raw data. Ian, who was still new to the field, had not thought it necessary to share such undigested data. Although Dr. Harden spent a few minutes talking about the tables Ian did have, at the end of the presentation, she chided him for not bringing his data. In short order, she made the following comments: "We need to see your data." "Everything depends upon your data." "We need to see your best cells and your worst cells." That, she argued, lets the audience see "What the noise level is." In these critiques, she made it clear that there are no shortcuts to quantification. Before summary statistics make sense, the basic facts must be established.

After the facts were settled, the next step was to translate the remaining indeterminacy into a problem with specific features. Later, when Ian presented another set of findings, he shared a complex graph from a multielectrode array showing the electrical activity of twelve cells over time. Blake asked him to hypothesize about a trough in the middle of the graph that occurred in cells eight through twelve. He did not have an interpretation he felt confident in but guessed that the cells were degrading. Dr. Harden corrected him; to answer that question, he would need to look at spike amplitudes. If the individual spikes were still strong, but were merely occurring less frequently, then the cells are fine. However, if the spikes were genuinely less powerful, then the cells were degrading. If so, Ian would have to discard all the data he had collected thus far. Zivah joked, "It's always extremely painful to give up a single unit!" Dr. Harden continued, "Don't go away unit! Don't leave me!" Although this exchange did not help Ian to explain the dip in his graph, it transformed an indeterminate situation into one with enough known elements that a hypothesis could be tested.

The immediate goal of engaging with thick data qualitatively is to get a sense of the system so meaningful tests can be applied. The ultimate goal, however, is the creation of predictable relationships. Yet this was daunting and rarely successful. I asked Stephan why experimentation was so difficult. He explained that there were inevitable differences between what he had planned to do and what was actually possible:

> Well, usually you design the experiment that you want to do. And you have a reason for that. You have all the specifics. But, then, as I learned, when you're actually doing it, you find out that the things you thought should happen—because you're making a lot of assumptions—just do not happen. Then you start trying other stuff. I was thinking of using a drug that would block cholinergic signaling. That doesn't seem to be doing anything. Okay. Then, let's see, it might be that I should block GABAergic signaling. It might be that I should block glutamatergic signaling.

When I asked why he thought the process was so unpredictable, he explained,

> You're trying to do something that nobody has ever done before. You think about it, and you write it down and you have your protocol and everything, it sounds like it's going to be easy work and you're just going

to do it. But, then, when you're actually doing it, you find out that many things actually go wrong. You come here and do a whole week of experiments and end up with nothing like what you wanted. So, then you have to change things, pretty much, one by one.

The description Stephan offers of altering things "one by one" is exactly the type of probing that is necessary when confronting an indeterminate situation. The goal of such probes is to find something, anything to measure, any way to transform the qualitative situation into something quantifiable. But quantification comes late in the process. For the majority of his experiments, there is nothing to quantify. He explained, "When we get to the quantification, it's because we know we already have good data. And we have a phenomenon that we can study. Then we can go into quantification. But before that, it's a lot of trial and error. Or, I should say, trial and failure."

However, as soon as the technology, research object, and skill are working together to produce a reliable reaction, Stephan explained that he will then produce as much data as possible: "Basically, if I get that experiment going all the time, then I'm going to do it ten times, fifteen times, and then I'm going to have a lot of things to quantify." He was currently in the process of quantifying some short video clips of cells reacting to a light stimulus. He told me that his interest was whether other cells react when one cell is stimulated: "So, one thing I can quantify is, how many cells? How many cells can I get a signal from? How often do I get a signal from them? What happens if I apply a drug? Do I get more cells? Less cells?"

Quantification

Qualification, although often a necessary step, was not an end-in-itself. Rather, its value was in discerning elements of the experimental situation that provided some actionable information. The goal, however, was to eventually produce data that no longer contained the ambiguity that demanded the hermeneutic eye. When Zivah and Emma shared some data from a set of studies they had been collaborating on, Dr. Harden immediately reacted to one of the graphs:

DR. HARDEN: "Oh my god! It's fit by a line! Oh my god, you have data that's fit by a line!" [laughter]

EMMA: "It's log linear."

DR. HARDEN: "I know. A log linear line. That's, like, practically an equation! Is that not an equation? That's an equation. I am so happy!" [laughter]

The effusiveness of Dr. Harden's reaction was an indication of both the value of such findings and their relative rarity. Later, Dr. Anderson confirmed this sentiment. She explained that Dr. Harden was very concerned with thoughtfully developing hypotheses and gathering good quantitative data but admitted that all of this typically came at the end of a more freeform and qualitative process:

Dr. Harden is very quantitative and, ideally, very careful. But I wouldn't say the lab is always so perfectly careful. I feel like often times, especially when you're starting a new experiment, you'll just kind of try stuff. You just try it and once you get anything that gives you any kind of interesting result you refine your method.

The process of "refining your method" is ultimately about transforming the context of data collection so that thick, ambiguous data can be thinned and made more interpretable. Although thick data can sound appealing (this is especially true for social scientists in interpretive fields), it is not hugely helpful, in itself, for experimental scientists. Major scientific discoveries are defined, instead, by the production of *thin* data—findings that represent robust, unambiguous relationships between variables.

In sciences with a limited ability to alter the site of data collection, data thinning cannot happen. Instead, thick data is made interpretable in the data analysis phase through statistical analyses which draw out simple relationships from complex data. The important thing to note about this is that nothing in the world has changed. The object of study has not changed in any way and neither researcher nor technical apparatus has improved. This is essentially a *post facto* intervention. The goal of this work is to uncover patterns where they are not immediately obvious. Pointing this out is not meant to minimize the significant contribution statistics makes to data analysis. But it is vitally important to distinguish post hoc practices from those that *change the possibilities of data collection.*

Rather than transform data after they have been collected, bench-building seeks to improve the data, to make them more perceptible and amenable to manipulation.[5] Through this engagement, the researcher observes the indeterminacy to discover its constituent elements and physically manipulates those elements to test the effect on the rest of the system. As I will show in the next section, this involves the co-evolution of material technology, embodied technique, and perceptive capacity.

BENCH-BUILDING AS CYBERNETIC EVOLUTION

The field of molecular neuroscience is, to some extent, an outgrowth of the Nobel Prize winning research of Alan Hodgkin and Andrew Huxley who were the first to outline the dynamics of nerve impulse propagation. Because early experiments with frogs proved too experimentally challenging, the pair moved to a new animal. Rather than working with a more common research animal like a rat or a monkey, they chose to experiment on the giant squid because it had neurons large enough to be seen with the naked eye. The larger neuron provided enough surface area to insert a thin electrode to record the first action potential (the neuron "firing"). In the subsequent years, the partnership invented several pieces of equipment to manipulate neurons in novel ways. The result of this was one of the earliest, and still influential, mathematical models in biology. In this case, the improved perception gained by using the larger neuron supported technological advances (recording the neuron) and led to a conceptual breakthrough.

Research in experimental labs takes place within an ongoing evolution of technology and technique. These are not independent. Rather, they represent the mutual refinement of hand, eye, and machine that leads to alternating phases of sharpening perception and novel manipulations. Bench-building is a stumbling process characterized more by trial-and-error (or, as Stephan explained, trial-and-failure) than brilliant flashes of insight. As such, its early phases are characterized by a predictable inelegance.

The most basic form of bench-building can be seen in the development of embodied skill. From the moment infants begin purposely exploring their environment, they begin a process of inquiry that will extend throughout the rest of their lives. As argued in the previous chapter, scientific inquiry is merely a self-aware, directed, and highly sophisticated version of this same process.

Hands

Despite sometimes being denigrated in favor of intellectual work, tacit knowledge remains important in experimental science.[6] As another ethnographer of molecular biology labs has pointed out, "What needs to be stressed with regard to molecular biology is that scientists act like ensembles of sense and memory organs and manipulation routines onto which intelligence has been inscribed; they tend to treat themselves more like intelligent materials than silent thinking machines."[7] Rather than detached experimentalists coolly recording outcomes from experiments, getting the experiments to work at all requires an intimate, bodily engagement.

The case of Ian is illustrative. Biology graduate students spend their first two years as traveling journeymen doing "rotations" in which they move from lab to lab to pick up new skills and develop interests. One of these students, Ian, entered the lab shortly after I arrived. The lab meeting before he arrived, Dr. Harden told us that Ian was coming but warned that his background was in computational neuroscience. Like theoretical physics, computational neuroscience was responsible for taking empirical findings produced in experimental work and creating better mathematical models. In physics, however, theoreticians have achieved dominant status through the development of powerful models and, most shockingly, purely theoretical predictions than ended up being borne out empirically (e.g., the Higgs Boson). Computational neuroscientists do not have a similar record of success and thus have not achieved a comparably high status.

What made Dr. Harden particularly wary, however, was Ian's lack of technical training. He had never conducted experiments. She told us, "He hasn't been tested." After an initial meeting in which Ian described the experiments he wanted to do in her lab, she felt skeptical: "I don't think he has a realistic idea about what it takes to do experiments." In the conversations, he displayed both the overly ambitious agenda and lack of detail that were portents of unsuccessful laboratory work.

She was proved correct. Ian struggled all semester and was unable to collect much data because he simply could not physically perform the experiments. Later, Ian told me that when he got into the lab, he had a very brief training session with Blake, one of the older graduate students:

> So, he initially trained me on how to do it. I dissected some mice earlier on another rotation and the very first time I did it he was like, "Oh, alright." It takes a nice touch and he expected me to just destroy [the

retina] and I got it out relatively nicely, but it was really kind of a sick joke on me because that beginner's luck just didn't persist.

After his initial success he began to have problems. Day after day, Ian continued to go through the hour-long process of dissecting the mouse and setting up the experiment only to discover that the retina was not providing a viable electrical signal. Students typically present their "rotation project" at the end of their semester in residence. Ian presented the limited data he had collected but had to admit that Blake did much of the manual work, "because my touch is not so good." Ian later told me that Blake "took mercy" on him and did several dissections for his project because he simply could not get a usable recording. Although he might have eventually learned, Ian was not asked to join the lab permanently.

The value of embodied skill was evidenced in the way lab members referred to "hands." At one point, Dr. Harden told the lab that a pair of researchers would soon be visiting. She said, "They're both technically outstanding, like, building things. It'll be good to have another pair of hands." "Hands," in the Harden lab, referred to the skill that allowed researchers to produce difficult to achieve, but desirable, outcomes.

In another case, Dr. Harden was talking with Alicia about an undergraduate who had applied to their PhD program. He had a neurological disorder that impaired his fine motor coordination. Previously, he had conducted some research using another student as a surrogate to do delicate physical tasks and thought he could continue using that system in Dr. Harden lab. She was dubious.

DR. HARDEN: "Could you imagine doing work in physiology with someone else being your 'hands'? It's bizarre."

ALICIA: "Does it work?"

DR. HARDEN: "I'm not quite sure it would work."

ALICIA: "You could get really mad at your hands, at least."

DR. HARDEN: [laughing] "I know! I already get mad at my hands but they're *my* hands. I couldn't imagine yelling at some student, 'Get that cell! I can't believe you didn't get that cell!'"

In addition to relatively rudimentary skills like dissection that serves as a barrier of entry into some fields, pursuing rarified skills at the research frontier can allow researchers to gather data that competitors cannot. For instance, one week during lab updates, Zivah explained that she was learning a new method of craniotomy which involved implanting an electrode into the brain of a living mouse. She noted that her skill with surgery was improving but admitted that it still took too much time to find the particular subclass of cells that she needed. She had problems even keeping the mouse alive during the process. However, she thought further improvements in skill would allow her to perform the surgery fast enough to gather data before the mouse expired and prevented the collection of hard to get data. In this example, the limits of the technology—the demand that the mouse be stimulated after traumatic surgery—created a space in which improved skill could produce high value data.

Tools

Although embodied skill is vital, bench-building is a *cybernetic* process because human intentionality—that is, our goal-directedness—is transformed by machinery. As we can trace the formation of sophisticated scientific skill to the acquisition of basic skill in childhood, we can trace the development of machinery back to basic tools: the stick that extends the hand or the wheel that extends the horizon. Although a site of extremely expensive and complex technologies, there were many mundane examples of human-machine cooperation in the Harden lab. For example, I was following Alicia one day through a routine set of experiments in which she needed to shoot a jet of controlled air at her tissue sample. The machinery used to do this was at the top of a rack that towered over seven feet. Alicia was petite, barely five feet tall, and she could not reach the button she needed to press to initiate the air pressure. Having faced this problem before, however, she had put a long glass wand (typically used for stirring solutions) next to the rig. When she needed the air, she used the wand to push the button.

At one point, I noticed that nearly all the members in Dr. Harden's lab used notebooks with graph paper. It seemed quite busy, visually, to me and made their words harder to read. I wondered why this would become a standard choice. However, their choice became immediately clear when they came across a data visualization they found important. The graph paper was a simple tool that allowed lab members to reproduce visualizations more quickly and accurately than if they were using regular notebook paper.

During a lab meeting, Dr. Renault, a postdoc who had recently come into the lab, explained that he stimulated the retinal tissue he was experimenting on with the flash from his iPhone. This provoked laughter, and Dr. Harden replied, "My retina can see an iPhone; I guess a mouse's can too." Dr. Anderson joked that the iPhone might be the solution to a persistent problem the lab had been having with standardizing their light stimulus. Emma continued, "You should just stick an iPhone in there!" Dr. Harden: "I know! What are we doing killing ourselves?"

Of course, the above examples—instances where human intentionality is given additional power through engagement with simple technologies—are not unique to highly elaborated research environments. However, they illustrate the basic logic that characterizes the more complex forms of human-machine interactions. What unites both the simplest technologies with those at the bleeding edge of science are the types of material transformations that each make possible.

These take one of two forms. The first are *scale transformations*. Like Alicia's use of the glass wand to extend her reach, technologies make human action more powerful, temporally exacting, or precise than even the most powerful or skilled human could achieve. Regular human senses are strengthened using technological aids. Things too far away are made to appear closer while things too small are made to appear larger. Sounds too subtle for human perception are amplified. Action that requires unrelenting attention or physical energy can be offloaded onto machines. The second are *modal transformations*. Like Dr. Renault's use of his iPhone flash, new elements are introduced that translate human action into a mode not naturally possible. Objects are transformed so that distinctions invisible to our senses are made manifest. Vistas in which all objects are similar in color are made to look distinct and are isolated and made available for intervention. Events that do not produce sound are made to produce them and yield previously inaccessible information.

For molecular biologists, scale and modal transformations extend and translate their intentionality. They become cyborgs whose technologies define their possibilities of action.[8] One cannot be a cutting-edge neuroscientist in the absence of cutting-edge equipment. During a presentation, one visitor explained the loss of identity that happened when she got her first faculty position:

> So, I went from [a well-funded lab with cutting-edge equipment], where we had multiple confocals and a two-photon each and all sort of equipment and then you go [to a far poorer university] and you have to reinvent yourself because there's no two-photon for another eight years and one confocal which was dead and didn't work.

The loss of these technologies forced her to "reinvent" herself within the limitations she faced. She was the same person, yet she was one researcher in a wealthy laboratory and another researcher in a poor one. She did not fall out of the field entirely, but she lost access to key pieces of technology that allowed her to stay at the cutting edge of the field. She ultimately made a career for herself on the outskirts of the field, answering questions far from the cutting edge.

The cybernetic connection between skill, technology, and identity means that researchers form personal relationships with their rigs. Although all the rigs technically belonged to Dr. Harden, she rarely conducted experiments anymore. Lab members using certain pieces of technology developed feelings of ownership over the rigs they used most often. In cases where only one researcher was using a rig, the area around it became a de facto personal space similar to a second desk.

Of course, rigs—especially, those that are new and have unique abilities—are often used by several parties at once. Yet rigs are often sensitive and demand time to learn their quirks. Getting into a productive setup with new machinery can be a challenge in itself, one easily undone by another researcher's recalibrations.

When I interviewed her about the relationship researchers develop with their rigs, Emma told me,

> It's true that if you use the same rig every day, you'll have much more reliability in being able to successfully execute your experiments. And, so, you'll collect more data more quickly. If you're the only one ever using it and no one ever comes in and puts a different profusion system on it or sets up a different triggering system to the computer or something like that that's going to make it so that you don't know what's going on any more then you're much more likely to have no issues and never have to fix anything and never have to spend a whole day wasting your time.

Not all issues stem from other people. Even when she was the only one using the rig, issues would arise: "Sometimes it's nobody's fault. It's just the entropy of these very delicate systems." Yet it was clear that having multiple people on the same rig is a predictable cause of problems, one that necessitated frequent group discussions that produced lab policies.

Not only must experimenters "sign up" for time on the rig, but they also need to communicate with others about it. Regarding her preferred rig, Emma explained to me, "If someone were to come on it, they would usually ask me to give them a tour of the rig and tell them how I'm doing everything. And then we would have communication throughout the whole time they're doing experiments about if they're going to change anything."

However, Emma noted that, even with good communication, there are tensions between different "styles" that are unavoidable:

> So, everyone uses different profusion systems, and they have, like different stuff set up on it that can mean that you can't get your recordings to work right. Everything gets tuned to your style. For instance, something that can happen on this rig that would drive me really nuts is if someone replaced this tubing [a tube used to apply gentle suction to allow a stable connection to a cell] and had it set up slightly differently so that you needed either more or less pressure in order to control the suction of the tip [for the patch clamp]. So, whenever I go onto a new rig that is one of the reasons why I don't successfully patch the first two or three cells that I try to patch because the suction is different enough, whether it's the length of the tubing or the thickness of the tubing can change how much pressure you need to apply to change the apparent pressure at the tip of the electrode. That's an example of something on any electrophysiology rig that's going to F you up for a little while.

Emma had learned first-hand the difficulty of sharing rigs during a training visit she made to a lab in Paris. She made the trip to learn a technique for uncaging glutamate, a process of activating glutamate release from cells through light stimulation. However, once in Paris, it took her a full week just to get acquainted with the new rig and get any usable recordings at all. Half the trip was spent just getting to the point where the technology would provide a stable platform for learning the new skill. In a conversation with Dr. Harden, Emma explained that her biggest problem was a simple technical hurdle, mastered by most first-year grad students—tearing through the inner limiting membrane to gain access to the cells. The Paris lab used a different type of manipulator which did not allow the electrode to be set at an angle. Instead, she had to learn how to tear through the tissue with an electrode pointed straight down, a challenge that was difficult enough to consume several days.

Sharing rigs became a problem in the Harden lab during a period with both Zivah and Mary, a student from the neighboring lab, both needing to use the only two-photon microscope. Zivah's problem was that when she came at the rig "cold," she could not get usable data. The first week on the rig was mostly spent getting it adjusted to her liking. Yet, right when she finally got everything to her liking and was able to start reliably collecting data, Mary would change the rig back again. Blake exacerbated the problem by announcing during a lab meeting that he was also going to need to use the two-photon for a set of experiments he was planning. Dr. Harden noted that the experiments Blake and Zivah were working on required similar set-ups and asked if they could tradeoff between themselves.

Despite the similarities in their experimental procedures, nei-ther Blake nor Zivah liked the idea. Blake argued that productivity increases the more time you spend on the machine. Dr. Harden asked if either could share the rig with the neighboring student. Neither was willing to do that either. Dr. Anderson asked what the ideal scenario would be: Would a whole day work or do you need to be able to reserve the machine for several days in a row? Zivah explained that she pre-ferred to have the machine to herself for a block of days. She admitted that she might not even run experiments on it the whole time, but she did not want anyone else to touch it while she was using it.

Blake suggested that what they need is the ability to reserve two-week blocks. Dr. Harden expressed sympathy with the need to get comfortable on a rig but told them "I'm not sure how to manage that because [Mary] is under a lot of pressure to get her results." However, she told Blake and Zivah that she would set up a system with three-day reservations. She conceded that it was not a perfect solution but hoped it provided each experimentalist with a reasonable amount of time to troubleshoot problems and get comfortable before running a series of experiments.

INNOVATION AND INTEGRATION

The intense focus on tacit skill and technology pays off in the inch-worm process of scientific development. On one hand, it is necessary to develop the skills and maintain the technical infrastructure to be able to participate at the cutting edge of the field. Thus, practices of integration help the lab keep pace with innovations in the field. On the other hand, technique and technology are the base on which to produce new innovations which, in turn, motivate integration from other labs.

These processes of innovation and integration describe how a field characterized by ongoing change can maintain its coherence and identity. For instance, Kohler has shown how drosophila geneticists developed a "moral economy" of unwritten but widely shared norms around issues of transparency and sharing materials.[9] These accommodations are necessary because asymmetries at the bench are the source of real social inequalities. Every lab wants to produce innovative, pathbreaking work, but, ultimately, the value in this type of work is typically not clear at the time of achievement. Rather, its importance only becomes clear retrospectively as the work becomes what has been referred to as an "obligatory passage point" for subsequent research.[10] Thus, innovation and integration are two sides of the same coin for the former is only recognized to the extent it motivates the latter. And integration is only attempted when it is believed that it will provide new possibilities for innovation. Central to this movement— production and reproduction, origination and replication, innovation and integration—is changing the conditions of data collection.

As I wrote previously, integrative replicators are interested in achieving specific ends and, so long as it meets that end, do not care about rigorously matching the methodology of the target study. If a new biological technique allows researchers to identify specific sub-classes of a cell, for instance, the goal is to achieve (or, better yet, improve upon) the same effect. If the same outcome can be achieved with less effort, *despite diverging from the original protocol*, that is success. This is not to say the original procedure is useless or untrue, only that its value lays in its ability to produce a particular end.

During a journal club in which the lab was reviewing an article relevant to an experiment they were about to embark on, Dr. Harden interrupted a lab member's summary of a section to ask, "Everyone see [the images in] A? Can we do that?" The two pictures showed the expression, in a genetically modified mouse, of a certain cell class both *in vivo* and *ex vivo*. She asked if the image was taken with an ophthalmoscope (an instrument for examining the inside of the eye). It was. She asked if any labs in the department had one. Emma and Dr. Anderson have each seen ophthalmoscopes in different labs. Dr. Harden wondered aloud if the lab could borrow one. Stephan did not understand its advantage other than producing beautiful images. Dr. Harden explained it would allow them to know, before dissection, whether a mouse was GFP positive. It would eliminate the need to genotype. Dr. Anderson pointed out that it would also let them know if an injection worked.

The type of small development referenced by Dr. Harden was not a major claim that might motivate a diagnostic replication attempt. Rather, it represented an incremental step that might provide a marginal improvement in perception. The goal was not to evaluate whether the authors actually produced the images they published. Rather, it is to use their methods because they would extend the lab's perceptive capacity (the ability to detect specific strains of mice much more quickly).

During another lab meeting, Zivah was telling the lab about a new method of securing tissue samples. Rather than using a slide to hold down the sample, a thin membrane would be used.

EMMA: "Did anyone look at how much they cost?"
DR. HARDEN: "I don't care how much they cost. I want somebody to do this. I think it's going to change everything."

She went onto to explain that it would allow them to "go anywhere on your retina instead of where the hole is." Currently, the lab accessed the retina by means of tearing a hole in the inner limiting membrane. The process was sometimes traumatizing to the cells underneath and meant that the torn hole was the total field of potential observation.

Blake wanted some clarification.

BLAKE: "So, you don't have a hole in the membrane at all?"
DR. HARDEN: "Right. You don't have a hole."
BLAKE: "That's a huge advantage too because the hole restricts where you can do your experiments, and it also provides a weak spot where you're likely to have detachment."

Carla points out that this method would provide a "big field" and Blake agrees: "Exactly. The worst thing ever is when you're on the edge of that hole and something interesting is just, like, over there [indicates just outside the hole in the innerlimiting layer], and you just can't get to it."

Once again, the advantage of the new technology was not earth-shattering. Despite Dr. Harden's enthusiastic statement that the new membrane would "change everything," the actual changes—providing a larger field for researchers—is the type of incremental perceptual advancement that is characteristic of bench-building.

Even when there are few concrete reasons why expensive, new equipment is needed, the mere promise of being able to accomplish novel manipulations can motivate labs to develop their capacities. During a period when Dr. Harden was looking to purchase some new equipment that would allow them to capture images more quickly and at a higher resolution, Stephan expressed doubts since none of the lab's current projects would directly benefit from it. Dr. Harden disagreed and noted several places where faster imaging might benefit current studies:

> If we do glutamate uncaging and look at dendrites that we want to image very quickly. So, you want to look at the rise time of your calcium signal. And you [to Stephan] will want to look at the rise time of your calcium signal. If you're going to use that as a way of looking at electrical coupling, if you're going to use calcium imaging, you want much better resolution than you have right now with the scanners.

Stephan admitted that while it might be useful for some future projects, he did not see the current value, but Dr. Harden explained that "It's the direction that imaging is going."

During a presentation by a prospective postdoc, he introduced a method he used called "dynamic clamp." Dr. Harden stopped him to address the room: "Did everyone understand that? This is the coolest thing, but it's probably new for some of you." She explained that the presenter's lab was, "doing a current clamp experiment, but they want to know how their conductance is changing as their membrane is depolarizing. So, you can't just put in a DC conductance. You have to have something that's changing. So, it's a really fantastic method for doing this." Kylie was not clear about the purpose of dynamic clamp and the postdoc candidate explained that it allowed researchers to test subtler features of the cell's activity within a circuit than is typically possible. Dr. Harden concluded, "If somebody could do that in one of their experiments, that would be great. We'll figure out a reason." Completely unmotivated by theoretical questions, the mere possibility of increased acuity in measurement was enough to direct the lab's investment.

In another case, Dr. Harden advised an undergraduate member of the lab to use a new method to locate gap junctions, a specific type of intercellular interaction. When Kylie pointed out that Alicia already tried this method but struggled making distinctions. Dr. Harden responded, "I think somebody needs to use it . . . and find something with it. [laughs] Because people are using it." Again, despite the struggle that her own lab had with the method, because "people are using it," she trusted the result and wanted to develop that skill in her own lab.

In the previous two examples, the mere presence of new technologies was enough to encourage adoption. Simply because "people are using it" the Harden lab was willing to "figure out a reason" to try it. Technological advancements drive the research agenda and are integrated because of their promise to extend the manipulative and perceptive capacities of the lab (even if it is not yet clear that it will be theoretically meaningful).

When the Harden lab wanted to reproduce a finding, the process frequently began as an integrative replication with shortcuts and substitutions. However, if these were unsuccessful, more attention was paid to reproducing the original finding more faithfully. In this way, what begins as integrative can become probative.

For instance, during lab updates, one lab member discussed a project which aimed to extend a finding from NIH molecular biologist Jason Stern. However, he was struggling to replicate the finding. The original study reported using a high dye concentration but did not report the exact amount. He had been using a dye concentration that seemed "high" to him, but it was killing all the cells. Emma asked how old his mice were. When he explained that they were between 30- and 50-days old, Emma noted that their age might be the cause of the problem. Cells dye much faster in older mice. She suggested he try the same procedure with much younger mice. He admitted that he was not sure what age he should use. Dr. Harden made it clear that she wanted, "Whatever Stern did. We want to do exactly what Stern did. We want his data."

The goal of this replication was not to "test" Stern. Rather, there was a belief that the results produced by Stern were real. Any inability to *re*produce them would be initially interpreted in terms of some lack of skill or equipment. However, if additional tries to more faithfully replicate the findings continue to fail, skepticism may increase. Yet, even as they may lose faith in a finding, there is rarely a bright line separating truth from falsity. There was a recognition that some findings may be real while being so technically challenging or dependent upon a very specific equipment setup that it might be extremely difficult to replicate while still being true.

They believed this because it happened to them. Zivah had published a highly intriguing study in which she was able to reverse neurons that were directionally selective (i.e., retinal cells that respond more actively from stimuli coming from a particular direction). The outcome was very difficult to achieve in the Harden lab, and the finding did not travel. Other labs had been unable to reproduce the finding. They acknowledged the replication failures as a real problem for the adoption of the technique while continuing to believe the technique to be possible.

Viewing bench-building in terms of integrative replication is important for two reasons. First, it highlights how utterly common replication is in technological fields in a way that science studies scholars have not understood. Rather than a confrontational verification of claims, integrative replication typically occurs as an attempt to incorporate new manipulations into one's practice. Second, integrative replication demonstrates the mundanity of bench-building. It is true that the ultimate shape of the frontier cannot be predicted. In other words, we cannot know what we do not know before we know it. Yet attempting to do what other researchers have already accomplished fixes the desired outcome and makes clear the easily intelligible processes that compose bench-building.

Constraints on Bench-Building

Bench-building requires control: not total control, but enough to extend the horizons of perception and manipulation. Yet this project is beset by challenges. Attention to detail is key. Remembering the temperature of a solution or the age of a particular mouse can provide the key to explaining an anomaly or suggest some intriguing new direction. Sloppy or inattentive practice is one constraint on bench-building. Unlike other constraints, however, this can often be overcome with sufficient rigor. This was Dr. Harden's message during a discussion of how light intensity differs on the lab's rigs.

> DR. HARDEN: "So, the brightest is [rig 1] with no filter? Then [rig 2]?"
> ZIVAH: "Yes."
> DR. HARDEN: "And if you normalize it per square millimeter because it's projected onto a smaller area than on the [rig 2]?"

Zivah admitted that it was a "very good question" but did not know which is the brightest. However, she had recorded some data in which she looked at both rigs with and without their filters in three different wavelengths. Blake noted that he has similar data.

Dr. Harden took a moment to criticize her lab: "This is something we've been very sloppy about in the lab is not knowing what we're stimulating with. Everyone should be very comfortable with knowing the intensities you need to do whatever is the experiment you're doing." The lab was beginning to incorporate some optogenetic techniques, and information about light intensity was no longer something that could be ignored: "When we start doing optogenetics you have to have a sense of, what are the intensities of light . . . like, have numbers in your head as to what these are because it will make a difference as to how you'll do your experiments and whether your experiments are going to work."

Later, Dr. Harden explained that the problem with not knowing these exact figures is that it appears that rods play an important role in the new experiments they want to run, but their current light levels might be "bleaching out" this input. Blake notes that these issues had been happening since he entered the lab. Two former lab members,

Yi and Jeremy, tried the two infrared filters in the lab and ultimately settled on the smaller one. Yi warned Blake not to use the other one because of the bleaching problems: "Yi was, like, 'Don't ever change this. Don't ever lose this.' So, it's annoying because we know that it works but we don't really know why."

However, vigilance alone cannot compensate for all constraints on bench-building. Much of the time, there is simply nothing on which to grab hold. When learning new techniques and introducing new technologies will no longer yield any additional purchase on the object of research, bench-building cannot occur. An indeterminate situation will remain indeterminate if probes produce random results, and its elements remain shrouded.

Unpredictability and non-standardization are two common reasons for this. Within the Harden lab, individual pieces of equipment would sometimes function inconsistently. For several months, the labs micro-pipette puller—the machine that pulled a melting glass tube until it narrowed and eventually broke producing the very fine glass point that was used when manipulating and measuring tissue—was beginning to require near constant calibration to produce standard pipettes. The lab finally bought a new one, and, after a week or so in service, Dr. Harden asked how the lab liked it. Zivah said it was much better. Emma agreed, noting that it was much more consistent. There were still issues, however, regarding the placement of the heating filament and the temperature that should be used the melt the glass. So, they devised a system whereby anyone using the puller records their settings on a Post-it note so that the lab could collectively work toward an ideal temperature.

Although bench-building is propelled by technological developments, new technologies were not always helpful. At times, they contributed to an inability to evaluate research. One of the areas that persistently caused trouble was the proliferation of new mouse strains. When Zivah and Emma were working on an experiment together, Dr. Harden told them about a new mouse that was being developed by the Kartoff lab that was supposed to make it easier to label a class of cells. However, Zivah and Emma were both aware of the mouse and were skeptical. They had heard through back channels that labeling the cells was done inconsistently. Dr. Harden replied, "Don't tell Kartoff that. He spent a lot of money to make this mouse."

Even more challenging were cases in which mice championed by different labs produced competing results. During a discussion about Zivah's experiments on directional selectivity, Dr. Harden interrupted to say that she had heard from a former student who now ran her own lab, that her student's lab has the directional preference of the mice wrong. After a pause, she continued, "Actually we don't know who to believe." A moment later, she explained, "Everybody questions everyone else's mouse. The field's a mess."

In addition to the lack of standardization in technology, researchers often struggled due to the limitations of the object of study. Because the Harden lab experimented on tissue—both *in* and *ex vivo*—they constantly brushed up against the limits of living tissue. When animals needed to be kept alive during experimentation, the lab struggled to reduce the speed and damage of experiments to attain usable data. When the experiments are focused on tissue, the lab tried to support the continuation of natural cellular processes long enough for manipulation and recording.

The delicacy of tissue foreclosed some experimental possibilities. During a presentation by Blake regarding some frustratingly vague research on spontaneous waves of neural activity that propagate across the retina, he told the lab that he was thinking about trying a new method that involved additional surgery. Dr. Harden was skeptical. She did not think he would have the time required. She explained that most of the samples die within 10 seconds after the type of surgery that he wanted to do. Thirty seconds would be lucky. Similarly, during another lab meeting, Dr. Renault, a recent entrant to the lab who had not worked with retinal neurons before, proposed a course of experiments to the lab. A more experienced lab member immediately criticized the proposal for being impractical because it would demand the Dr. Renault make four unique tears in the inner limiting membrane, a prospect he deemed "a nightmare."

Deciding whether problems constituted potential hurdles on a path of eventual success or evidence of insurmountable problems is a key aspect of scientific judgment. Solving a particularly challenging problem could lead to professional success, but investing time and *not* solving it could derail a research career.[11]

One lab member spent a year attempting a manipulation to increase the activity of an enzyme (protein kinase) in starburst amacrine cells (a subtype of retinal amacrine cell). He had just begun to see some movement. Out of the nine cells he had run in the previous week, he had accomplished the desired manipulation in two.

Rather than being pleased, however, Dr. Harden expressed skepticism: "Is it reliable enough?" Two out of nine is a weak success rate, and one of the cells actually reduced protein kinase activity. Moreover, there were still several competing hypotheses for what was actually occurring. She asked him pointedly, "Do you want to keep doing these?" Dr. Harden explained the dilemma: "It's great that you see something, but if you don't see it consistently, it's almost the worst-case scenario because you could waste a lot of time." While he thought it over, she addressed the rest of the lab and told them that, if they ever find themselves in this situation, she will be supportive either way. There are times when diligence and patience are needed to make a breakthrough. However, there are other times when you need to cut your losses and move on: "Sometimes the biology doesn't intersect with our efforts in the way we want."

Ten months later, Stephan's question had evolved to looking at the effect of acetylcholine on retinal waves by stimulating tissue and (in the experimental condition) blocking its expression. Yet his experiments were still yielding little interpretable data.

During his presentation, he showed a recording of one of his experiments to the lab. The video was dark and grainy. The video looked a bit like a car's windshield on a rainy night. Lights from passing cars illuminate part of the windshield before moving across the glass.

Despite its graininess, Dr. Harden was immediately impressed with the image quality and asked to see it again. As he played the video a second time, she asked him to pause: "Look at the upper right corner. There's a cell that goes on late." She reminded him that there were different subclasses of the cells on the screen and delay was one of the ways they are distinguished. As excited as Dr. Harden was by the videos, the following slide was deflating. Stephan showed a plot with the actual data from seven tissue samples. Despite blocking the cholinergic waves, he found no perceptible change in the number of cells involved, an outcome he found "disappointing."

Rather than dismiss the experiment as a failure, however, Dr. Harden wanted to spend a few minutes with the plot. She pointed out that two of the tissue samples in the experimental condition seemed to have significant increases in cell activity

STEPHAN: "Yeah, But I have two that go down."
DR. HARDEN: "But those go up more than those go down. What are the numbers? The highest effect, do you remember? Was it forty-five over . . ."
STEPHAN: "The highest effect was around the twenties."
DR. HARDEN: "Uh huh. So, around twenty-three over twenty?"
STEPHAN: "Or, twenty-six over twenty-two. Something like that."

After this exchange, Stephan moved on to another set of unimpressive findings. The following is a direct excerpt from my field notes:

Somewhere around here, I begin to realize that this talk is a funeral march for failed experiments. He hasn't presented anything of any value so far. Basically, he gave some background, described his experiments, and the presented data that showed his manipulations were having little effect. There just aren't a lot of "findings." He seems somewhat apologetic, and the room is relatively quiet. There just isn't much to talk about when everything fails.

When experimental manipulations do little to sharpen perception or make manipulations more precise, there is little opportunity for progress.

The scientist plans, nature laughs. But not always.

Yet what would become of a science in which such plans were continually frustrated? What if, rather than standing on the shoulders of giants, scientists found only clay idols that could not support their weight? What would a laboratory that engaged in little bench-building look like? The most apparent difference would be the relative absence of cutting-edge technology and sophisticated embodied skill. This is largely what we see in psychology labs.

4

UNBUILT BENCHES IN
PSYCHOLOGY LABORATORIES

I n experimental science, bench-building is the extension of human
intentionality via the introduction of new technologies and the
development of new techniques. Through a cycle in which sharpened perception leads to new manipulative abilities which produces new
indeterminate situations which, in turn, requires sharpened perception
to assess, the horizons of possibility are extended. Bench-building is a
messy process of cybernetic evolution that rarely (but sometimes) yields
new, reliable manipulations. Because it manifests as embodied skill and
research technology, any constraints on bench-building should be visible in relatively low levels of technique and/or technology.

Developmental psychology and social psychology show low levels of development along both dimensions. The growth of psychology was fostered by the emergence of new occupational roles that
drew on physiological methods to empirically address philosophical
questions.[1] This move away from what has been derided as armchair
philosophizing was premised on the idea that the same experimental methods used by physicists would provide a sure path forward.
Yet the history of technological progress in this area has not mirrored
that of the natural sciences on which it is modeled.

Understanding psychology's struggles with bench-building is essential to understanding the difficulties psychology has had in making
technological progress.

THE OBSERVABLE MANIFESTATIONS OF BENCH-BUILDING: TECHNOLOGIES AND SKILLS

Bench-building extends the researcher's capacity to manipulate and/or perceive their object of study through improvements of technique and innovations in technology. There is, of course, a huge diversity of embodied skills and research technologies across scientific laboratories. However, their presence—and their ongoing refinement, elaboration, and transformation—is the most visible indicator of bench-building in labs.

Both skills and technology lend themselves to significant differentiations. Take, for instance, running. As soon as a child begins to walk, they begin falling forward as their exuberance exceeds their ability. Once they gain the dexterity to thrust their back foot forward in time to catch themselves, they have learned to run. This is a basic skill that occurs naturally during development, one that is acquired at a young age and, in most contexts, does not lend itself to much differentiation. Besides sports, there are few times when running particularly fast or slow has any effect on one's life. There are, of course, some specialized contexts in which running is differentiated. American football professionals, for instance, may be expected to have 40-yard dash times at par with others who play their same position. Beyond even this elite level, however, there is a frontier of professional running in which the very boundaries of what is possible for a runner to achieve are pushed. Every move the athlete makes and everything they put into their bodies is tweaked until maximum performance is achieved. New records are still being set, and we do not yet know the limits.

Or, as an example from technology, take the camera. The average consumer can purchase a digital camera that will take beautiful pictures of a graduation or vacation for a few hundred dollars. A professional photographer has higher demands, however, and requires more elaborate camera technology. It may have a higher pixel count, be able to take photos in conditions of low light, or take photos very rapidly. Although these technologies are far superior to consumer cameras, they have definite limits. Beyond this professional grade, however, there is a cutting edge of camera technology in which the possible is continually getting refashioned. For instance, a 570-megapixel camera the size of a refrigerator is currently perched in the Andes helping astronomers look for dark matter, and there is no reason to believe it represents the upper bound of camera technology.

One way to understand the different roles that skill and technology play in laboratory practice is to frame each in terms of floors and ceilings. By floors, I refer to the point at which skills meet "competence" or technologies are "good enough." By ceilings, I refer to upper bounds of skills or technologies. Some have limited room for growth, while other skills or technologies compose the "cutting edge" of a field and have possibilities that are not yet known.

Put together, the floors and ceilings of skills reveal a typology that includes lay skill, professional skill, and, at the frontiers of possibility, the somatic frontier (Figure 4.1).

Lay Skill. Lay skills are those that involve little training and cannot be greatly improved upon. Competence *is* mastery. For instance, when undergraduate volunteers were allowed in the molecular biology lab, they were often recruited or allowed to participate because they brought some specialized skill. They were programmers or had previous experience in bio labs. When they did not, they were given

		Ceiling	
		Low	High
Floor	High	Professional skill	The somatic frontier
	Low	Lay skill	

FIGURE 4.1 The Floors and Ceilings of Embodied Skill

menial tasks appropriate for their lack of skill. For instance, some undergraduates were given dissected retinas by lab members which they then dipped in various solutions in a process, I was told, that "doesn't take very much skill."

Professional Skill. All competent members of the lab are expected to have certain, specialized skills. Being able to set up rigs and dissect their own animals was a requirement. Such professional-level skill does not indicate any unique ability. *Mere* competence is a requirement of participating but not an indicator of excellence or special ability. Moreover, once these basic skills have been achieved, there can be limited room for improvement.

The Somatic Frontier. Although many lab skills do not allow for displays of virtuosity, there are situations in which having "golden hands" is considered very valuable. Basic dissection is an area where competence is easily achieved. However, more advanced surgical techniques allow researchers to accomplish challenging procedures. Building, debugging, and repairing equipment is another area in which skills can be differentiated. Although everyone can tighten a screw when a lever comes loose, far fewer can open the machines or build them from components. Because the somatic frontier is, by definition, unsettled and tied to an individual body, it can create problems in both communicating and diffusing the skills.

In a parallel typology, the floors and ceilings of technology include consumer grade, professional grade, and, on the bleeding edge, the material frontier (Figure 4.2).

		Ceiling	
		Low	High
Floor	High	Professional grade	The material frontier
	Low	Consumer grade	

FIGURE 4.2 The Floors and Ceilings of Technology

Consumer Grade. Most of the items used in all labs are essentially consumer grade. Computers, cameras, and audio recording technology are all technologies that could be purchased "off the rack" and do not represent either a high barrier to entrance or an opportunity for differentiation. The quality of the data in a video-recorded social psychological experiment would not be markedly improved if the experimenter used an expensive, high-resolution camera rather than a mass-produced personal camcorder, for instance.

Professional Grade. Some pieces of equipment may be quite expensive, specialized, and considered necessary for entrance into the professional field, yet, beyond minimum standards, they are not differentiated by quality. Many support technologies in the cell biology lab were like this. For instance, manipulators were machines with dials used to precisely maneuver the electrodes. Although the breakdown and wonkiness of even professional grade equipment was a constant issue, there were rarely discussions about getting the "newest" or "best" equipment in this domain since, like consumer-grade equipment, "good enough" is all that is needed

The Material Frontier. At the material frontier, the very possibilities of technology are pushed. Technologies that extend perception create images or sounds that are clearer and more nuanced. Technologies that extend human action are made faster and more exacting. Technologies are combined in ways that create entirely new modalities of perception of action. Pieces of professional grade technology can be given new functionality through the ongoing integration of new technologies. Thus, the ability of a microscope changes with the inclusion of new genetically altered animals, dyes, and stimulation technologies.[2]

In the previous chapter, the cell biologists spent an enormous amount of effort developing and refining their skills and buying and building new technologies. They were constantly pushing into the unknowns of the somatic and material frontiers. For psychologists, on the other hand, the situation is entirely different.

PSYCHOLOGICAL TECHNOLOGY

Edward B. Titchener, who was responsible for importing William Wundt's experimental psychology into the United States in the late nineteenth century, was deeply interested in the material culture of psychology laboratories. At the turn of the 19th century, Titchener lamented that no article had done the work of describing how psychology laboratories function. This was essentially significant, he argued, since the introduction of the experimental method into psychology brought about a "revolution, radical and far-reaching."[3]

In one passage, as striking for its confident prescriptions as it is for its advocacy of old-timey experimental technologies, Titchener gives advice for starting a psychology laboratory on a budget:

> If I were compelled to name a definite limiting sum, I should, I think, make it £30. For £10 you can get one or two good pieces: the Ellis-Helmholtz harmonical, or the Marbe colour mixer, or a Zwaardemaker double olfactometer with solutions, or a triad of colour wheels and a reliable aesthesiometer, or a Stumpf interval apparatus, or a set of Appunn forks; and the remaining £20 will go some distance towards a series of instruments for drill work, more especially if you have a carpenter at hand and make your memory-drops and fall chronometers and so forth at home.[4]

In the two decades that followed, Titchener's interest in the material aspects of laboratory work did not wane. His magnum opus, *Experimental Psychology*, was subtitled *A Manual of Laboratory Practice*.[5] Rather than focus on the major psychological findings of the day, it contained detailed sketches of the equipment involved in early, influential psychological experiments (e.g., Figure 4.3).

However, in the intervening century, the condition of most psychological laboratories remained so comparatively underdeveloped technologically that one commentator argued that, as it stands,

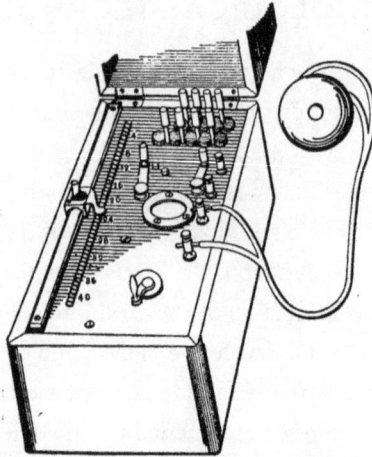

FIG. 9.—Seashore's audiometer. Sold by
the C. H. Stoelting Co.; price about $50.

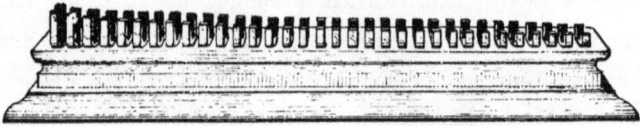

Fig. 5.—Appunn's series of high forks, for the determination of the qualitative
TR. The forks are actuated by bowing across the tops of the tines.

FIGURE 4.3

"The lab is a virtual space and, in most respects, co-extensive with the experiment."[6] Although both social and developmental psychology labs were, in general, less elaborate than the biology lab, there are telling differences between the two.

The Material Culture of Social Psychology

As evidenced by the increasing use of online experiments,[7] much social psychological research is not confined to a specific space. Moreover, the desire for more "naturalistic" data often leads social psychologists out of the lab. For instance, one study conducted by a graduate student of Dr. Wagner's attempted to elicit pride from undergraduate subjects by taking them out of the lab and walking them near important landmarks at their university.

Yet even when social psychological studies did take place within the lab, there was little that was specific to the lab-space. It was merely a room where the researcher could set up some chairs, a table, and a video camera. Of course, every social psychological experiment involves *some* form of material technology. At the most basic, it might be a pencil and paper. However, there are domains of social psychological methodology which involve move advanced forms of technology. There are new computer programs that promise to standardize the collection of FACS data (i.e., the coding of expressions based on facial muscles). Implicit association tests, which attempt to measure implicit bias by comparing reaction times to pairs of descriptors, require computers and specialized software.

Some researchers have worked with software developers to create applications for smartphones. This allows them to query subjects throughout the day rather than be limited to questions within a laboratory setting. One of the graduate students I observed gathered some simple, non-invasive physiological data before the experiment (although the equipment, from medical and research supply company BIOPAC, was largely a black box to those who used it).

The comparatively minor role of technology was evidenced in a brief discussion that occurred at the end of a lab meeting in late December. Dr. Wagner told the room that he had $12,000 left to spend on a grant that was expiring at the end of the year. He asked the room if they had any suggestions. Derick, a graduate student, suggested the lab buy more machines that measure physiological responses. Ellie agreed and recommended buying a kit to start measuring the hormone oxytocin. Dr. Wagner asked if they needed to improve their audio/visual equipment. Dr. Schmidt, a postdoc, argued that their microphones could use an upgrade. The ones the lab owned were room mics that picked up a lot of ambient noise. She suggested they buy lavalier microphones (the small clip-on microphones used by TV news anchors). Dr. Wagner asked if they needed new computers. Derick said they only have one working computer now. They could use another. Ellie said the problem was that everyone stores all their data on the computers. Rather than new computers, she suggested they invest in cloud storage. Derick wondered if cloud storage might violate some privacy rules. Ellie replied that other labs store their data in the cloud, but Derick pointed out that other labs store survey data which is more anonymous than the types of video data their lab uses.

At the end of this back and forth, the lab members had made their pitches. They asked for new biological tests, better audio recording technology, newer computers, and more storage. Only the first, the oxytocin test, would open the lab up to a new research area. The problem was that Ellie, who would soon be graduating, was the only member of the lab who used the physiological equipment the lab already owned. The other purchases solved minor annoyances which, as I discussed last chapter, are in integral part of bench-building. However, all of these—audio, computers, storage—represent low-ceiling technologies. The goal was not to get to the cutting-edge of audio or computer technology but only to achieve a baseline of functionality. Moreover, they were not in the service of *other* cutting-edge technologies. The Harden lab's purchase of a new pipette puller was not going to open new experimental vistas for them. It was just one piece of low ceiling technology. Yet it was in service of other pieces of high ceiling technology. The same was not true in the social psychology labs I observed.

Although these social psychology labs relied little on material technology, their practice was heavily organized by non-material technologies. I refer here to things like the scales, tests, prompts, and primes frequently used by members of the field. Although these tools were frequent sources of frustration, they provided a measure of integration for a field which has little in the way of methodological orthodoxy.

However, the nature of these technologies actually served to disincentivize technological advancements. Rather than objects of ongoing focus by researchers hoping to refine and end their power, the mere presence of these popular experimental technologies made researchers less likely to either develop competing measures or hone existing ones.

For instance, Deng, a graduate student in the Wagner lab, wanted some feedback on a study he was planning. The study was concerned with perceptions of time. The only scale already in use was created by a highly regarded social psychologist. However, when the lab collectively looked at the scale and its questions, they were very critical. They felt the questions were repetitive and did a poor job of capturing the different facets of time perspective. Hannah exclaimed, "It always gets me when you see a scale in print and then you see the items and, it's like, that's not measuring that at all!" Dr. Wagner sympathized that it happens "All the time." They briefly discussed developing their own scale but there was little enthusiasm for this. Later, when I asked Deng about it, he explained his reservation:

> Developing your own would take forever. Another five studies and then publish it. Then go through reviews. That would be a year or two years. Forget it. I'm not going to do that [. . .] Hers is well used. A lot of people use it. It's a big name person. Nobody can give you crap about using a big name person's scale even if it's not quote unquote the best scale.

Rather than improve the scale, a risky proposition, he believed it made more sense to simply use the flawed scale because of its ubiquity and acceptance. Of course, this gamble, between following traditional research trajectories or pursuing innovative research strategies,[8] exists in every science. Yet the possibility of only marginal improvement over previous technologies creates a disincentive to pursue them.

Importantly, investments in technology were sometimes seen as risky, since figuring it out, setting it up, troubleshooting, and collecting potentially hard-to-interpret data all diverted attention away from more standard forms of productivity. For instance, Ellie's request for oxytocin tests would demand that the lab devote major resources to learning how to use a new technology and how to interpret the data it produced. Ellie, herself, had already undergone a similar struggle when learning to use the BIOPAC system which she had to learn mostly on her own: "I dealt with a lot of it on my own which, in some ways, is really exciting because it makes me feel pride, but, in other ways, it's been very painful and has hurt my publication record because I took way longer than if I was just asking people to fill out surveys and stuff." Similarly, Mary, who had a background working in a biological laboratory before beginning her PhD in psychology, was initially interested in learning fMRI imaging in addition to more traditional psychological methods. However, she had come to the realization, "I can't do both."

The Material Culture of Developmental Psychology

For infants a few weeks or months old, experimental techniques are very limited. The most popular choice in the labs I observed measured the infant's "looking time" when presented with stimuli. However, Dr. Deborah Collins, who helmed the largest developmental lab I observed, studied a range of children from newborns to four- and five-year-old kids. The older the child, the more inventive and interactive the study could be. Rather than merely observe their looking time, older subjects are active participants in the experiment. In one experiment, for example, a researcher hid a toy in a box with twelve drawers in order to see if children of different ages could remember the placement after some intervening tasks. In another, the experimenter put four buckets in a room and then showed his toddler subjects a map which revealed which bucked contained a toy to test if the toddler could understand the map's symbolic representation. Neither experiment required any specialized technology.

Like social psychology labs, psychologists who do research on toddlers sometimes "create" their lab space anew for each experiment. An empty room is transformed into a "lab" by the presence of an experimenter, a subject, an object that serves as focus, and some recording technology. However, creating experiments for toddlers has its own technical challenges. Specifically, it was necessary that the experiment was both easy enough for the toddler to accomplish while being challenging enough to maintain their interest. If it is too easy they get bored. If it is too difficult they get frustrated.

In one experiment, which was basically a shell game designed to test executive function (i.e., the ability to control one's attention), the toddlers were having trouble taking the lids off plastic cups that either contained a toy or were empty. When the kids chose a cup and couldn't take the lid off, they then tried a second cup to see if it was easier. This made coding difficult because coders were unsure exactly what to label a "choice." The team running the experiment spent a few hours loosening the lids to ensure the problem would be avoided. In another case, Sarah was demonstrating a memory task for toddlers involving cups with toys in them taped to a Lazy Susan. However, she told Dr. Collins that the infants were getting distracted by the tape and would not engage with the experiment. Dr. Collins said "Let me be a baby. How does this work?" They then went through the experiment slowly together and developed a number of suggestions including putting a more desirable toy in the cups and replacing the distracting tape with Velcro.

Although experiments need to be easy enough for the subjects to understand, they also had to be complex enough to keep their attention. In one study, researchers were planning on comparing the abilities of toddlers, three months apart, to successfully complete a reasoning task. To their frustration, the experimenters could not keep the older children interested and they were, counterintuitively, performing worse than the younger subjects. Dr. Collins suggested hiding the object in a recently created experimental device specifically designed to be more motivating for older toddlers, the "jingle box." Dr. Collins explained, "These kids love the jingle box. It's hilarious."

When the research aims to experiment on younger populations, options are reduced, and developmental psychologists tend to turn toward more standard methods like measuring looking time. For instance, the Hill lab only studied children up to twelve-months-old. Rather than emphasize flexible spaces, their two experimental rooms were designed around permanent pieces of research equipment— plywood puppet stages with outward-facing cameras built into them. Different experiments altered the action on the stage but the stage itself remained unchanged.

Although many of the methods in developmental cognition studies have become relatively stagnant, at times developmental labs integrate new technologies. A third developmental psychology lab I observed, run by Dr. Geller, had purchased an "eye tracker" which promised to automate coding and provide more detailed information about eye movement than simple "look/no look" which was how most of these studies were coded. Similarly, the Hill lab bought brain imaging equipment. However, in both these cases, the new technologies proved difficult to integrate.

After getting the eye tracker set up, they ran some test subjects to see what sort of output would be produced. When asked for a progress report by Dr. Geller, the graduate student in charge of the project complained that they were having problems transferring video from the hardware to the computer. More troublingly, she noted that it was producing lots of "pretty charts" but no interpretable data. Specifically, moving from a binary coding scheme to a far more complex scheme created a good deal of ambiguity regarding what counted as a "look."

Similarly, the Hill lab had received a grant to purchase a near-infrared spectroscope (NIRS) which tracks changes in the concentration of hemoglobin on the cortex. These changes, in turn, are associated with neural activity. Although NIRS is a limited method due to its inability to detect changes below the cortical surface, it is non-invasive and allows the subject to move during the experiment which are both requirements when experimenting on infants. It looks like a shower cap with electrodes spaced every inch or so connected to a rack of signal processing machines. Unfortunately for the Hill lab, it also produced data that were hard to interpret. Dr. Hill paid for Cassandra to attend a conference and training session on NIRS.

Three years after purchasing the eye tracker, the technology was used in just one of the 31 papers the Geller lab published. Over that same period, NIRS data had been used in zero published studies by the Hill lab, and the machine was gathering dust in a closet.

Naturally, not all labs have such struggles. The Collins lab also purchased an eye tracker, and, although it produced the same frustrations that all technologies do, several lab members were able to use it fruitfully. Two points need to be made in reference to this, however. First, labs were not required to integrate the new technologies. It allowed them to enter new niches, but it was not necessary to their survival. Even members of the Collins lab who knew how to use the eye tracker were dissuaded from using it when it did not contribute in some fundamental way to the experiment because it took more time to set up and created more room for technological error.

Second, and more importantly, as in social psychology, making use of new technologies often requires that researchers have specialized skills. This can take time away from more professionally profitable endeavors. Members of the Collins lab who worked effectively with the eye tracker had learned to code in MATLAB, technical software used by scientists to visualize and model data. However, when the technology is not necessary to success in the field, there was a risk of devoting too much time to learning technical skills and troubleshooting janky technologies rather than running original studies using easier and more widely accepted methods.

For instance, when she was a postdoc, Dr. Kidder had done some experiments which, as one measure, included data on the subject's heart rates. Although she was still interested in gathering physiological data, she noted that it was "very labor intensive and time consuming" and, thus, she avoided using those methods because "I had to get tenure." Likewise, Sarah had done neuroimaging studies in the past and was interested in using those methods as an offshoot to purely behavioral projects. However, she did not know when she would have the time to do that: "I've got enough going on here!"

TECHNIQUE IN PSYCHOLOGY

In the conclusion of Titchener's account of the psychology laboratory, he admits the field still lags behind the natural sciences in the production of great theoretical discoveries: "There is nothing epoch-making about current laboratory work: Psychologists have not yet discovered their argon or their Röntgen rays: but it is none the less work, work whose methods get discussed and assimilated, and whose results gradually alter the face of the science. In brief, the two things that come out of the physical or chemical laboratory, precisely those two things come out of the psychological,—trained workers and original work."[9] Even in the absence of major theoretical advances, Titchener argued that the production of technically sophisticated psychological experimenters still represented a major product of the field. In this section, we address the meaning of technique in experimental psychology.

Harry Collins, who popularized the concept of tacit knowledge within science studies,[10] noted that in the intervening decades the term has been used to describe such diverse forms of behavior that there was a pressing need to clarify the concept. In response, he developed a typology that included "somatic" and "collective" forms of tacit knowledge.[11] Somatic tacit knowledge is the paradigmatic form described in Michael Polanyi's (1958) classic example of learning how to ride a bike. Explicit instruction is insufficient to teach a somatic tacit skill. Simply put, almost no one learns to box, play an instrument, or build a TEA laser without prolonged practice boxing, playing, and building[12]. Certainly, guidance is helpful, but without physical engagement, learning will typically not happen. Crucially, this does not mean these behaviors are somehow beyond mechanization. Just because humans cannot learn some skills through explicit instruction does not mean that explication is impossible. The nature of physical actions, even highly skilled behaviors, is essentially mechanical and, therefore, explicable.

Collective tacit knowledge, on the other hand, is akin to learning what Pierre Bourdieu called a habitus, a way of life embodied and enacted.[13] If the paradigmatic example of somatic tacit knowledge is learning to ride a bicycle, collective tacit knowledge might be compared to learning to ride a bicycle through a city. This involves learning the subtle rules of appropriateness that govern specific contexts. Bikers may be physically able to ride full speed through a crowd of pedestrians, but they will elicit anger if they do so.

Unlike somatic tacit knowledge, which is based on physical activity, collective tacit knowledge is rooted in the fluid dynamics of collective judgment. This is the elusive form of tacit knowledge that allows individuals to be skillful social actors; to be graceful, tasteful, polite, and germane. Collins argues that it is currently inconceivable to explicate or mechanize collective tacit knowledge.

Significantly different patterns of development of non-cognitive, tacit knowledge between fields has been overlooked. Collective tacit knowledge—the skills involved in designing convincing experiments, framing findings, and otherwise learning how to operate successfully within a field—is a concern in all fields. However, the role of somatic tacit knowledge is far more limited in the psychological fields I observed than in molecular biology.

Tacit Knowledge in Social Psychology

I asked several social psychologists if they had any technical skills. Dr. Wright, a postdoc whose work has been summarized in the *New York Times*, *PBS NewsHour*, and other popular media outlets answered "no" and added, "I don't think I got trained in anything. One thing I got trained to do was to think like a social psychologist and learn how to write papers." Social psychologists rarely get training meant to increase their somatic tacit knowledge. They learn the habitus of their field, the collective tacit knowledge that will allow them to be full members of their community. They learn to "think" and "write papers" like social psychologists. They develop statistical skills, and some may become excellent at designing novel experiments. But these skills do not produce reliable manipulations. Unlike molecular biology, where physical and technical skill is vital, the research practice of social psychologists is largely disembodied.

Although my observations generally support a kernel of the sentiment expressed by the postdoc above, it is a bit of a simplification. When I asked other social psychologists about their skills, they mentioned a variety of skills they had or were hoping to learn including new statistical techniques, programming, and methods for collecting and analyzing physiological data. Others responded by telling me they had good organizational or "people skills." In general, social psychologists have few *embodied* skills, and, in the rare cases where they do, they tend to be low-ceiling skills. That is, they gain skills where mere competence is all that can be achieved.

Although the lack of technology and physical engagement with their research object make *embodied* skill a rarity, the social psychologists I studied did learn other sorts of skills beyond statistics (which was a common skill among all labs studied). Several members of Dr. Wagner's social psychology lab were trained in the Facial Action Coding System (FACS).

FACS is a method for coding human facial expressions and is the integration of two lines of research. The first, developed by Swedish anatomist Carl-Herman Hjortsjö, is research on expressions and facial muscles. The second, from psychologists Paul Ekman and Wallace V. Friesen, looks at the cultural uniformity in expression.[14] Coding mainly revolved around recording changes in "action units" (AUs) and their intensity. There are 46 AUs, and most are based on facial musculature. For instance, AU 12 is the "Lip Corner Puller" that is activated by a contraction of the zygomaticus major, a muscle in the upper cheek used when smiling. In addition to coding AUs, which tells researchers where on the face activity is happening, intensity coding produces a measure of strength. It ranges from A (trace), B (slight), C (Marked or Pronounced), D (Severe or Extreme), to E (Maximum). Additionally, there are head movement codes, eye movement codes, visibility codes (if certain things are not visible), and gross behavior codes (things like sniffing). FACS has since been modified and used for research in other primates including chimpanzees, macaques, gibbons, and even non-primate mammals like dogs.[15]

The primary function of FACS training seemed to be as a signal of competence. Although a psychologist could learn FACS and successfully apply it without getting certified, without the certification, they could not claim to have used the method. Thus, the certification allowed researchers to lay claim to a type of expertise. It is significant to mention that, although FACS was considered a rigorous way of coding facial expression and emotion, it was not the only way of coding. In cases where the lab member was not FACS certified, he or she would typically train undergraduate coders to simply judge instances of an emotion of interest. Thus, although FACS training was considered helpful, it was, in no way, necessary to the work that the lab was doing.

Although not common in the labs I observed, a few lab members were trained to collect basic physiological data. Unlike FACS, there was no official certification. Two things should be noted, however. First, these sorts of noninvasive measures are old, crude, and do not support displays of technical virtuosity. This is not meant to demean. Many old, crude, and mundane skills are extremely important for research. Yet this is not an active frontier of development in these labs.

Second, basic "physio" was never a central variable. The primary outcome of interest was never, for instance, heart rate. Instead, the outcome of interest may be, say, excitement with heart rate serving as one indicator among others captured through visual coding and subjective reports. Moreover, because it was such a specialized skill within the lab, it rarely became a topic of collective focus even when such variables were available. For instance, when Ellie, a graduate student of Dr. Wagner, detailed a set of studies she was running, she waited until after explaining the entire experiment before casually mentioning that she also took "baseline physio" before each experiment. During the lab meeting that focused on her project, those measures were not discussed at all.

Perhaps the clearest evidence that much of social psychology is characterized by disembodied practice is the growing use of online experiments in social psychology.[16] Using platforms like Amazon.com's Mechanical Turk (MTurk), researchers gain access to a large, geographically diverse population. This method is attractive because it is far less expensive and easier than recruiting live subjects while providing a population that is more representative and, thus, not limited to the narrow subject pool of undergraduate subjects psychologists have traditionally relied upon.[17] The use of online research platforms was described as a "game-changer" by several members of social psychology labs. Instead of spending an entire semester collecting data for study, they could run dozens of subjects in a few hours. As Allison explained, "In my first year in grad school, there was no MTurk, and running a study would take a semester just to get eighty people into the lab to fill out a survey. Now, it takes an afternoon, and you can analyze that data that night and have an answer for your advisor in the morning."

However, by embracing this remote source of data-gathering, they have committed themselves to filtering all aspects of their experiment through the medium of the internet, the restrictions of the online platform, and the subject's equipment and environment. They lose all "hands on" access to the object of their inquiry. Greta, a graduate student in social psychology, was running a study on MTurk that involved the subjects reacting to a recording of a laugh. She explained that she was unhappy that some subjects might be listening to the laugh on cheap laptop speakers in a loud room while others may be listening through expensive headphones, but she acknowledged that there was little that she could do about it. When she presented her data to the lab four months after our exchange, she did not mention these concerns.

Tacit Knowledge in Developmental Psychology

In my observations of molecular biology labs, the term "hands" was used to denote the high levels of somatic tacit knowledge necessary to dissect animals, build equipment, and perform experiments. In contrast, "hands" is colloquially used as a synecdoche for generic, unskilled laborers (e.g., "all hands on deck"). In the developmental psychology labs, this is the role that many members have. For instance, because running experiments on infants required workers to help send out recruitment mail, schedule and confirm subjects, babysit siblings, and clean up the lab, Dr. Hill frequently referred to her ongoing need for "warm bodies" to keep the lab running. There were tasks that required some limited training, but the functioning of the lab required a reliable stream of undergraduate volunteers to do the many ongoing tasks that involved little to no research skill. The lack of skill among many of her volunteers did not bother Dr. Hill. She explained that her lab accommodated the interest level of the volunteers. Those who were excited by the work or interested in potentially going to graduate school were taught to run experiments—in rare cases, promising undergraduates were even allowed to collect their own data for senior theses. Those less interested, on the other hand, would be given less-intellectual tasks.

Because of the need for warm bodies, I was often recruited to work in the developmental psychology labs. Although the physical skills needed to perform these tasks varied, none could be deemed challenging. For instance, when the volunteer scheduled to be a second coder didn't show up for an experiment, I was enlisted. Dr. Parker explained my role in about fifteen seconds. I was to look at the monitor and press a button on a computer keyboard when the infant was looking at the stage and release the button when they were not. The following is an excerpt of my field notes from that first day:

> The job was stupidly simple. When the experimenter (Jen) said "go" we watched our monitors, holding the shift button that had a small, paper happy face taped onto it whenever the child looked at the stage and releasing when they looked away. After the trial (usually thirty seconds to a minute or two), a beep would indicate we could stop coding until the next "go." This was literally the extent of my job. Carly (and later, the other undergraduate coder, a girl named Emily) did a bit more. They pressed a button on another computer to indicate that a certain trial was over and also made some marks on a coding sheet to indicate if anything strange happened. For instance, our first baby sneezed during a trial and she wrote that down. The whole time we're working, a DVD is recoding the monitor.
>
> When I sat down, the first child began his trials. He was just three months old and was accompanied by his mom who looked educated and middle class. The coding was extremely difficult. He was fussy, crying off and on, and was generally pretty fidgety. I was told that three months is about the youngest psychologists can test and that's the youngest they deal with in that lab. The experimenter repeatedly tried to get the infant's attention by banging on the stage and making odd clicking sounds with her mouth. They did the same thing with the older child later. Only once the child was looking did the experiment proceed.
>
> At some point during the test, the experimenter signed to Jen that I needed to move so she could see my monitor. I guess she uses it to see what the baby is doing.
>
> When the first baby wasn't working, they gave the mother a chance to feed him. Jen made a comment that he was a "horrible" baby prompting Cassandra to jokingly (but somewhat seriously) tell her that no

babies were "horrible," indicating that the parent was just outside the room and could potentially her them. Jen quickly corrected herself, saying he was a difficult subject.

Meanwhile, another infant boy was in the main room, and Cassandra went out to talk to them. She complemented the baby saying, "He has the biggest smile ever! So cute!" The dad of this boy (an elven-month old boy) asked if they really notice differences between babies. Cassandra tells him that they're not looking for differences between individual babies. I guess this means they're only interested in differences between classes of babies where class is reducible to objective time.

The 10:30 baby (the three-month old) was still getting tested at 11:15 which made the other baby wait. She needed to change his diapers and did it on the counter in the lab.

During the experiments themselves, they ask the parent to close their eyes during the test. Lindsay told me this was for publication. I guess they are worried about the mother's subconsciously guiding the child's attention.

[. . .]

It's difficult to say how hard the coding is. After the two babies left, we had some down time, and Alissa told me what I'd scored (the computer calculates reliability immediately after the trial). On the first baby (the three-month-old), we got 87 percent reliability which is below the threshold. I think they were planning to recode it. The second, however, we got a 97 percent reliability which is pretty good, and she said I'd be fine.

Admittedly, there was a bit of a learning curve. We did, after all, fail to reach the 90 percent threshold for intercoder reliability in my first try. However, I only ever dipped below 90 percent twice after my first time—once, when I had not realized that the experiment had started and a second time when the child was extremely fidgety and frequently fell out of frame. Later, I was trained to perform the lead coder role. It was the same as second coder with the addition of some document management tasks.

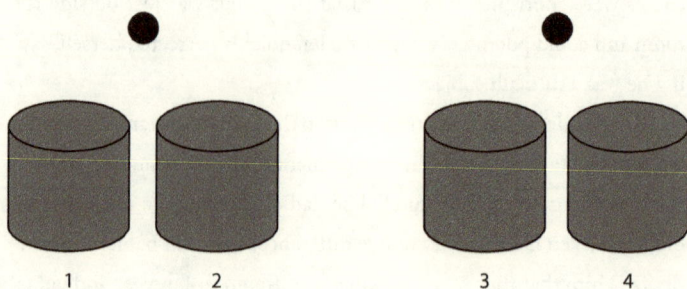

FIGURE 4.4 Four Empty Buckets and Two Balls

Running experiments is more challenging than coding looking-time experiments, but it is not a rarified skill. For instance, in Dr. Collins' lab, I ran an experiment designed by Vani, one of her graduate students. The task involved hiding two balls in a set of buckets and seeing if a seventeen-month-old child could infer which bucket the ball was in. The goal was to play a "game" with the child in which she wants to find the ball with some clues from me. I began by sitting cross-legged on the ground while her parent held her on her lap. Then I showed her two buckets to my left and two to my right (Figure 4.4).

Then I put a long cardboard divider in front of them and took out two balls to show the subject. After the subject sees the balls, I put a ball in one of the buckets on the right with that hand and, at the same time, put the other in one of the buckets on the left (Figure 4.5). This occurred behind the screen, so the child did not know which bucket each ball was in.

Then I lowered the screen and tilted one of the empty buckets toward the subjects before replacing it (Figure 4.6).

I asked the subject to find the ball (Figure 4.7).

Finally, the parent was told to let the child get up to find the ball.

At this point, the logic can be laid out. There are two balls and four buckets. One of the balls is in either bucket one or two and the other is in either three or four. However, I showed the subject the

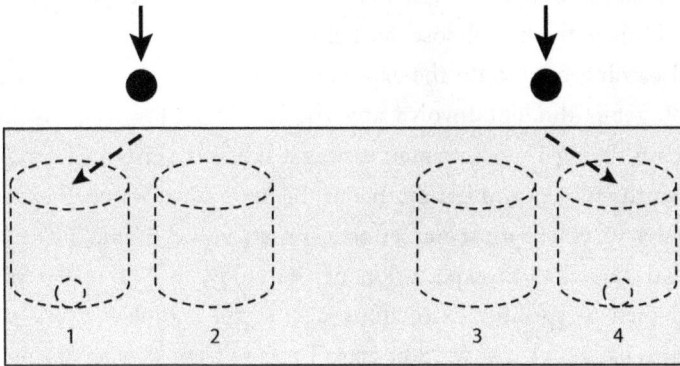

FIGURE 4.5 The Two Balls are Put in the Buckets Behind the Partition

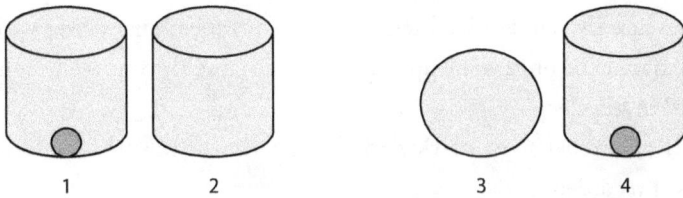

FIGURE 4.6 Revealing One Empty Bucket

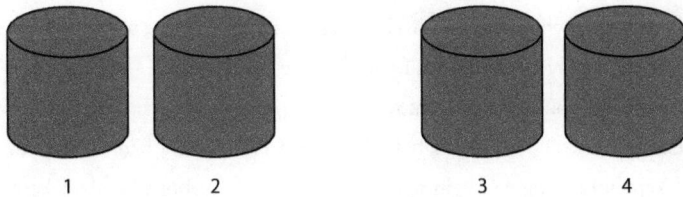

FIGURE 4.7 Two Balls Hidden in Four Buckets

empty bucket three. Given the available information, she only has a 50 percent of finding the ball by searching buckets on the left side and 100 percent chance by looking on the right and utilizing the knowledge that bucket three was empty. Vani's question was, can seventeen-month-old toddlers do the simple logical operations that would allow them to choose most efficiently?

Learning how to do the experiment was more challenging than coding but did not involve any special skill. However, my first attempt being the experimenter was a mess. It started as soon as I met the subject and her mother at the door. I had watched experimenter after experimenter effortlessly steer the interaction from casual chit-chat to explanation of the study, to IRB paperwork, and then to specific instructions. Yet, in the moment, every part our exchange felt awkward because I was self-consciously trying to complete every task. Later, in a conversation with Vani and Sarah, another graduate student, they sympathized with the first-time jitters. Sarah explained that she overcame the awkwardness by having a heavily standardized script that she practiced many times. She joked that she once woke up her partner because she was reciting her spiel in her sleep.

If my exchange was awkward, the experiment was worse. Here is how I recorded it:

> After two pre-trial tests I moved on to the test. Like the interaction with mom, it felt like a mess. I had a hard time getting the barrier between the child and the two buckets to stay up. I forgot to remind the mom to hold her child until I gave her the "all clear" and she jumped at the buckets as soon as I removed the barrier (before I showed her the empty bucket). I accidentally looked toward the hand I had the ball in. I kept forgetting to begin with the ball equally in both hands. I kept using the same tone of voice I use with my dog ("Where's the ball?! Can you find the ball?!). Overall, I just kept noticing mistakes as they happened, feeling terrible, and trying to continue as though everything was copacetic.
>
> Either because of my incompetence or her age, the subject didn't enjoy the game much. The first round of "trials" she came too soon (when I forgot to tell the mom to hold her). Then, she stopped coming

over to look for the ball altogether. She just headed for the black curtains that divided the room and hid equipment set up for a different
experiment. I tried to get her back by playing the simpler game of
rolling the ball back and forth again. She started playing with me and
I decided to give the test another shot.

On this try, she just wandered around for maybe forty-five seconds
and eventually stumbled toward the correct bucket. Later, when Vani
and I were reviewing the recording (a painful event) she counted it as a
successful trial. Did she know what she was doing? Frankly, I'm highly
dubious. She didn't even seem like she was going "toward the bucket."
She looked like she was walking toward the curtain and suddenly saw
the ball in the bucket when she was on top of it.

In the next try she got it immediately. The next two trials didn't
work at all. She had clearly lost interest or simply didn't understand the
game and just wandered around the room. The video is focused on me,
so Vani didn't know what was going on, but the subject just kept wan-
dering in the back of the room, out of view of the camera.

After we got through the four trials, I said it was over, and we left
the room.

When Vani and I looked over the tape, she criticized me on a couple of protocol failures. I was only supposed to use three, precisely
worded phrases ("Look!", "Watch this!", and "Can you find it? Can
you find the ball?"). Instead, I used natural language to direct the
child. Also, I was supposed to change the location of the hidden ball
in an exact sequence, predetermined to avoid perseveration, an outcome in which a subject gets fixated and could result in them choosing the same bucket over and over again. But, although I felt like
it had been terrible, Vani said it was mostly a good experiment and
complemented my "child voice." When I reran the study the next day,
I used her phrases and remembered to change up the buckets. After
I was finished, Vani told me it was "perfect." My physical skill in that
domain had achieved proficiency after less than an hour of practice.

Even the creation of the experimental equipment is not a particularly specialized skill. Dr. Hill told me that her husband, a non-psychologist, had built all her stages during a period of unemployment. Many of the props used for stimuli were purchased from toy companies. For props that needed to be specially created, there was a bookshelf full of crafting items.

Of course, the ability to conduct research on children at all can be thought of as a skill. After a practice job talk by Shanti, a post doc in her lab, Dr. Geller criticized her for not highlighting her skill in getting usable data working with infant subjects. Because her interview was in a department that primarily housed linguists and cognitive psychologists who studied adults, she told her to emphasize the fact that children are a unique population who provide access to particular types of data. Moreover, children are a very difficult population: "To find a behavior that allows measurement—that's a science and art in and of itself." There was marked variation between researchers in their skill in handling children. Some seemed to be uncomfortable with children and spoke primarily to their parents. Others were far more at ease and could quickly establish rapport.

In some ways, this differentiation of skill appears similar to the differences in tacit skill long discussed by science studies scholars.[18] However, this is a facile comparison. While one may improve being "good with kids" by learning various techniques, the personality of the researcher was an undeniably important element. Warmth and extroversion were especially crucial. More to the point, however, even the researchers who were the most skilled at dealing with children did not control them or reliably manipulate them. The very idea of a "frontier" of technique in this area is plainly wrong. It is a low ceiling skill. It is telling that none of the labs in developmental psychology offered any explicit training for working with young children.

Interactions as Skill, Interior Design as Technology

Neither social nor developmental cognition studies *require* highly elaborated lab spaces or advanced skills. Yet it would be a mistake to limit the discussion to specific research technologies. Inasmuch as it is oriented toward producing an experimental end, the entire lab environment can be considered part of the experiment. This includes at least two other categories not addressed—scripted interactions designed to manipulate subjects and research environments designed to elicit desired states.

Scripted interactions. Because many social psychology experiments attempt to manipulate subjects, they require that research assistants act as a type of social machinery. In either the role of "experimenter" or as a confederate subject, the research assistant becomes a type of interaction machine that uses the guise of natural interaction to produce some change in the subject.

In one experiment, two "subjects" (one actual subject and one confederate posing as a second subject) were performing an "experiment" (a decoy task meant to obscure the real experiment) on two computers facing opposite directions. When the subject's computer "broke" (a planned part of the experiment), the other person "fixed" it (pressed a sequence of keys programmed to allow the computer to return to the fake task). The actual experiment was looking at how subjects expressed gratitude. The air quotes highlight the fact that the experiment depends upon creating a false reality for the subject, one with features that can be manipulated.

Allison described these types of experiments as a "An hour-long play that happens on the hour every hour where the experimenter has a set of lines that they need to deliver." However, interactions can only function as technologies if the subject believes they are occurring naturally. Once the subject's suspicious is raised, once the subject begins to think that their "partner" is actually a part of the experiment itself, that becomes impossible. Thus, Allison explains, "The confederate has to be believable every time. And then they must have a pretty controlled interaction with the participant every time." Yet there is a natural tension between these two. Natural interactions are organic and unpredictable while experiments are supposed to be neither.

Writing scripted interaction and being able to perform them in a way that does not immediately arouse suspicion is a skill. Writing them requires a sensitive intuition of how subjects will react to specific types of situations. Performing them means being able to "act" in a way that will not be detected. These are low-ceiling skills, however. While it is important to be able to perform these actions competently, there are obvious limitations on the power that either a script or confederate can exercise. When developing a script, it might be run through in a lab meeting to make sure it makes sense, but once its deemed "good enough," work on it stops. The perceived ease of playing a confederate in these scripted interactions can be gleaned from the fact that this job was typically given to undergraduate research assistants who had no special training.

Designed spaces. A final aspect of the lab's material culture that is worthy of mention is the actual design of lab spaces. Rather than cause specific effects, the interior design of labs is often geared toward creating a neutral space that does not interfere with experimental manipulations. If biology labs are designed to create a sterile environment that prevent the contamination of living tissue, much of the material culture of developmental psychology was designed to create a sort of emotional sterility in its young, fickle objects of research. Despite being in two separate regions of the United States, it was striking that the physical similarities between the three developmental cognition labs I observed extended beyond research technologies and into the waiting rooms. The brightly colored furniture and cartoon animals painted on walls made the labs look like daycares, and the dolls, games, toys, and books were used to keep the child awake and engaged but not overstimulated. The experiment rooms, on the other hand, were typically barren. In some labs the room would be dark expect for the one stage light to draw the child's attention. In others, black curtains were used to create a completely plain room where the experimenter became the only source of stimulation.

When the experimenters left this carefully crafted environment, they often faced trouble. For instance, Dr. Collins' lab was within walking distance to a museum that catered to young children. Members of the lab would sometimes conduct experiments there since it would be possible to recruit many subjects in a single day. However, it was known among lab members that subjects were more focused and, thus, were better subjects, in the lab since there were less distractions. Older kids (five to eight) might have enough self-control to participate at the museum, but younger children would get overstimulated in the crowded environment. Like doing surgery in a field, the lack of environmental control produced a greater chance of "contamination."

The Limits of Iteration

Bench-building occurs as a process in which an indeterminant situation is probed and observed attentively until its elements begin to appear. In the Harden lab, this took a predictable path. Research ideas stemming from either the literature or the lab's own previous research would lead to an experiment. A small amount of data would be gathered and discussed at a lab meeting or in hallways. Adjustments would then be suggested—new techniques or technologies to try. The researcher would then return to the bench and collect more data. This iterative process would continue, repeatedly, until (a) the bench-building led to a productive data-gathering opportunity or (b) the researchers concluded that additional work was unlikely to yield additional purchase on the research object (Figure 4.8).

This is a truncated picture of a cycle that could cover a dozen lab meetings extending over months or even years.

Lab meeting 1: ➡ Data collection ➡ Lab meeting 2:
planning experiment   presentation of data

Data collection ➡ Lab meeting 3:
presentation of data

Data collection ➡ Lab meeting 4: ➡ Preparation for
presentation of data   publication

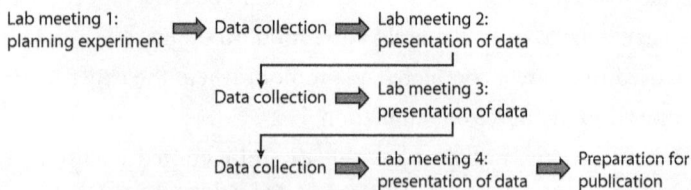

FIGURE 4.8 Iterative Scientific Practice

Multiple cycles of iteration only make sense, even in the Harden lab, when there is a belief that they can be profitable, that what was thick, multiplex data could be thinned and made legible. Lacking the belief that iteration may produce incremental improvements in perceptual or manipulative capacity, spending excess time at the bench becomes wasteful. It makes more sense to take what data can be gathered and move on (Figure 4.9).

In this scenario, researchers may choose to spend more time analyzing data and framing findings.

Thus, a lack of investment in technique and technology can be viewed as an entirely rational response to a situation in which bench-building is constrained. The previous sections make clear that bench-building is not completely absent in psychology laboratories. I participated in several informal sessions where researchers would "try out" new methods or experiments on each other to make sure they elicited the desired response. One advanced graduate student in cognitive psychology had a hypothesis about word order affecting fluency in a reading task. He read it to the group to get their impression.

Non-iterative data collection

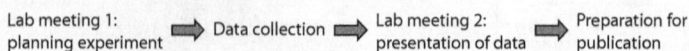

Lab meeting 1: ➡ Data collection ➡ Lab meeting 2: ➡ Preparation for
planning experiment   presentation of data   publication

FIGURE 4.9 Non-iterative Scientific Practice

It did not create the effect he wanted so he decided to develop a better stimulus. In developmental psychology labs, researchers often presented new stimuli during lab meetings to see if their colleagues thought it would capture a subject's attention.

However, this sort of bench-building is limited compared to what I described in the last chapter. Word order can only be rearranged in a few ways. There is only so much you can do to hold a toddler's attention. Repeated trips to the bench offer diminishing returns. Logical and clever experimental designs are important in every field, but only some fields benefit from repeated iterations of data collection.

In experimental social sciences like psychology, powerful manipulations are generally rare. The debate regarding the validity of social priming methods is informative.[19] John Bargh and colleagues published a seminal study showing how stimuli that are presented to subjects below their level of conscious awareness can activate stereotypes and alter behavior. In one of the most surprising experiments, subjects who were unconsciously primed with words associated with stereotypes of the elderly walked more slowly when leaving the experiment than those primed with a control.

The implications of the study were massive. If humans can be made to act elderly simply by unconsciously having a stereotype activated, it suggested a phenomenon of breathtaking pervasiveness turning us hither and yon all day every day. Not since Freud's original discovery of the unconsciousness had such a vast mindscape been opened for exploration. And explored it was. The article became a cornerstone of a burgeoning subfield. Yet when Belgian psychologists failed to replicate Bargh's highly cited priming study,[20] he dismissed the replication and subsequent news coverage as products of "pay-as-you-go publications and superficial online science journalism."[21] This quickly descended into a squabble between Bargh, the authors of the replication, science bloggers, and online commentators. For my purposes here, it is irrelevant whether Bargh or his critics are right. An op-ed in the *New York Times* about the dust-up points out that the effect sizes in Bargh's article were not very large to begin with, and thus failed replications should not be surprising.[22]

What is significant, however, is that Bargh defended his work by arguing that the replicators had introduced "critical changes" to the experiment, like slightly different subject instructions and priming procedures. This type of critique against a failed diagnostic replication is a familiar strategy. Naturally, experimental paradigms on the bleeding edge of science are fragile. At the research frontier, tacit knowledge is necessary, and replications may be difficult to achieve. Yet psychologists who face a couple of stubborn constraints limiting their ability build more robust and reliable interventions.

ETHICAL AND ONTOLOGICAL CONSTRAINTS

The studies being debated above are not at the bleeding edge of a research frontier: they were published almost twenty years ago. Why have these methods not been refined? Why have new technologies or methods not provided new vistas and united the lab with other sciences and outside institutions? What makes bench-building so hard to achieve when the object of experimentation is human behavior?

The easy answer is complexity. Human behavior is the product of billions of years of evolution which has shaped a genome which continues to baffle scientists. The 86 billion neurons in our brain develop in an eddy of interpersonal, political, economic, and cultural currents. That any science should struggle in the face of such astounding complexity should hardly come as a shock. Scientists themselves often rely on the language of complexity when they face persistent problems in making widely acknowledged progress.[23] Yet complexity can imply a mere quantitative limitation, as if all we needed to make progress was more data and the computational power needed to analyze it. Although the language of complexity appears in the following chapters, the experimental constraints on psychologists can be better described using different language.

Specifically, these constraints have ethical and ontological dimensions.[24] On one hand, the ethics of experimenting on human subjects limits the types of strategies social scientists can use. Bench-building involves an intimate relationship between researchers, tools, and objects of study, and anything that inhibits the evolution of this relationship will limit the ability to develop reliable manipulations. Certainly, there are good reasons for the oversight that accompanies experimental studies of human subjects, but it is not surprising that some of the most famous and illuminating studies in social science—from the Milgram and Stanford Prison Experiments to Humphrey's Tearoom Trade—were also the most ethically questionable. The very methods that tell us the most about human behavior are the ones that are the most immersive, invasive, and manipulative.

The effects of these restrictions were especially evident in psychology labs studying infants and toddlers. Due to legal and ethical protections, researchers were limited in their control over subjects. As I have discussed, in experiments with infants, they were expected to remain seated on their parent's lap looking at a stage. Researchers then directed their attention toward the stimulus, so their faces could be recorded for coding. However, it was an inevitability that some subjects would get antsy and begin to stand on their parent's legs or lean out of frame. Because the experimenter's goals were mediated through the parent's hands, flawless adherence to protocols was sacrificed for the comfort of the child. Researchers had few options to remedy this, so they simply adjusted. They would give the parent and child breaks in the middle of an experiment if the subject was getting fidgety. When the child leaned out of frame, the coders could no longer see the face to measure looking time. Yet they continued coding based on the position of the body or some other cue. Because control of the subject was limited, environmental control was frequently compromised as well.

However, even if social scientists could attain better experimental control, they would still face a problem that confronts them as an onto-logical gulf: they deal with objects of study that are abstract and multi-valent. As Peirce explained, "Men who are given to defining too much inevitably run themselves into confusion in dealing with the vague concepts of common sense."[25] For instance, "power" is a phenomenon that occurs between nation-states and also between children on a play-ground. One instantiation is not "purer" than the other. Nor is finding their common essence a matter of complexity. Instead, understanding "power" involves the capacity to draw out commonalities between these cases. In the physical sciences, on the other hand, objects of study are usually better understood when reduced to their components.

This results in a confounding research situation for social scien-tists. The very methods that bring physical sciences closer to their object of study pull social scientists farther away from theirs. Natu-ral science often becomes more abstract and technical as it evolves. As Robert K. Merton noted, "With the increasing complexity of scientific research, a long program of rigorous training is necessary to test or even to understand the new scientific findings. The mod-ern scientist has necessarily subscribed to a cult of unintelligibility."[26] Certainly, this distance between expert and popular languages may be exacerbated by scientists as a rhetorical strategy to enable them to maintain authority over a domain,[27] and lay citizens can advocate for inclusion in seemingly technical areas.[28] The distance between tech-nical and lay knowledge is contestable and semi-porous, but it is real.

Yet this same trajectory of unintelligibility is rarely seen in the areas of social science concerned with the human experience. Researchers in the Weberian tradition argue that social scientific concepts take their meaning from specific historical and cultural circumstances.[29] Abstracting a concept of social relevance from its context degrades and deforms it. In cell biology, "thinning data" transforms an uninterpre-table complex system into something tractable and "real" in a strictly physical sense. In psychology, "thinning data" produces thin data.

To be clear, psychologists rarely, if ever, discuss "ontology." Nor are the issues involved in translating everyday concepts and experiences into scientific language treated as anything other than solvable problems requiring the right insight and effort (at least publicly). Yet these issues arise continuously as psychologists design and interpret their experiments.

For instance, one of the infant cognition labs was running experiments looking at infants' ability to discriminate between groups of people. Laura, an advanced graduate student, was investigating whether infants based their perception of "groupness" on similar appearance or collective action. Clearly, this work had implications for understanding things like the development of racial attitudes, an inspiration she acknowledged. However, instead of using images of actual people (or even realistic representations of people) as measures of "difference," she used cartoon objects made of red circles and yellow triangles with faces on them: these cartoons were easy to standardize and maximally different to make them easier to distinguish. The initial idea was translated into a doable project through standardization and control. But it also became more abstract and farther removed from the rich concept that motivated the investigation.

Although challenging research conditions are not unique to psychology, the ethics of human subjects' protection and the complex ontological status of cultural and psychological objects constrain bench-building in fields that take human thought and behavior as their primary research object. These constraints—the ethical and the ontological—are useful for understanding the limitations of modern experimental psychology. Yet neither should be considered permanent. Research ethics are a product of historically situated legal, regulatory, administrative, and epistemic cultures; they may become more or less constrictive under different circumstances. Limitations to access or control in human science can, in principle, be overcome. New methods that collect biological measures or real-time social media data may push these boundaries. However, the far more challenging issue is whether ontological constraints can be overcome. This question—which is concerned with the political, legal, and cultural conditions that enable and constrain the production of psychological knowledge—will be addressed in the conclusion.

Modern psychology is torn between two incommensurate realities—the demand for theoretically interesting scientific knowledge about human thought and behavior and the struggle to produce rigorous, replicable experiments. In experimental psychology, the ethics of human subjects' projection and the stricture of good science meets the ontology of evolving, contentious cultural forms (both lay and scientific). What is outlined in the following chapters is recognizable as experimental science. These communities follow all the phases of experimental research with their own, evolved culture of research and methodological ethics, yet their products are deeply debatable.[30] What follows is not an exhaustive categorization of responses, but three ways such a challenge has been met.

5

MAN AT POINT ZERO

Developmental Psychology and the
Production of Normal Science

Folktales across Europe and Asia tell stories of ghost lights, will-o'-wisps, and hobby lanterns. These are phantasmic lights that appear at night over bogs and marshes to lure travelers off of safe paths. As they pursue the light, it draws ever farther away, leading to the traveler's demise. The pursuit of scientific knowledge can be compared to following one of these phantoms. The safe path of what is known is abandoned in favor of slogging through a swamp to chase a forever-receding horizon. Famously, Karl Popper once used a similar metaphor:

> Science does not rest upon solid bedrock. The bold structure of its theories rises, as it were, above a swamp. It is like a building erected on piles. The piles are driven down from above into the swamp, but not down to any natural or 'given' base; and if we stop driving the piles deeper, it is not because we have reached firm ground. We simply stop when we are satisfied that the piles are firm enough to carry the structure, at least for the time being.[1]

Even the most productive science is built on piles driven into a murky, uncertain foundation. At best, it is "firm enough as a basis for further exploration" but not necessarily true in an ultimate sense.

Popper's emphasis on theories differs from my focus on scientific practice, and the metaphors of driving piles and erecting structures becomes much less metaphorical in the context of bench-building. Rather than justified belief, I have argued that the production of scientific knowledge involves physical changes at the point of manipulation and data capture. Trusted technologies become the piles on which further structures are erected.

The promise of experimental psychology is based on the alluring ghost light that the same method which produced impressive technological accomplishments in other fields could be imported to the realm of human affairs. However, as the previous chapters demonstrated, some domains resist bench-building. The swampland is too soft and unstable to steady the piles. In psychology, a confounding mix of ethical and ontological problems frustrates the efforts to extend perception and develop new manipulations. These swampy fields are characterized by interpretive ambiguity and a lack of environmental control.

The difficulty in interpreting evidence and manipulating research objects does not *prevent* scientific activity. Proposing hypotheses, collecting evidence, developing theories—all of these can occur even under the most challenging circumstances. That being said, it is important to acknowledge the challenges that this form of scientific activity takes and the ways that it undermines bench-building. This chapter is concerned with the way that developmental psychology struggles to produce statistical significance in a swampy field. "Swampy" is not meant as a derisive label. Rather, it is meant to indicate the fundamental tension between two facts. First, although all experimental sciences are erected on the swampy foundation of nature, the intensity and character of the challenge differs. All experimental frontiers present indeterminant situations, yet some are easier to build on than others. The various challenges associated with experimenting on infants makes developmental psychology particularly challenging. Second, despite these challenges, researchers attempt, in good faith, to produce what they see as legitimate, ethical, and rigorous science.

Something has to give.

The psychologists detailed in this chapter make clear choices that allow them to pursue scientific psychology. This involves adopting a package of theory and methods that provides both open questions and concrete ways to answer those questions.[2] Although I have thus far discussed my observations of the Hill, Geller, and Collins labs in terms of "developmental psychology," these labs represent a particular theoretical position within developmentalism. They are proudly and explicitly nativist. That is, they believe that sophisticated human cognition cannot develop through sensory experience alone. Rather, they argue than humans are born with a set of fundamental concepts about numbers, language, physics, morality, and a variety of other domains. Within this theoretical framework, they make the infant meaningful to the scientific gaze and provide a foundation for "normal science."

However, this does not solve the basic problem of the field. There are obvious challenges to experimenting on infants that limit the scope of bench-building. Infant subjects are inviolable and inscrutable. The ethical and ontological constraints are formidable. Yet experimenting on humans at "point zero" also provides some advantages. It allows developmentalists to claim that they are tapping into universal, pre-socialized phenomena. However, the decisions made to turn a baby into a legible scientific object produce ongoing and seemingly unbridgeable divisions between their work and that of other subfields.

THE HUMAN AT POINT ZERO

Psychology in the early 20th century was largely the study of the standardized, white rat.[3] It was assumed that they represented a simplified model of human behavior while offering "experimental convenience and control" that human studies could not match. They were inexpensive, abundant, and could be freely manipulated. Yet as the limitations of equating rodent and human behavior became increasingly apparent, psychologists began to experiment more on human subjects.[4]

The strategy of behaviorist researchers to make human behavior legible by selecting an object of research deemed to be a simpler version continues in developmental psychology. In fact, trying to study "man at point zero," a term philosopher Maurice Blanchot used to characterize anthropological research on "primitive" groups, represents one of the oldest and most common strategies for establishing a field of study in the human sciences. This involves getting to the "essential" or "foundational" aspects of humankind by going to an ontogenetic, phylogenetic, or cultural "source" and building a science from only what is deemed fundamental. This strategy links early anthropological ethnographies, behaviorism's focus on animal studies, and infant psychology. In each of these fields, a group or organism that is supposed to be less developed and, consequently, less complex is supposed to offer the researchers a chance to get to the "roots" of contemporary culture or psychology.

In developmental psychology, the infant became viewed as a pre-programmed human. A critic of developmental psychology explains, "By virtue of being very young, and having had less opportunity to learn, the infant is seen as close to nature, devoid of the trappings of adult training and (Western) 'civilisation.'"[5] This is precisely what appealed to many of the developmentalists I interviewed. For instance, Alice explained that, although she was originally a political science major as an undergraduate, she became frustrated by the complexity of culture: "When you're studying adults there's so much more to control. And when you're trying to get to the issues of what we start off with, it's really hard to work back from adulthood. You have to peel away so many more things."

Another graduate student, Sharon, took a different trajectory. Originally studying animal behavior, she came to the study of infants because of the similarities in the two approaches: "Originally, I got involved because it seemed like another good way to study innateness. The methods go together really well." Ultimately, however, the switch to studying human neonates allowed her to explore her interests in "these very concrete things that make us human" concluding, "Yes, culture changes us, and yes, we differ according to our experiences, but, at some level, we're really all quite similar."

But it was also clear that some saw the distinction between the infants they studied and adults as a yawning gulf. When I asked Dr. Daniel Freneaux, a postdoc in the Collins lab, if he felt he had any special insight into human behavior given his psychological training, he quipped, "I'm not really studying human beings. I'm studying babies."

Therein lies a key theoretical struggle at the heart of developmental research. By moving to a simpler object, they create an interpretive gap between their object of study and their theoretical interest. To some extent, this is part and parcel of all experimental science. The map is not the territory, and the laboratory experiment is not the natural system. Yet in fields where bench-building is common, technological developments at the point of data capture provide concrete evidence that *something* is bridging this gap. Of course, just what this something is can be hotly debated within fields, but a reliable intervention means that something is definitely happening. And further interventions help constrain theories and adjudicate between competing hypotheses. Indeterminacy is given shape.

In fields with limited bench-building, on the other hand, the interpretive gap is a persistent irritant and threat to productive work. In "misbehaving" fields that are unable to settle their own controversies,[6] other means are used to quash disagreement. For the developmentalists I observed this included a package of theoretical and methodological concepts that go by the name of nativism. Thus far, I have refrained from discussing internal theoretical and methodological distinctions within developmental psychology to focus on broader practice-oriented questions about bench-building. However, the fact that the three developmental psychology labs I observed were nativist in orientation is significant to understanding their particular approach to experimental science. Rather than a "specialty," nativism was something closer to an identity that associated researchers with specific networks within the field. Although I will later address how nativists defined themselves negatively—the "they" who are not "us"—for now, I focus on how they defined themselves positively.

Theoretically, nativism provides researchers with a basic puzzle—which concepts are innate to humans and how do more complex concepts arise from these beginnings? To confront these questions, two central goals in nativist studies are to (a) show that particular forms of knowledge appear in younger infants than ever before and, thus, edge ever closer to the human's zero point or (b) to extend "what babies know" into new domains. So, for instance, an experiment shows that five-month-olds already have expectations about how liquids should act when a glass is tipped over, begs an obvious question—are they born with that knowledge or did they learn it in their five months of experience with liquids? Although it cannot be answered definitively, one way to support the nativist interpretation of such a finding is to find the same effect in even younger infants. Conversely, showing that infants already have expectations about, for instance, fairness in social relations, can open a new domain of concepts that can be argued are innate. This shared orientation helps these labs develop common interpretations of the inherently ambiguous phenomena of infant behavior.

Yet this is just one problem of studying humans at point zero. We cannot, as Dr. Hill was fond of saying to the parents of infant subjects, ask babies to write us essays explaining all they know. This was a cute way of acknowledging that infants are not helpful research objects and do not yield information in ways tailormade for experimental purposes. Researchers attempting to break new methodological ground often face this problem. For instance, Carey, a graduate student in the Geller lab was working on the development of prepositions in toddlers and had discovered a massive database in which researchers had installed recording equipment in the rooms of toddlers to record every word said. This was a particular thick set of data, but she was having troubling figuring out what to do with it. She lamented, "I'm swimming in it."

Infant and toddler behavior is characteristically "thick data" in that it is rich with implications but open to multiple interpretations. As Burman argues, "Developmental research, with infancy as its proto-type, can be seen as a paradigm example of both experimental inge-nuity and ambiguity [. . .] Overall, debates in the literature have been preoccupied with the problem of determining between competing interpretations for the same experimental result."[7]

The benefit of using standardized methods is that it avoids being overwhelmed by data complexity and structures the data capture. For nativist developmental psychologists, looking-time paradigms have become a staple method. However, because it limits the data capture to information about one dimension—eye gaze—the method essen-tially limits the findings to two types of effects—novelty effects and familiarity effects. In some experiments, researchers expect infants to look longer at something that surprises them. This could be because its new or because it changes along some dimension. In other experi-ments, researchers expect that infants will look at objects with which they have been familiarized. I once saw a graduate student ask Dr. Collins about it and she explained that younger subjects tend to show more familiarity effects while older subjects tended to show nov-elty effects. However, she conceded that both may be operative at any one time and could even cancel each other out: "Obviously, it's really hard to tell if it's balancing out or they're not showing a preference."

In nativist developmental psychology, there are additional practi-cal challenges to interpreting data. Adjudicating between competing interpretations is often challenging because multiple skills are often involved with the development of a single behavior. For instance, one branch of developmental psychology has looked at the emergence of the child's ability to understand other people's minds. When do children realize that other people have their own beliefs about the world? However, children's "executive function" (i.e., their ability to control their own attention) abilities are also developing, and it remains an ongoing debate in the field whether the experiments meant to test false belief are merely testing executive function. That is, it is easy to argue that the reason why a very young subject fails to infer another's thought is not because they lack the ability. Rather, they fail because the experimental paradigm is too taxing. It would be similar to testing whether eight-year-old children understand the properties of multiplication by asking them to figure out the product of 893 and 78. A child who gets an incorrect answer may still have a basic knowledge of multiplication and be able to solve many simpler problems.

Nativism helps narrow down a set of theoretical questions around a common set of theoretical concerns and experimental approaches which helps bracket the various ontological problems involved with studying human beings. Later, I will show how these theoretical decisions (that is, made away from the bench at the field and lab levels) create the opportunity for profound, unsurmountable disagreements between subfields to emerge.

But first I want to highlight that these theoretical decisions do not address the fundamental problem of bench-building in the field. Working with infants presents practical problems that serve to constrain development of new techniques and technologies. The biggest benefits of working with infants—that they are unsocialized, uncultured humans with, purportedly, generically human responses to stimuli—are also the biggest problems. Given that they are unsocialized and uncultured, they do not participate willingly. And, because they are highly protected subjects, they cannot be forced to do anything. Thus, in addition to theoretical problems, developmental psychology faces profound practical problems.

Infants As Research Objects: Frustrating and Costly

Psychologists who work with non-human animals can breed them, control all aspects of their environment, restrain them, and run an unlimited number of studies on them. Adult human subjects, on the other hand, can usually be convinced to participate with the experimenter's wishes, eliminating the need for physical control. Infant subjects maintain a liminal space since they are as unpredictable and resistant to instruction as animals and yet bear the rights of a highly protected human being. The practical necessity of getting parents to assent to all experimental procedures prevents researchers from doing anything to the infant that is unpleasant.

During a lab meeting in the Geller lab, one graduate student was telling another about an experiment in which a psychologist did not allow her own child any access to pictures until she was nineteen-months-old to test if the child still developed the ability to have representational cognition. The other grad student sarcastically replied, "Awesome!" The reply was an attempt to confront the fact that such a study probably yielded very hard to get data while also being deeply troubling. Although a researcher may be able to take such liberties with their own children, for the rest, they had little opportunity to engage in major experimental interventions like this.

Because of these constraints, simply getting subjects to participate at all was a constant challenge. The Geller lab was attempting to reuse one of its standard experimental paradigms on a younger-than-usual subject and were running into difficulty keeping the toddlers focused. One of the experimenters was recounting her frustration to the lab by explaining how she had to continually prompt the subject: "Can you give me . . .?" "Do you see a . . .?" Another, who was also working on the experiment, joked, "Do something!"

In addition to infants being generally challenging subjects, they are also difficult to access. In contrast to adult subjects who have historically be drawn from a pool of readily available college students, infant subjects must be recruited from off campus in a process that is expensive and time-consuming. During a presentation given to members of a cognitive psychology lab at the same university, Dr. Hill lamented that an earlier version had to be scrapped after it was discovered that the data were useless. The visual stimulus was obscured from certain angles meaning that some of the infants could not see what was being presented to them. She lamented to the group, "Do you know how hard it is to collect thirty babies, two-month-olds?"

Simply getting neonates into the lab was an ever-present pressure in developmental labs. The flow of infants—how many, what ages, and who got access to them—was one of biggest practical concerns. Much like access to extremely rare and expensive particle accelerators is a choke point, limiting research output for particle physicists,[8] infant subjects were a valuable and limited commodity in developmental labs. For instance, Dr. Freneaux struggled early in his graduate studies due to a lack of subjects. He explained that the scheduler in the department was not invested in the job, "So, you would get two babies a week." That meant it would take months to gather data for a single experiment (which may, in the end, not even work). The lab eventually hired a new scheduler, and it changed his experience: "We could get ten babies a week because she was really doing the job. That makes a huge difference. That just changes the speed of work. That's the fuel of the car."

Early in my observations of the Hill lab, I registered surprise at how few subjects the lab tested on any given week. During one week, for instance, Dr. Hill told her lab how happy she was getting thirteen subjects. (This may seem like a paltry amount given the lab ran experiments for three weekdays, but cancellations were very common.) I calculated just how much money was expended in their pursuit of subjects. While helping send out solicitations through the mail one week, Dr. Hill remarked that the postage that week alone was going to cost them $400. With a generous average of thirteen subjects per week, that equates to about $31 per subject.

Additionally, subjects who actually responded and participated were given a $20 honorarium. That means over $50 is spent per infant in direct costs. This calculation did not include the costs in getting the names and addresses from Experian (a credit agency that sold the contact information of new parents to researchers) and other costs the lab incurred.

Later, I asked Dr. Hill if she ever calculated how much money each child costs the lab. She told me the industry standard was about $100 per child. She explained that this cost could be further adjusted up depending upon whether the lab pays its student volunteers, employs a lab manager, etc.

One of the reasons why the lab is a warm, welcoming environment is strategic. It encourages parents to return. Because recruiting is money and time intensive, having return subjects is a huge benefit. It is cheaper, and, after developing personal relationships, the cancellation rate is far lower. For this reason, labs will go to great extents not to upset parents. When subjects cry or need to be changed or when siblings are unruly, there is never any pressure put on the parent to "control their child."

Because of this, a premium was put on making the lab look responsible and well-organized beneath the unavoidable chaos of any place housing infants and toddlers. I only saw Dr. Hill, a friendly and informal adviser to her undergraduate assistants, get cross with them once—when the volunteer got confused and showed up to lab an hour late. Although Dr. Hill remained nonplussed in front of the rest of the lab (and the parents), as the volunteer went to leave at the end of the day, Dr. Hill scolded her across the lab, "By the way, don't pull that shit again!" Later, another undergrad in the lab told me that Dr. Hill had only one "ironclad rule": If the parent showed up and you are not there to meet them, "you're fired."

Joanna, the Collins lab manager, told me that one of her main jobs was to make sure graduate students (who ran most of the experiments in the Collins lab) showed up for their appointments. When the lab scheduled subjects in the early morning, she would even make "wake up calls" to remind them. Despite this, however, she had multiple situations in which subjects arrived and the experimenters were not there.

The extent to which developmental labs go to maintain a professional image and foster good relations with parents can be seen in this exchange in which Joanna describes what happens when the experimenter does not show up for an appointment:

AUTHOR: What do you do when that happens? Do you just apologize?

JOANNA: Apologize. I am skilled at running fake studies. So, I have several studies up my sleeve that I can fake for any given age range.

AUTHOR: That is hilarious! They come in and you just pretend . . .

JOANNA: I just run a fake study and, honestly, they don't know the difference. The studies that I run are real studies. It's just we're not going to use the data. The kid might not be in the exact age range we need. But the parents don't need to know that. So, the rule of thumb is make it seem like nothing's wrong. Which can be difficult sometimes.

AUTHOR: That's hilarious!

JOANNA: Yeah, I know! It is. It was actually one of the questions they asked me during my interview, when I interviewed for the place. They asked something like, "A family comes in and it turns out they had the wrong appointment time. What do you do?" My response was to apologize profusely. They were like, "Okay, that's good but what we actually do is pretend like nothing's wrong." [laughter] And it actually happened on my very first day here. So, a family showed up. They didn't have an appointment. There had been some scheduling mistake and we ran them in a fake study.

AUTHOR: You got practice quick I guess.

JOANNA: I got practice quick.

The importance of maintaining relationships with parents was significant enough to engage in the farce of running a phony experiment.

STRATEGIES FOR BUILDING ON
A SWAMPY FOUNDATION

Getting infants into the lab is costly and time-consuming. However, once that hurdle is surmounted, a more fundamental problem confronts them—a research object that is both oblivious to the goals of the experimenter and cannot be seriously manipulated. In contrast to the cell biologists who engaged with thick data in an attempt to discover its elements and, eventually, make it legible, there was little hope that either new skills or new technologies would markedly improve the quality of the data. Instead, the goal was to make the best out of a challenging research environment. If improving the quality of data collected was not likely to succeed, achieving statistical significance within existing experimental protocols was, at least, a potentially doable goal.

In the following section, I illustrate how difficulties associated with experimental research on infants have led researchers to adopt a series of mostly unstated solutions. Not mentioned in the published reports, these strategies are vital for maintaining productivity in the subfield but also make the literature harder to interpret.

Protocol Flexibility

Experimenters in developmental psychology utilize what might be referred to as a bend-but-don't-break philosophy of protocol adherence. The validity of experimental data may be conceived of as a continuum. On one side, there is data that comes from an infant who is calm and focused, allowing the experimenter to capture the necessary data for proper analysis. On the other side is data that simply must be thrown out. This happens when the infant never stops crying or never shows any interest in the stimuli. Other times, the experimenter causes the failure. During one study, for instance, an experimenter hidden behind a stage was supposed to slowly turn a plastic barrel back and forth above the stage. Instead, she accidentally dropped it. The barrel landed on the stage with a thud and then rolled off the stage, crashing loudly on the floor. The data from that subject was thrown out. But between these two extremes lies an expansive gray area of minor violations that force researchers to decide whether to proceed or not.

Protocol violations tended to be context specific, yet there were several regular situations in which rules were bent. Some seemed relatively inconsequential. For instance, as a routine part of the experiments, parents are asked to close their eyes to prevent any unconscious influence on the child. Although this was explicitly stated in the instructions given to parents, during the actual experiment it was often overlooked. The parent's eyes would remain open. Moreover, on several occasions, experimenters downplayed the importance of having one's eyes closed. One psychologist told a mother, "During the trial, we ask you to close your eyes. That's just for the journals so we can say you weren't directing her attention. But you can peek if you want to. It's not a big deal. But there's not much to see."

Other violations had more potential to bias the data. For instance, studies were often stopped part way through so the parent could change, feed, or calm down the infant. Later, the parent and child would reenter and begin again. Of course, at that point, the infant had already been exposed to some portion of the stimuli. Another time, an insistent older sibling demanded that he be allowed to join the mother and subject in the experiment room. During the trial, the mother had to tell the sibling to be quiet and still several times which drew the attention of the infant away from the stage.

Because most of the props for stimuli are homemade and most of the people actually running the experiments are undergraduate assistants, it should not be surprising that experiments can be less than smooth. However, as long as problems did not completely derail the experiment, it went on. For example, the Hill lab was looking at an infant's expectations regarding how liquids and solids move. There were two sets of stimuli, a cup of colored liquid and another cup containing a solid which, when vertical, looked identical to the liquid. During the experiment, the child would be shown the liquid being poured back and forth, from cup to cup, until they habituated to it and lost interest. Then they would be shown the solid being "poured" out of the cup and into another. Rather than smoothly pour out, however, the solid slid out of the cup in a single piece. Although the goal was to measure whether the infant would be "surprised" when the "liquid" did not pour like a liquid. However, when sliding the solid from cup to cup, it made a loud sound that often startled the subjects. After one experiment, the mother of the subject actually mentioned it to Dr. Hill, but she dismissed the concern and told her that the subjects were showing a preference for the water anyway. Regardless of the soundness of this explanation, the larger point—that an experiment based upon measuring infant attention was being contaminated by an attention-grabbing distraction—was ignored.

Outside of the experiment itself, the coding process was also full of ambiguity that was overcome through protocol violations. In order to measure looking time, the studies are coded by two "independent" coders (nearly always in the same room) based upon a closed-circuit video feed of the infant. However, there were many times when coding from the video became challenging. Very young infants would often fall in and out of frame because they lacked the strength to control their heads. Shadows made it difficult to read small or dark eyes. It could be hard to tell whether the subject was actually looking at the stage or just staring off in that general direction.

When two assistants coded, they often negotiated a joint solution to these problems. Half a dozen times while coding, I was asked by the other coder, "Is that looking?" "Are you marking this?" "Do you think that's a look?" This was especially necessary in situations involving "visual sticking points." That is, when a subject's eyes are scanning across a stage, seemingly following its action, it is not problematic to assume there are looking at the experiment. In these situations, the two coders can match up, perhaps falling out of sync for a moment here and there as the child's eyes wander away and back. However, when the subject was still or showed great focus, coding often became far more difficult. For instance, when a subject stared intently just off-center it became a challenge to code. Should it be coded as a look the entire time? Or are they never looking? The problem is that if one coder makes the decision that the subject is looking and the other decides they are not, they would badly diverge. Thus, "checking in" to establish a general role about what constitutes a look was done to avoid this problem.

Although problems that arose during the studies were sometimes simply ignored, obvious breaches to procedure were noted on a sheet that the coder or experimenter filled out. One coder wrote "playing with shoes" next to the third and fourth trials on her sheet. Several experimenters wrote "fussy" to classify an entire experiment. But this data is not thrown out. The computer data output, sheets filled out by both experimenter and lead coder, and consent form were filed away together. Long after the experiment was run, when the data was analyzed, the researcher, who was often not present on the day of the experiment, decided whether the subject would be excluded because they were "distracted" or "fussy."

Stacking the Deck

In written reports, psychological experiments have a coherent narrative structure. A hypothesis is developed. Subjects are exposed to the stimulus, and their response is coded. When a predetermined number of subjects have been run, their data is then analyzed, and conclusions are drawn.

However, in actual lab practice, the experimental process is fluid. Instead of waiting for data from a set number of subjects to draw any conclusions, infant researchers have an ongoing relationship with data that begins as soon as the first subject is run. After coding a child who had just been run on a new experiment, a graduate student came into the coding room and asked to see the data. When she saw the computer print-out, she began to jump up and down, squealing with joy. After she left, I asked the other coder why she was so happy. The coder explained that it was the first subject run in her new experiment, and the infant had responded as she had hoped. While her reaction was unusually expressive, it is indicative of the relationship that experimenters have with data, even at very early stages in the experimentation process.

This was not unique to graduate students. I saw an undergraduate assistant come into Dr. Hill's office after video-coding an infant run on a new study. She told the professor the effect was "12.4," which meant the infant looked at the experimental condition for 12.4 seconds longer than the control condition. Dr. Hill then smiled and told me that 12.4 was a "huge effect." Before the undergraduate left, she told the professor that she had looked at the data from two other infants in that condition and both had shown similar effects.

Rather than waiting for the results from a set number of infants, experimenters began "eyeballing" the data as soon as babies were run and often began looking for statistical significance after just five or ten subjects. During lab meetings and one-on-one discussions, experiments that were "in progress" and still collecting data were evaluated based upon these early results. When the preliminary data looked good, the test continued. When they showed ambiguous but significant results, the test usually continued. But when, after just a few subjects, no significance was found, the original protocol was abandoned, and new variations were developed.

During one meeting, Dr. Collins was asking a post doc about his new experiment. It was not going well. The post doc had run just three subjects and described the reactions of each in detail. One supported the hypothesis, one contradicted it, and one showed no preference for the experimental or control conditions. The professor responded, "Well, you can't tell from just three babies," but she gave him advice on how to alter the protocol slightly and instructed him to stop after ten subjects if the study still was not working. In another meeting, the psychologist asked a new graduate student about a study. He told her he was reluctant to run statistics before all the data from all sixteen subjects were in. She told him that if there was going to be an effect it should be visible after twelve subjects, so he should run the statistics to find out.

Experimenters carefully attend to the computer printouts and run statistical tests long before they are finished collecting subjects. These serve as early signals that the experiment will be a success or a failure. Early signs of failure lead to adjustments so as not to waste time and resources. This makes sense from an economic standpoint. However, when a lab chooses to only complete the studies that show effects after a few subjects, they are essentially beginning each experiment with a head start. As the next section makes clear, however, this does not guarantee a successful study.

Experimental Failure is Made Useful

Papers in infant cognition from a nativist perspective often demonstrate some ability in a certain age group (e.g., seventeen-month-olds) and contrast it with failure from a younger age group (e.g., fourteen-month-olds). This can be used to demonstrate how knowledge develops in a particular domain. However, this need not be the order of actual research. In developmental psychology, failure often precedes success.

Because experiments are very costly in terms of both time and money, throwing away data is highly undesirable. Instead, when faced with a struggling experiment using a trusted experimental paradigm, experimenters would regularly run another study that had higher odds of success. This was accomplished by varying one aspect of the experiment like the age of the participants. For instance, when one experiment with fourteen-month-olds failed, the experimenter reran the same study with eighteen-month-olds which then succeeded. Once a significant result was achieved, the failures were no longer valueless. They now represented a part of a larger story: "Eighteen-month-olds can achieve behavior X but fourteen-month-olds cannot." Thus, the failed experiment becomes a boundary for the phenomenon.

In rare cases, the situation is reversed. For instance, in one case from a lab meeting in the Geller lab, they were failing to replicate an earlier finding from their lab, even with older subjects. This was the exchange between Dr. Geller and her trainee:

DR. GELLER: Is this the same procedure as Geller 2009?

MILA: Yes.

DR. GELLER: So it's safe to say we're not replicating ourselves.

MILA: Yes.

DR. GELLER: Hmm, I'm wondering why we don't replicate ourselves.

Another graduate student mentioned that the subjects were older than the subjects in the published study. Rather than assume that something might be wrong with the original study, Dr. Geller responded, "So, there's something about this task that doesn't work with the older kids." She asked if anyone has anyone can come up with a reason why it would be harder for the older kids. Members of the lab laughed, and the meeting moved on.

In other cases, the experiment is simplified to increase the chances of a success. Dr. Freneaux was struggling to get an experiment to work. The experiment was an extension of a set of experiments that Dr. Collins had done several years ago. In them, an object moved behind a barrier and, after a pause, either that object of a different object emerged from behind the barrier. This indicated whether infants of different ages can differentiate objects based upon whatever features the experimenter chooses to vary (e.g., size, color, shape, etc.). Dr. Freneaux and Michel, a grad student, extended the experiment in a couple of ways. First, rather than do the experiment live on a stage in front of the subject, it was represented as a brief animation sequence that was projected onto a screen. More significantly, instead of shapes, Michel and Jan were using cartoon people to see if infants could detect changes in individuals.

Dr. Collins told the pair to run ten infants but to stop if the data was not coming out: "We need a goddamn method check. The method has to work." Michel wondered if he should go back and conduct a closer replication by replacing the cartoon figures with inanimate objects to see if the method worked. Jan suggested that they just have both guys come out, go back in, and then drop the screen. Michel designed the experiment and didn't love the changes. However, Dr. Collins seemed open to them since they had to do something to simplify the experiment. Jan suggested that one of the guys be dressed in a hat and cape. Dr. Collins says, "And is black." Jan: "And walks with a limp." While they were joking, there was an important kernel of truth in this exchange. They needed to create the easiest version of the experiment possible because, as Dr. Collins explained, they would need at least one successful experiment to move forward. She told them to "throw everything" at the babies to produce at least one experiment with statistical significance. She suggested they stop what they were doing and run ten babies with the extremely distinct cartoon men. Then either result could be considered interesting. Either they would detect the difference and Michel's experiments can continue, or they would fail and the lab could claim that infants have an odd deficit in individuating people.

In another case, a graduate student was conducting an experiment modeled on a previously successful study from a psychologist from a different university. However, the experiment was not working because the stimulus was boring, and most of the subjects were "fussing out." The psychologist told him, "It's important to interpret a failure in terms of a success" and suggested he simplify his methods in order to achieve some significant result.

The strategy of finding virtue in failure is another economic decision to get as much utility as they can from the data.[9] If any success can be achieved, failures can be framed around it. One statistically significant finding can be the linchpin that holds a series of (mostly unsuccessful) studies together.

Working Backward from Statistical Significance

It is difficult to get statistically significant results working with infants. However, it is even more difficult to get significant results that bear directly on the hypothesis that motivated the experiment. Often, statistically significant results present more questions than answers. Instead of conforming to the motivating hypothesis, the significant results are unpredicted, and their meaning is unclear. Roughly half of the regular lab meetings I attended (e.g., meetings concerned with research issues and not administration, planning, job searches, etc.) were dedicated to the discussion of statistically significant, but ambiguous, findings.

The structure of these meetings was similar across labs. A professor or graduate student would email a short document to the lab a few days before and then hand out those same pages at the beginning of the meeting. Usually, they would contain a couple of box plots or bar charts. The experimenter would then point out where statistical significance was reached and then ask the lab for help figuring out what could be argued from the results. The lab would attempt to collectively craft a story out of the significant findings.

This should be contrasted to how the phases of research activity operate in the molecular biology lab. Although it is very common to bring a hermeneutic approach to thick data, the point of this practice in the biology lab was to provide the researcher tools with which they could return to the bench to attempt to produce better data. By comparison, in the developmental psychology labs, the processed rarely pointed researchers back to the bench. Rather than use the meetings searching for clues that could be used to grapple with the indeterminate situation back at the bench, these meetings were attempts to take positive signals from the bench and solidify them into unimpeachable arguments that could withstand peer review.

Thus, when a clear and interesting story could be told about significant findings, the original motivation was often abandoned. I attended a meeting between Alice and Dr. Collins where they were trying to decipher some results the student had just received. Their meaning was not at all clear and the graduate student complained that she was having trouble remembering the motivation for the study in the first place. Dr. Collins responded, "You don't have to reconstruct your logic. You have the results now. If you can come up with an interpretation that works, that will motivate the hypothesis."

In another one-on-one meeting, Sharon was reviewing a set of recent studies she had been running. As a whole, the experiments were concerned with separate aspects of an overarching question—do people naturally infer efficient movement to others? That is, if I assume a man is walking to a tree, do I believe he will make a beeline toward it? And, if he does not, if he zigs and zags, do I then interpret that as some irrationality? Or are there other forms of movement (e.g., dance, play, etc.) that do not follow this logic of efficiency? Although some of Sharon's experiments had produced statistical significance, others had failed, and she was having trouble interpreting the successes and failures. Rather than attempt to interpret all the studies together, Dr. Collins replied, "Let's step back and look at the whole argument of the paper. Do you need this [study]?" She asked Sharon to outline the entire argument that was originally meant to unite the studies. Afterward, Dr. Collins explained to her that she did not "have to nail that in this paper" and offered a competing way to frame the successful studies. Sharon was relieved and left to write the article.

A blunt explanation of this strategy was given to me by an advanced graduate student: "You want to know how it works? We have a bunch of half-baked ideas. We run a bunch of experiments. Whatever data we get, we pretend that's what we were looking for." Rather than stay with the original, motivating hypothesis, researchers in developmental science learn to adjust to statistical significance. They then "fill out" the rest of the paper around this necessary core of psychological research. Vani explained the strategy in similar, although less colorful language during a discussion of selectively reporting positive findings: "Everyone selectively reports. Isn't that right?" She asks this to Sean who agrees. She continues, "You run ten studies and you publish the one that works."

Like protocol flexibility, there are ethical limits to this sort of post hoc theorizing. During one meeting regarding a significant, but unclear, finding, Dr. Collins and her graduate student went back and forth for fifteen minutes discussing various hypotheses for the findings. Finally, the professor said, "I don't see a terrifically clear story coming from this," and they moved on. In another case, Dr. Collins and a postdoc were working on a grant application that contained some initial findings. One of the measures they were using was a composite of several tests. However, although the composite measure was significant, only one of the tests was driving the results. With it taken out, the composite measure was no longer significant. Unfortunately, the test was unrelated to the motivating hypothesis of the grant. For over twenty minutes, they struggled to find a way to legitimize the composite measure. However, the professor decided that "It's a little dishonest to report the composite score if only [Test A] is doing all the work." They decided to leave both the composite measure and the highly significant test out of the grant application.

The Challenge of Integrative Replication in a Swampy Field

The problem with researcher freedom, according to recent critiques of psychological methodology, is that it casts doubt on the published literature. Simmons and colleagues argue that false positives are "perhaps the most costly error" because "once they appear in the literature, false positives are particularly persistent."[10] All of the strategies discussed above have dubious reputations among psychologists precisely because they increase the likelihood that false positives will enter the literature. A high volume of experiments (that are flexibly altered and abandoned) means that psychologists simply collect data until they begin to find statistical significance. Not every protocol violation is going to radically sway experimental outcomes, but some will. Building a story around significance does not always help enshrine a false positive but sometimes it does.

Developmental scientists are well aware that there is an elevated risk of false positives in their field. The reason is simple: In swampy fields, producing any effect is a challenge. Producing one that will reliably replicate is something else entirely. I asked Sarah what knowledge she wished she could have imparted to herself when she started graduate training. She said, "Don't count on studies to replicate." She clarified that she was referring not just to "other people's" but "your own studies, too." The relationship with published research was complex in these labs, and they developed local knowledge regarding the validity or invalidity of articles, methods, and other labs based upon previous experience. Thus, claims become evaluated within a matrix of indicators. Like the molecular biology lab, they engaged in integrative replication as a way to evaluate new studies and see what new methods and techniques they could glean from them. However, because of the inherent challenge in studying infants, there were serious limitations to this project.

Labs will use methods innovated by outside researchers when moving into new research areas. However, when these experiments do not produce statistically significant results—when the infants are unable to sit through the experiment or when they show no awareness of the changing stimuli—it is not often clear why. To simplify somewhat, there are three possible hypotheses for failure. (1) The extension of the experimental paradigm may simply show that the proposed relationship does not exist. For instance, an outside lab may have used a specific method to demonstrate an ability in six-month-olds. Trying the same experiment with four-month-olds may fail because the subjects are just too young and have not developed that ability. Although the extension failed, the original method may still hold some positive value for researchers. (2) The source study may simply be a false positive and, thus, impossible to replicate. This may be due to chance, sloppiness, or malfeasance but the result is the same. It provides nothing of value to the lab.

These two hypotheses are opposite sides of the same bad penny. They each embrace a dichotomy between True and False findings and share an intellectualist focus on claims rather than technologies. In the first hypothesis, the finding is true, but its application is limited. In the second, it is simply false. Although there are cases where a finding is cleanly replicated and others where, due to fabrication or malfeasance, a finding can be called obviously fake, the more typical and interpretively challenging situation occurs when hypothesis three is raised.

(3) There may be deeper problems with the way the experiment was carried out. The new experiment may differ from its model in dozens of unintended ways and not be a "true" replication. This is a classic dilemma that arises during replication attempts. As I argued earlier, when replication is driven by the desire to integrate rather than diagnose truth, replicators often cut corners in an attempt to replicate the outcomes as simply as possible. Only when a slapdash replication fails do replicators do the more exacting work of replicating the experiment exactly.

However, in swampy fields, there are expectations that the conditions of the original finding and that of the replication *cannot* be matched. When the two diverge on issues of skill or technological setup, they can be bridged. However, when the divergence is due to the inability to gain control over the object or conditions of research, then there is no reason to believe that such a challenge can ever be bridged. (Significantly, this is true not only for the differences between labs but even within the same lab.)

In order to sift through these competing explanations, psychologists who find their studies failing often conduct exact replications to test the method. This is a test for the first hypothesis. If the exact replication works, the experimenter may conclude that four-month-olds are simply too young to make the distinction asked of them in the new study. The child may truly be incapable at that age, or the stimuli may be too complex. Either way, the success of the replication provides some contrast for understanding the new experiment's failure.

If an exact replication fails, researchers begin a more thorough interrogation of the original study and its methods. Because developmental scientific reports present skeletal descriptions of the experiment, many aspects of the procedure are left out. Thus, when psychologists were having trouble getting a replication to work, they would call or email the author of the source study to get a more detailed account of the experiment. A member of the Hill lab told me about a case where the original author, a professor at a neighboring university, actually visited the lab and watched as the experiment was being performed. It involved an experimenter manipulating objects on stage with a mechanical arm. She gave a series of instructions that were not in the original paper regarding how experimenters should pick up the objects and which way they should be looking during trials. The experiment still did not work, however, and did not produce any publishable studies in the two years following the exchange.

Like integrative replication in molecular biology, copycatting methods leads to the growth of local knowledge regarding the validity and/or robustness of an article or line of research. If a source study came from a well-established lab yet could not be reproduced, the first thought is to assume fault. The experiment was treated as basically valid but difficult to reproduce. I heard these referred to as "fragile" paradigms. The very idea of a fragile paradigm was, in some sense, to acknowledge the fundamentally problematic nature of bench-building in their field.

On the other hand, when the author was relatively unknown, or the experiment still did not work after several attempts, the original study became marked as dubious in the lab. During one conversation, a graduate student was discussing an article from an unknown lab that pertained to her project. Her advisor dismissed the article because "no one's been able to reproduce it." Because negative findings are rarely published, this knowledge does not diffuse across the field through the medium of journal articles. Instead, failures become known within the lab and across labs through networks.

MAINTAINING THEORETICAL COHERENCE

Swampy fields produce ongoing problems for experimental study. The constraints that researchers face impede the development of new techniques and technologies. In the previous section, I argued that researchers can continue to operate in such experimentally challenged fields through the use of strategies that bend findings toward statistical significance and, thus, allow them to maintain an image of normal science even if bench-building is uneven or absent. Rather than view the literature as a set of true and untrue claims, experience taught them to embrace a more nuanced view of what could be built upon.

In addition to these empirical problems, however, constraints faced by developmental psychologists also result in theoretical problems. Panofsky has outlined how the inability to resolve theoretical debates in behavioral genetics led to an "archipelagic" organization in which subfields are isolated and mutually skeptical.[11] This same dynamic organizes developmental psychology.

This stems from the original ambiguity of trying to interpret infant behavior. Vani explained, in infant studies "where your data is in terms of looking times, it's not always 100 percent clear what the data you're seeing actually mean. And, you do read papers where people are interpreting the same results in drastically different ways depending what their theoretical stance is." The wide latitude in interpreting the human at point zero fosters the need to embrace a theoretical space in which infants can become legible. However, different decisions can be made, and this produces ongoing, seemingly unresolvable tensions.

The three labs I observed were committed to different versions of nativism. This is the belief that humans are born with certain forms of innate cognition. This prompts questions about what types of native knowledge we have (e.g., do we have innate theories of physics? Numbers? Identity? Justice?) and how these forms evolve or manifest over time. Nativism is typically contrasted with empiricist theories which, broadly, argue that we develop our cognitive structures through experience. Nativism is a type of species universalism. This led the developmental psychologists I observed to downplay potential issues of subject diversity. If an innate theory of addition is part of the biological inheritance of all humans, the biographical details of individual subjects are just noise.

Subject Diversity

Studying humans at "point zero" is supposed to avoid one of the fundamental challenges in experimental science—the selection of a standardized experimental object. Lorraine Daston and Peter Galison have argued that the selection of such "working objects" is necessary because "unrefined natural objects are too quirkily particular to cooperate in generalizations and comparisons."[12] Pre-socialized infants are prized as representations of raw, essential humanity. Yet, in practice, it was often clear that even these supposedly fungible research objects, were already showing significant signs of cultural diversity.

I once asked Dr. Hill if she had any data on who actually participates in her studies. She said she gets about 80 percent white, college-educated parents. However, when she increased the "hono-rarium" paid to the parents from $5 to $20, the number of minority and low education parents improved markedly. They now make up 50 percent of the participants. She said she was pleased with this because the federal government requires you gather data on the race/ethnicity as well as the educational attainment of the parents to get a representative sample of the surrounding area.

Yet, besides meeting a federal mandate, she did not express any belief that the diversity would have any significant benefit to her studies. In fact, I several times heard Dr. Hill dismiss the role of cultural difference in the basic categories of infant cognition using the same example: She argued that infants learn the basic dynamics of falling objects regardless of if the object is "a silver spoon or a pack of ciga-rettes." She noted that she also had an undergraduate math major vol-unteer who once looked at the influence of race/ethnicity and parental education level on the finding, yet they found little difference, so she felt justified that she was truly finding something universal.

Yet in some contexts cultural differences became either explana-tory phenomena or an object of interest. Despite mostly claiming that their working objects were fungible, it was often clear that they were not. If such differences are randomly distributed, they may be ignored as scientifically unimportant. Yet developmentalists often spoke of systematic variations.

At times, these could be considered happy accidents. For instance, the Collins lab was in an affluent, highly educated city and their sub-jects were largely drawn from this population. One of the lab mem-bers told me that they were often able to elicit behaviors from infants weeks or months earlier than other labs because their subjects live in enriched environments with lots of interaction and engagement. In a field where simply demonstrating the presence of an ability in younger and younger subjects is considered a publication-worthy contribution, drawing on a population of advantaged subjects is an unambiguous benefit.

In other cases, systematic differences were presented as necessary background information. I attended a planning session for a project on noun acquisition by toddlers in the Geller lab. That is, if infants learn a blue widget is called a "snork," will they generalize "snorks" to red and white widgets as well or will they assume that "snork" refers to, say the color blue or that specific widget rather than a class-of-all-widgets? During the discussion, Dr. Geller told her lab that white, middle class, urban parents do not use abstract concepts when classifying objects for their children. She clarified, "That's our population." The purpose of this interjection was to help design a study that would be targeted for the types of subjects they expected. Yet, such practical adjustments undermined the idea that infant subjects could be treated as universal, standard objects.

Class was not the only variable. In another case, Dr. Collins was meeting with two grad students, Sarah and Kristie, who were struggling to extend a popular study on imitation in young toddlers. In their experiment, the experimenter fails to accomplish a task with a toy (pull apart two Lego blocks). Then the toy is provided to the child to see if they will imitate the initial action but, rather than imitate the failed attempt, infer the goal and complete it. Although the pair were achieving some imitation, it was far less than the original study, a situation Dr. Collins called "worrying."

The students then showed Dr. Collins an example video clip to provide information on how the experiment is set up. The subject was an Asian boy who performed the task perfectly. After patiently watching the experimenter fail, he immediately completed the task. Dr. Collins notes how good the subject is and tells a story of an experiment she did earlier in her career that looked at linguistic differences between English and Mandarin speakers. She remembered that the Chinese subjects were far better at the task than the US subjects. They focused and engaged in the task while the American kids wriggled around, getting distracted. She said that the Chinese may have greater executive function and suggested it might be attributable to either genetics or socialization.

Theoretical disagreements produce experimental differences which, over time, create professional divisions.

Nativism v. Empiricism

Normal science requires a shared theoretical framework that can organize thought and establish a set of open research questions. Yet the absence of a successful bench-building program which disciplines fields around material interventions, theoretical frameworks take on a more important role. Moreover, because different theoretical commitments lead to different sets of questions, multiple such frameworks can co-exist. Practical clarity is achieved through distancing rival communities both theoretically and socially.[13] This allows for the production of a type of intersubjective agreement which, under the right conditions, looks very much like objectivity.[14]

Developmentalists across labs frequently brought up the tensions between nativism and empiricism in developmental research. Empiricism was used to indicate a cluster of not wholly congruous specialties like Bayesian learning theory, dynamical systems theory, connectionism, and associationism. What united these perspectives, when evoked by nativists, was their inability to recognize that knowledge development in infants cannot be a purely statistical process that organizes what William James referred to as the "blooming, buzzing confusion" of infant experience. In contrast, nativists believe— "believe like we have blood in our veins" according to Dr. Geller—that infants begin life with some pieces of foundational or "core" knowledge.

For instance, when I asked Alice about Bayesian research, she explained that "I and a lot of people in this department would think there's no way you can build up those concepts from nothing. It can't just be probabilities. It has to at least be weights that are set differentially." She continued, saying that Bayesian learning models violate their own principles by smuggling in pieces of knowledge that the system itself would not be able to learn on its own: "People who are nativists saying, well actually look what you've built into that model. You've kind of made it smarter than you're saying. You kind of took a lot of things for free."

Interactions with empiricists were often awkward for nativists. For instance, when Alice recently visited a prestigious psychology department famous for empiricists, she felt "uncomfortable," explaining that "there's kind of an east coast/west coast gang mentality in developmental psychology." Despite everyone occupying a niche within a niche in psychology—cognitive development—she found it impossible to connect with the people she spoke with: "I kind of felt a little lost, and no one's questions really matched my own. Although they were also really interesting, I didn't feel like I could actually contribute to anything there or engage other people in the kinds of questions I wanted to ask there."

The differences between the fields produced a context in which nativists felt they could neither understand nor communicate with developmentalists they considered to be empiricists. Vani, for instance, told me, "If you go and talk to people in [empiricist labs] it's hard to even have a conversation with them because of how empiricist they are." She later explained that this was due to differences in vocabulary and theoretical assumptions. Sean, another graduate student in the Collins lab interested in the formation of fundamental cognitive concepts, was more critical of "the people who just kind of ignore the problem completely and are more empiricist." However, he had to admit that "frankly, I don't know what exactly they think because I haven't talked to them too much, and whenever I read their papers they don't make any sense to me. Like, they make claims that I just don't understand." As an example, he cited an article by Dr. Jones which purported to solve a classic philosophical problem on the development of common nouns. Yet after Sean read the article, he argued that Dr. Jones had missed the point of the original philosophical argument and "solved some other problem."

To avoid what they see as an unproductive conflict, scholars tend to sort themselves into like-minded groups. For instance, Vani explained that nativist/empiricist arguments rarely arise in her department "because everyone's a nativist. And the people that are working in the fields that we work in are also nativists, so all our conversations and arguments are all with other nativists."

Several times, I watched Dr. Hill criticize empiricist arguments and steer graduates toward nativist interpretations. On a day when the lab was not running subjects, a graduate student from another lab visited to speak with her. He sat on the red pleather couch while she pulled up a small, wooden chair meant for a child. He told her that he was becoming "increasingly convinced" by radical empiricist arguments. Dr. Hill was polite and jovial with him, but she criticized his position after which he backtracked. He no longer claimed to be "convinced." He then said he was "compelled." Still, she pushed, talking about how, in domain after domain of knowledge, nativism was the only position that makes sense.

Another time, Min, a graduate student who had recently joined the Hill lab was discussing a course she was taking with another psychologist in the department. Dr. Hill was frustrated that the student was learning nativist arguments from an empiricist. Min, who had little exposure to the nativist/empiricist debate, queried Dr. Hill on her opinions regarding other theories she is learning. Min asked her about dynamical systems theory. Dr. Hill called it "crap" and asked if they were looking at the work of Dr. Jones, a noted empiricist. Dr. Hill told Min the Jones work was little more than behaviorism since it lacked any system of internal representation and was unable to address the development of complex skills like language.

Similarly, when Sharon was discussing various postdoc opportunities, she mentioned another well-known empiricist. Dr. Collins responded immediately, "What on earth do you have in mind; in the case of [empiricist professor]?" Sharon explained that she was interested in theories of Bayesian learning. Dr. Collins dismissed the idea, arguing that their interests are too divergent to be a good match. Sharon conceded that she had not put much thought into the choice.

Distrust was not one-sided. When I interviewed non-nativist developmental psychologists, they expressed a similar inability or willingness to intellectually connect across their disciplinary divide. Dr. Jones, a frequent target of criticism from nativist developmental psychologists, explained "I don't really feel like I'm in opposition to these people. I, like, have nothing to do with them. Except that I bother them." Like criticisms coming from the other direction, there seemed to be a basic inability to meaningfully engage. This has both theoretical and methodological dimensions.

Dr. Kidder, a developmentalist trained in dynamical systems theory, explained that she feels separated from nativists because of their theoretical commitments: "I would say that they have a theoretical perspective that's driving their research and their ideas of what babies know, more or less. I wouldn't say it's sloppiness. I would say, with their perspective, those are the kinds of conclusions they're going to draw." Dr. Jones was more critical, arguing that nativist psychology was rife with "*a priori* philosophical commitments," explaining, "Would you want your cancer researchers to have ontological commitments? Shit no! Okay? It's a really bad idea. These people are doing a kind of philosophy."

Critiques of nativism were not limited to their theoretical stance. Rather, the entire paradigm of looking-time studies was implicated. Dr. Jones told me,

> I've used preferential looking, too. I know exactly what these methods are. They're a mess. This is why non-replicability is such an issue. Everybody knows on the street what's not replicable. There's a lot of stuff in the journals that's not replicable. Because preferential looking is a terrible, terrible method. But what's bad about it is that people don't care how preferential looking works and they don't care how habituation works.

Similarly, Dr. Kidder who does research specifically on attention, suggested that, although she could advise nativists on crafting better studies, she did not believe any suggestions would be taken seriously. Specifically, she argued that the studies needed to be complicated, using different habituation procedures, yet she believed that such advice would fall on deaf ears.

> If I said, "This is how you should be doing your experiments. You should use ABC and D as your stimuli and you should have one group of babies habituated to A and another to B and another to C and another to D. And then test them on those contrasts later on." They would say, "You don't have to do that. You can just habituate them to A and test them with B. That's all you need to do." They would think it was unnecessary.

Thus, profound theoretical and methodological differences are present. Dr. Jones summarized the estrangement:

> No, they can't understand me, and, like I said, I can't understand them. That says it's incommensurate. We're not in opposition. We're doing different things. We happen to be in the same subfield and publish in the some of the same journals. I often feel like, just don't cite me, I won't cite you. Just let me do my stuff.

Dr. Collins, vowed nativist, conceded that these divisions may be insurmountable: "Every generation an associationist, empiricist movement gets developed under a new name like connectionism or system dynamic theory, and those debates are never going to go away. It's very hard to give absolutely knockdown arguments that everybody agrees with."

Escaping the Swamp

In developmental science, researchers face a tricky balancing act. On one side, there are psychology's ideals regarding what constitutes good science. By modeling their field on an idealized conception of scientific research in the natural sciences, psychology has produced an unforgiving culture where experimental designs must be flawless and must achieve statistical significance. On the other side, however, is a room full of infant subjects perpetually riding the razor's edge between a stormy tantrum and a sound sleep.

Working with infants demands researchers frequently use local, contingent decision-making. What separates this from the local and contingent aspects of typical research environments is that there is little hope of ever reaching "interactive stabilization" (Pickering 1995) between researcher, research technology, and research object. Neither improvements in technology nor more embodied skill will make an infant controllable.

Nonetheless, these nativist developmental psychologists have chosen to stay in the swamp, uncontrollable indeterminacy all around them, in order to pursue a model of normal science. Experiments test theories. Claims are made and extended. Findings are replicated. Yet the problems at the point of data capture are profound and create both empirical and theoretical issues that highlight just how different this version of science is from what I outlined in the chapter on molecular biology.

Gouldner once called normal science the "fusion of intellectual vices and virtues" because, while it was a mode of productive research, it typically avoided interrogating its own foundations.[15] By shielding themselves from both empirical and theoretical problems, they are able to create a productive space of "doable problems."[16] However, this model represents just one way to do science under these challenging conditions. The social psychologists I discuss in the next chapter have forged a very different path.

6

THE VERTIGO OF FREEDOM

Social Psychology and the Dynamics of Interest

The nativist developmental psychologists discussed in the previous chapter attempted to avoid thorny ontological issues by focusing on what was assumed to be the basic, universal architecture of human cognition. Choosing a "pre-socialized" research object, embracing a specific theoretical orientation and set of methods, and overlooking routine violations of experimental protocols enabled them to produce a culture that supported both mutual critique and a growth of knowledge even in the face of minimal technical elaboration.

Despite its benefits, working with infants and toddlers limits the types of questions that can be asked. Number, causality, size, color—familiar developmental topics lend themselves to studies of the evolving cognitive abilities of young children. However, researchers interested in topics like power, love, identity, trust, or justice require subjects who have some familiarity with these rich, socially embedded concepts. Thus, socialization, far from being avoided, becomes a necessary condition for research. Yet trying to fashion a science out of the crooked timber of lay concepts creates its own difficulties.

The characteristic challenge in cell biology is trying to extend perception and control over living systems at microscopic scales. For developmentalists, it is wrangling useful data from newborns and toddlers. In contrast, the central difficulty for social psychologists is making everyday life amenable to scientific scrutiny. That is, how can lay concepts be defined in technical terms? How can they be operationalized? How can experiments be interpreted and generalized? These may seem like simple problems, yet they occupied an enormous amount of time in both the labs I observed.

While the developmentalists adopted a self-consciously normal approach to science, much of the psychology detailed in this chapter can be described as a churn of non-paradigmatic experimentation. Rather than settle on a stable set of concepts and methods, the social psychologists operated in an epistemic environment with few clear standards and nearly limitless possibilities. This was both vexing and exciting

SCIENCE WITHOUT A PARADIGM

Experimentation is what separates social psychology from other domains of expertise that seek to establish authority over everyday life. Political pundits, philosophers, and sociologists write about "power," yet social psychologists have transformed "power" into a variable that can be manipulated as a component within an experimental system. Like biologists doing experiments on mouse retinas, there is a learning process in working with these types of psychological "variables." As Deng, a graduate student, told me, "When you run the experiments, you learn what works. You're going to take that manipulation with you for the next one. If it doesn't work, then you drop [it]."

Yet experimenting on humans provides an uneven ground for developing the sort of somatic expertise and technological control that enables researchers to extend their perceptive or manipulative power. Continuing, Deng admitted that there were limitations to learning that are unavoidable:

DENG: As long as you're dealing with humans, manipulations are not
   perfect. Maybe you read [an article in the *Journal of Personality and*

Social Psychology] and it worked for them, but you bring that in, and it won't work over here. That happens.

AUTHOR. Why do you think that is?

DENG. People, man. You're just dealing with people. Different time periods. Different day. People come in with different moods. You're trying to induce moods sometimes—they come in with sadness, and you're trying to induce happiness. Stuff just doesn't work. When you're dealing with people, you're going to run into stuff like that. Stuff just isn't going to work.

Experimental work, by definition, is neither consistent nor predictable. However, this is not what Deng is pointing out. Rather, his argument is that there is a ceiling on his tacit knowledge because even the "best" manipulations in social psychology will not become reliable technologies.

For instance, many experiments in the social psychology labs used "primes"—methods used to induce specific psychological states. For instance, a researcher may ask a subject to recall a time when they felt powerful or powerless and then write a paragraph about it. Having manipulated the subject's subjective sense of power by having them recount it, experimenters would then have the subject participate in various tasks to see if their performance was affected by this change. Yet despite being widely used, these sorts of primes were notoriously fickle. When I asked Allison, an advanced grad student, about it, she told me,

It's messy. It's noisy because there's so much variability in what people bring into the lab and in how they think about their life experiences. You could recall something from last week and I could recall something from when I was five-years-old. There's so much variability [. . .] It's a quick and dirty manipulation. It can be effective, but it has issues.

An unstandardized, idiosyncratic research object coupled with limited environmental control combine to present a formidable challenge.

Facing this, an experimental community could redirect its attention toward the bench. When complexity is believed to be tamable in some way, researchers may invest their time and resources to build their bench, overcome these limitations, and, in doing so, produce tools which may be taken up by others in their field. Yet if researchers believe engaging with this complexity will be fruitless, a lab's attention may shift away from the bench because time spent developing skills and integrating technologies is seen as producing diminishing returns. Instead, focus goes to other, more profitable, phases of the research process.

Cell biologists often produced dense, hard to interpret data like jagged graphs. This motivated experimenters to return to the bench to refine their methods or introduce new ones. However, if there is little faith that the return trip will be worth it, the jagged graph becomes an end product. Then the question becomes how that imperfect data can be framed and presented. Revisiting a figure from chapter 2, we see how attention can be rebalanced (Figure 6.1).

In nativist developmental psychology, there is a good deal of attention given to coding, data cleaning, and narrative creation in service of crafting something usable out of the data the infants provided.

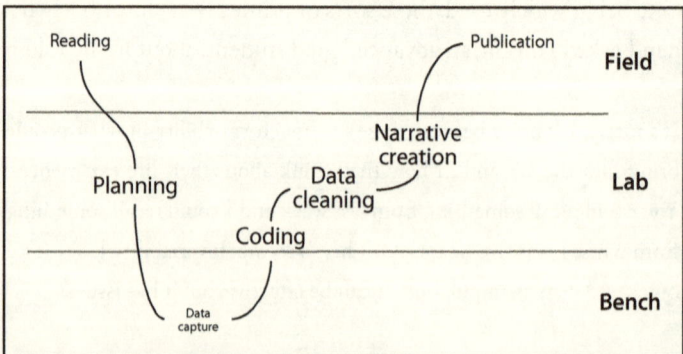

FIGURE 6.1 The Reorientation of Field, Lab, and Benchwork in Social Psychology

However, by embracing stable methods and theories, the types of experiments, theoretical approaches, and narratives were constrained. However, in social psychology, with its proliferation of theories and methods, both the planning and narrative creation phases have few natural bounds and can be disorienting scenes, overflowing with theoretical, methodological, and analytical options.

Most lab meetings were exercises in navigating this sea of choices. After several months of observing lab meetings that left presenters overwhelmed with disconnected or conflicting advice, I began to ask members of the labs how they interpreted it. Ellie, an advanced grad student, admitted that presenters usually get peppered with "a ton of ideas" that "go different directions." To combat information overload, she explained that she had tried to heavily structure her presentations: "If I don't, I end up being, like, what just happened?! I see that look, especially on younger students' faces, where they almost look upset because they feel confused and lost." Another grad student explained, "[The] first couple of times I presented, I was on the verge of tears." She continued, "you feel the lab slipping out of your control and suddenly they're on a crazy tangent, and they want to run their own study based on it, or they have this idea, their own angle on the question."

The dizzying nature of these meetings is the unavoidable outcome of the epistemic approach adopted by these labs. When there are few theoretical and methodological constraints, the possibilities can be both thrilling and overwhelming. In the next two sections, I detail two lab meetings I attended to highlight how this flexibility manifests at different stages of the research process. The first meeting details the planning phase in which a new idea was presented, and the lab helped the presenter operationalize an embryonic concept. The second meeting took place during the narrative creation phase. An article had been rejected by a journal and the group's attention was directed toward figuring out the best way to generate a compelling narrative from the data already gathered.

Operationalizing Lay Concepts in the Wagner Lab

In this section, I provide an extended account of a single lab meeting in which a graduate student presented an idea for a study. The initial idea for the experiment was relatively straightforward—a study of how a culture of kindness within a workplace might affect staff turnover. However, the conversation that resulted was freewheeling and presented the student with dozens of possible directions such a project could take.

His idea was initiated by an observation that the administrative faculty in their department had undergone an unreasonable amount of turnover. This led him to the question: why do people come and go from jobs? Naturally, money was a factor, but is it possible that they also do not like the job culture? If this is important, then what are the aspects of a good working environment? Kindness? Courtesy? He explained that a cursory literature review on the topic revealed that people who expressed positive emotions about a job typically end up staying.

He returned to his question, what constitutes an environment that makes someone want to stay? He suggested that it might reflect a sort of general positive emotion at the job, a phenomenon he labeled "environmental kindness" (EK). His question for the lab was how to design a pilot experiment. The following are direct quotes from my fieldnotes from the beginning of the meeting:

> Dr. Wright asks, "What is environmental kindness?" Deng admits he's not sure how to operationalize it (or even what the theoretical components are). He suggests that things like compliments and helping behavior are sure to be a part of it. His question is how to do a pilot study to get a better grasp on how to do a fuller study on this project.
>
> Holly notes that Linda George has done some work on career satisfaction and is a really nice person to talk to. She suggests he could talk to her on the phone to get a sense of the work that's been done in this area. Deng acknowledges this suggestion.

Marlene asks why he's focused on kindness that's not directed toward the subject. Deng is worried the notion of reciprocation would be too overwhelming then. She asks if he's looking for an idea like "community," and Deng says yes.

Holly asks if Deng is planning on controlling for how the subject is treated in their environment. If he truly wants to avoid the reciprocation charge, he'll have to figure out a way to separate out environmental kindness and kindness directly experienced.

In the first three minutes, the lab leapt between questions of how to define the core concept, how it related to current literature, and how to operationalize it. This was not a sloppy amalgam of issues that are better kept separate. The three goals—which include defining lay understanding, situating the work within the field, and creating an experiment—are intertwined. Commitments made in one dimension constrain the others. For instance, Deng's initial focus was looking at EK as an element of job satisfaction. The commonsensical notion of "good work culture" immediately put this study in the domain of previous studies on the psychology of work which, in turn, already contains a set of well-used methods (e.g., employee satisfaction surveys).

When any element in this package is viewed as unpromising, it necessitates changes that may ramify across the entire study. For instance, very quickly, the lab head dissuaded Deng from pursuing a study of work culture. Dr. Wagner told Deng, "We have five or six ways to measure this. There could be some very innovative ways." He explained that the literature on work was already very dense and would not provide much room for new, exciting theories or methods: "I think if you go into organizations you're bumping up against three-tiered models and just a huge stack of literature." Ellie was also concerned that the study was getting bogged down in a very competitive area: "One of the broader concerns is this sounds like a giant literature." "It is," agreed Dr. Wagner.

With that warning, the initial proposal became just one idea in an unrestrained discussion focused on defining the theoretical concept "environmental kindness," situating it within or against current literature, and investigating it experimentally. Like most lab meetings, talk ricocheted chaotically between these three domains. By the end of the meeting, the possibilities available to Deng were kaleidoscopic.

First, the original idea of looking at EK as a feature of work environments, was given several twists. For instance, rather than employee retention or happiness, Ellie suggested looking at which sorts of work environments people choose to join. She thought that Deng could contrast "good culture" with variables that people typically associate with employment choices like money in order to "create a tension" within the literature.

The idea of studying "joining" was then decoupled from the employment realm by Dr. Wagner who suggested an experiment in which subjects could choose to join a nice group or a group with some other characteristic (e.g., smart or funny). At this point, the conversation was free-flowing enough for people to begin suggesting radical transformations to the original idea. Why study work at all? After all, it is a crowded literature. Dr. Wagner asked if Deng could look at the cultures of softball teams or neighborhoods. Dr. Schmidt, a postdoc, suggested looking at how people choose graduate programs. Deng was swept along by the rapids.

Punctuating this discussion of operationalization were two other conversations. The first concerned the definition of EK. Dr. Wright asked Deng a series of questions about the meaning of this term. Deng explained that his interest was not in the quality of particular relationships but in actions that establish a sense of community. Marlene noted, however, that the exact same actions can have very different interpretations. For instance, a boss giving an employee a birthday cake can seem like a warm gesture if authentic, but it is an empty gesture if mandated by company policy. Dr. Lee, a postdoc, asked if power played a role. That is, does EK come from the top down (e.g., bosses to employees) or is it a phenomenon that emerges between equals? Is there a difference between EK and altruism? Just these two questions opened several, distinct interpretations. For instance, Deng could have defined EK as an authentic culture of kindness by coequals or as a set of behaviors that communicate kindness (authentic or inauthentic, it does not matter) from those in a position of power to their subordinates.

The second conversation concerned strategizing how to fit EK into current literatures. In addition to the research on employee retention already discussed, lab members mentioned many other literatures that seemed relevant to various dimensions of Deng's project. Ellie advised that research on system justification and low self-esteem could explain why people choose to stay in jobs with little EK. Dr. Wagner noted that EK could be a foil to behavioral economic models of decision-making. Jansen, who was a PhD student in the business school offered to send Deng articles on the "affective tone" of organizations.

At the end of the meeting, Deng, shell-shocked, said, "I was looking forward to something I could do on the internet really fast." This provoked laughter from the room.

Two points are important to make about this meeting. First, once the original idea (cultures that make workplaces more appealing) became translated into a variable (environmental kindness) there emerged a staggering diversity of possible projects including everything from people choosing graduate schools to whether people decide to move out of neighborhoods. Theoretically, the study could be narrowly focused on concrete issues of worker retention or could address abstract issues of self-esteem using laboratory experiments. Second, when evaluating which of these projects Deng should pursue, members of the lab were strategically interested in selecting projects that avoided areas that were already highly elaborated. Those with "three-tier models" and crowded literatures were to be avoided. On the other hand, Dr. Wagner specifically advised Deng to ponder his choice because an "innovative" method might be possible.

It might be objected that the lab meeting described above involved a nascent project, and, as such, it should be characterized by a creative exploration of many possibilities. Certainly, it can be argued that research planning should emphasize originality rather than the dogmatic application of tired methods. Yet it is clear from the discussion that there were few constraints of any type on the project. It was not clear which theory would be appropriate nor which type of experiment would be best. And, significantly, researchers much further along in the process face the same set of issues.

Framing Results in the Church Lab

Deng's presentation involved the introduction of an embryonic idea and, thus, could be expected to result in the lively scene described above. This section describes a lab meeting which focused on a set of four experiments that had already been conducted in the Church lab and the attempt to craft from them a compelling, publishable narrative. Even though they already had the data and, thus, were limited in what they could say, this meeting was marked by a similar flexibility.

For the study, Dr. Church and her grad student Hannah were examining the dynamics of romantic relationships. The first draft had recently been rejected from a prestigious journal and the pair was looking to rework it and send it back out. The set of four experiments, which ranged from in-person studies with couples to experiments with online participants, looked at the effect of what they called "understanding" on two outcomes in romantic relationships—feelings of authenticity and relationship satisfaction. The main finding in the original study was that understanding was important for both outcomes but only when there was conflict.

The reviewers focused their critiques on a few issues. For one, they thought the authenticity outcome was vague. Dr. Church admitted being irritated by this but conceded that the article was "cleaner" focusing solely on the relationship satisfaction variable. Additionally, the reviewers argued that the research had been done before. They were preparing to send it out again and brought the article to the lab to get help streamlining the study and emphasizing its originality.

Thus, the lab meeting began with the inversion of the problem that Deng faced. Rather than create the theoretical and empirical possibility for useful data, Dr. Church and Hannah already had their data. Operationalization was done. The data gathered was about romantic relationships and no amount of reframing was going to make this a project about racist stereotypes or cognitive dissonance in political discourse. However, although it constrained the interpretation, the results did not *dictate* their framing. Working from the data, they turned back toward the world of lay knowledge and social psychological literature to search for an appealing way to frame the results they had.

Allison began by asking whether "responsiveness" might be a better concept than "understanding" since their main outcome focused on periods of conflict (a period when responsiveness might be increased). Dr. Church agreed that that might be true but objected that framing the article like that made the finding seem obvious: "The problem I have with that is the problem I always have. It's, like, no kidding responsiveness is good! Arg!" Dr. Church made the strategic goals clear. The right concept must not only fit the pattern of data, but also not diminish the findings by making them seem obvious.

Nicole wanted to know if "understanding" was different than "perspective-taking" which, she noted, already has a rich literature. Hannah agreed the original term used in the rejected draft was not well-received but seemed reluctant to engage that crowded field. Instead, she asked if there was "a concise word or phrase that we can use over and over again that captures that?"

Nicole suggested "validation," a word that would allow them to mostly avoid existing literatures. However, this idea was quickly rejected:

HANNAH: I fear using that actual word might bring up a different literature.

DR. CHURCH: Yeah. There's no way we can use that word.

HANNAH: But I think that is what it is. Maybe we can talk about it a little
more in that way to make it clear.

CHURCH: Maybe in the discussion. But, yeah, we can't use that, or we're
going to get killed.

Although novelty was a goal, thumbing your nose at current research
would likely not be well-received by reviewers (who may well be
authors working in the snubbed literature).

Hannah asked the lab if it was a good idea to change the central
concept to "responsiveness," a concept already established in the literature. Mary thought it was possible but cautioned that the reframing
raised a potential problem. Previous research had argued that responsiveness is composed of three components (understanding, validation, and support). This framing would demand that Dr. Church
and Hannah show how their findings met these criteria. Because the
study was not designed with this in mind, meeting this bar might be
impossible.

Dr. Church brought attention back to the data and asked the room
what they thought of the central finding of the four studies, that "feeling understood buffers you against the negative effects of conflict."
Dan said that he found the study surprising because he would have
guessed that feeling understood would be universally helpful: "My lay
belief is that having a partner who's understanding is always good."
"That's good for us," she told him. Dr. Church continued arguing
that, in order to make the paper more appealing, they needed to do a
better job to "set up the counterintuitive notion." Referring to Dan's
comment, she made a suggestion: "This two-paragraph section would
need to start off with, not literally this but, 'Everyone thinks that perceived understanding is great.'" After asking the lab and making sure
that this belief was common, she continued, "but then we would need

to argue that it's unclear under which circumstances it helps." She reiterated, "It's setting up the counterintuitive notion."

Hannah then asked whether framing the article would be easier if they dropped one of the experiments and only presented data on three. While the first three experiments were all based on questionnaires, the fourth involved actual couples who were videotaped during a task and Hannah admitted that its inclusion was done with a "strategic" motive: "We were thinking people are going to like this observed, behavioral piece." Dr. Church was frustrated that the outcome—which showed that having a responsive partner improved relationship satisfaction—was "so obvious." However, she dithered: "But it's behavior. That's the cool part." Hannah suggested that they could cite the video as evidence of "behavioral indicators" of validating and understanding (two of three components of responsiveness according to Mary). That would allow them to use responsiveness.

The meeting ended with nothing settled. Compared to the previous example, the discussion in this meeting was more constrained. Rather than an abstract idea, the authors already had results and a framing. Despite this, the central concept in the paper was not settled and could have been labeled understanding, perceived understanding, validation, empathy, affirmation, self-verification, perspective-taking, or responsiveness. This choice would have necessitated changes in how the article was framed within the literature. The data, although providing Dr. Church and Hannah with the multiple points of statistical significance they would need to publish, did little to adjudicate these problems. Additionally, the inclusion or exclusion of the fourth experiment provided additional flexibility in defining their concepts.

THE CONSTRAINTS OF "REALITY"

After her presentation with Hannah, I asked Dr. Church whether theoretical and analytic flexibility provided room for strategic choices about the framing of her findings. She rejected this. "Reality constrains you," she countered. However, when she elaborated, it was clear she had a very specific concept of "reality": "You can't really do whatever you want because you're bound by shared knowledge and reviewers will eventually see your work. You don't really have a choice in the matter, right?"

The constraints imposed by "reality" in social psychology are not the same ones that the molecular biologist Dr. Harden was describing when she lamented, "Sometimes the biology doesn't intersect with our efforts in the way we want." This is not the constraint of a natural system which is uninterested in our attempts to make it legible and enroll it in the pursuit of our goals. Rather, Dr. Church was referring to the constraints of a field's collective judgment. Yet without an evolving frontier of technical possibility which settles facts by building them into experimental subroutines, the concept of "shared knowledge" that Dr. Church referenced is as fractured and contradictory as the lab meetings.

This is why Mark, an advanced graduate student, told me, "What gets published are things that work. That seems to be the only standard as far as I can tell. It just has to be a consistent story that makes sense given the past literature and has findings to back it up." That is, if a set of studies contains statistically significant relationships that can be framed in a way coherent with previous studies, a paper will find a home. Yet without a dominant theoretical paradigm nor clear methodological standards, making research "consistent" with and fitting it into the "past literature" can be taken as literary exercises rather than serious constraints. As Dr. Wright told me, "To me, it always felt like there's a little bit of creative, a little bit of fiction to what we do. The most cynical part of me feels like we write science fiction, and the plot is data." In this section I look at how both the plot and the data can be creative resources for social psychologists.

Playing Games with Language

For social psychologists whose research objects include lay concepts, the amorphousness of natural language is both a frustration and a strategic resource. Using phrases like "supportive working environment" or "validation in intimate relationships" in casual conversation would rarely elicit a request for clarification. Yet the same concepts in the context of an experimental laboratory demanded an enormous amount of the lab's attention. Endless discussions revolved around choosing the best word to describe a phenomenon and debating the meaning of terms. This was *the* characteristic challenge in the two social psychology labs I observed.

It is a practical problem with its roots in a philosophical conundrum. Everyday language is a flexible and evolving medium, and the words we use to understand our lives may not correspond to what philosophers call "natural kinds." That is, they may not reflect divisions in the natural world. For instance, even psychologists who claim that human emotions have evolved for specific reasons and, thus, can be separated into a limited set, tend to produce lists that hardly cover the totality of emotional experience. For instance, Paul Ekman's original formulation included anger, fear, happiness, sadness, and surprise. Yet much of our emotional life exists in complex admixtures that cannot be neatly reduced to these. What of giddiness? Or yearning? Or resentment?

Researchers interested in trying to manipulate emotions in subjects often faced the issue that emotions are rarely independent. For instance, in developing a method to prime subjects to feel awe, Derrick complained that he was unable to generate awe without also producing happiness: "It's basically just a mix of good emotions." Conceptually, it is possible to separate them. For instance, an immense storm might produce a feeling of awe, but happiness would likely not accompany it. Yet, empirically, it is hard to isolate because any experience of awe, a profound emotion, is probably going to elicit other emotions (in the case of the storm, terror).

Even common forms of experience proved elusive. Dr. Schmidt was investigating the effect of humor on a game in which one participant allocated money to the other. Her idea was to have two subjects come into the lab, engage in a cooperative task while she measured the amount of humor generated by the dyad, and then test if the level of humor predicted the amount of generosity in the allocation game.

Despite the relatively straightforward premise, the study raised many thorny questions, and the lab spent much of Dr. Schmidt's presentation wrangling with the concept of humor. To summarize just one line of questioning:

Does merely *making* jokes count as humor?
Does it need to produce a reaction from the other subject?
Does this reaction have to be laughter?
If so, is the study about laughter, then?
If so, what about laughter that seems disconnected from humor
    (e.g., nervous or polite laughter)?

When I interviewed Dr. Schmidt later, I asked about the difficulty associated with trying to define such a common concept. She explained, "Humor is broad. There's positive humor and negative humor. There's irony. And, you don't even have a uniform definition of humor. Some say that sarcasm is a part of humor. Some say, no, it's different. [. . .] Everyone seems to know what humor is but, actually, nobody does."

But, of course, everybody does know what humor is. At least, if tell a friend I saw a funny movie, they understand what I mean. What people *cannot* do is give a definition of humor that both meets our understanding of the concept and can be operationalized in a way appropriate for scientific experimentation. Charles S. Peirce reminds us that "No words are so well understood as vernacular words [. . .] yet they are invariably vague."[1] Natural language does not evolve for scientific purpose and, thus, is poorly equipped to be translated into technical terminology.

Thus, while people can argue about which definition of humor is better, there is no reason to believe that any one is *correct*. As Nick told me,

> A lot of times, it comes down to semantics [. . .] I think it's important to clearly define what it is that you the researcher means by that term so that other researchers can see if what you're working on fits with what they're working on. But it's problematic. It's frustrating trying to figure out the right terms to label the things that you're talking about and trying to figure out how they're similar or different than all the other constructs that seem very, very related and overlapping.

However, if wrestling with concepts seems to be just "semantics," its effects are anything but. Conceptual differentiation can have social ramifications as research traditions splinter and grow around particular social networks. Shan, a graduate student in the Wagner lab, lamented that "people might use the same term, but they refer to different things or they might be talking about very similar things, but, because they have their own subfield term for it, those groups never meet. You'd never even know that there's a whole existing thing because you don't know what to search for."

Like the mutually incompatible nativist and empiricist traditions in developmental psychology, conceptual differentiation can produce research traditions that, while obviously occupying the same theoretical space, are seemingly blind to each other. Dr. Wright lamented, "Everyone's trying to differentiate themselves. They're all doing different things. They don't collaborate." He continued,

> You can get a sense of this by two relevant literatures—social status and social power. Very, very relevant to each other. How much status you have. How much power you have. They never cite one another. They're

so busy thinking about what distinguishes them from others and want-
ing to create their own identity that they're not referencing the other
literatures.

These types of divisions are found in many places. For instance,
regarding a similar split within her area of interest, Ellie told me
that, "There's work on 'prevention and promotion' which is pretty
much the exact same thing as 'approach/avoidance.' Are you focused
on preventing bad things or promoting good things? Do you want
to avoid bad things or approach good things? [. . .] They exist in
different labs. They don't cite each other." And Shan described an
incident from a qualifying exam in which she was attempting to
understand the difference between the literatures on "uncertainty"
and "sense of control": "They're so hugely overlapping. When do
you feel a loss of sense of control? When you feel uncertain. When
might you feel uncertain? Well, part of the subjective feeling of
uncertainly is that you don't have control. Yet because you have
careers built on one thing versus another, I think you highlight the
differences a lot more."

Conceptual differentiations produce social divisions, and, with the
flexibility inherent in labeling and defining concepts, aligning yourself with or distinguishing yourself from an existing tradition can be
a consequential strategic decision. Both moves come with trade-offs.
Aligning with an existing tradition can help if members of that group
review the article and value the expansion of the field. However, they
can also be especially critical of new work in their specialty. It was for
this reason that Deng was advised to avoid the literature on employee
satisfaction.

On the other hand, attempting to distinguish research by making a break with current traditions can make research seem novel and
exciting. Conversely, it can anger reviewers who feel such "innovation" represents little more than a shallow rebranding. Dr. Church and
Hannah recognized this threat when they dismissed the idea of using

the new term "validation" over more established concepts in the literature on romantic relationships.

Renaming a research tradition is more palatable when its members have retired or are peripheral scholars. But this can result in the repetition of research. Ellie told me, "people don't realize there's work that has been done and then redo and think they're the first people to have done it. This is always a problem in psychology. I've found articles that I think are scarily similar to mine from, like, the 70s." She recently discovered an article from the 1990s that anticipated a currently popular psychological model on the benefits of positive emotions: "I do think psychology has the weird thing where sometimes we allow a reinvention of the wheel."

Going Fishing

Conceptual flexibility provides some room to move narratively yet does not solve the problem of bench-building which occurs at the data capture phase. To ensure that they have something to bring to the stage in which concepts become important, social psychologists can provide themselves with data that can be analyzed in multiple ways to improve the chances of producing statistical significance. In some cases, this meant keeping data that might be excluded for various reasons to see if they made a difference to the final results.

In online experiments, for instance, subjects who fail "attention checks"[2] can be automatically excluded from analysis. However, in a discussion in the Church lab, Lauren advocated a different strategy: "You should be telling them, 'You failed this attention check. Answer it again.' [. . .] That way you don't have to exclude them. It just lets them know." Hannah replied that she still would not want to use that data since such unmotivated subjects would probably just learn to better detect attention checks rather than focus on the substantive questions.

DR. CHURCH: Well, she can figure that out.

HANNAH: She can't because then they start answering them correctly.

DR. CHURCH: I know. I meant she could analyze the data with and without the failures.

Thus, although it would be impossible to figure out if the data were actually improving, such warnings would allow the researcher to keep the data and decide whether or not to exclude them.

In many cases, however, the goal from the start is to build a dataset with flexibility. Some used the language of "casting a wide net" to refer to the practice. For instance, Ellie explained that, for the experiments that would form the backbone of her dissertation, "My goal was, by casting a large net of things to code, I would give myself the best chances of finding effects." Similarly, during a presentation in the Wagner lab, Daphne was previewing a planned study which used pictures posted on Facebook as its primary data. She told the lab, "I'm casting a wide net based upon what we can get at in the photos" and described dozens of variables she was planning on having her research assistants code.

Casting a wide net was an especially common strategy for in-person (as opposed to online) studies. Experimenting on live subjects was a risky endeavor due to its financial and labor costs. Spending eight months planning an experiment, training research assistants to run it (and, perhaps, perform as confederates in it), collecting data, and analyzing it only to find nothing could hobble a career still in the starting gates. Thus, these studies in particular tended to be dense with variables to code.

When I asked Allison, one of Dr. Church's graduate students, about an in-person study she was currently running examining the effects of social rejection, she explained that choosing a rich data source provided more options in the data analysis phase: "I have a lot of options which is how I design my studies deliberately. That's something I was trained in at one point! Throw a million DVs [dependent variables] in there because you never know what's going to work." Dependent variables are things measured that are supposed to be altered in some why by the independent variable [IV] that the experimenter manipulates. Having more DVs provides more opportunities for statistically significant findings. She continued,

> I have a lot of self-reports. A lot of different scales. A lot of different ways of asking the questions about expectations for acceptance and worry about rejection. And then I'll have a seven-minute video interaction for each participant, with the participant and the confederate so you can code for a million different things. Not a million. That's an exaggeration but, maybe, 20. So, things like a global assessment—how warm was this person? How interested did they seem in social connection? How friendly were they? And then more specific behavioral things like nonverbals—like eye contact and smiling, mimicry and synchrony. Like, if I were to do this [mimics my posture]. It's a subtle movement that matches your partner and increases rapport. And then verbal things like, do they laugh? Are they saying things like "uh huh," "yeah," "good idea"? Are they responding positively to the person as they're doing this problem-solving task together.

When I asked if she maximized the number of dependent variables because it was a time-intensive experiment with live subjects rather than an easier to run experiment with online participants, she agreed: "Exactly. Just the cost in terms of time and labor is very high compared to someone who runs a very simple study. But, yes, hopefully the richness will pay off."

Although it was openly discussed in the lab, there was also an acknowledgment that such analytic flexibility should not be publicized. When Hannah was preparing job market materials, she used one section of her research statement to highlight a new study. However, she was concerned this new line of inquiry would appear "too narrow" and wanted it to "seem like it could go a bunch of different directions." She continued, "I basically have sets of IVs and DVs, and you can mix and match." Dr. Wagner warned her not to say that. Such options might be practically helpful, but to admit to designing a study for that purpose seems unfocused.

Like the flexible practices that developmental psychologists engaged in, these activities should not be considered "good" or "bad" in themselves. Decisions made in analysis—for instance, whether to combine measures or exclude subjects—can be either legitimate acts of expert discretion or researcher misconduct depending upon context and motivation. However, it was clear that the area in-between was vast and murky. Dr. Wright explained how he perceived the tension:

> I think that would be an ideal that you go in a priori, knowing what you're going to measure, measure that thing, and then test for an effect. Strategically, that doesn't always work. Let's say you videotape people in a room, and you're interested in what people do in that room. You could have decided, "Hey, I'm going to be affecting whether people smile or not" but you don't get an effect there, but you've got 800 different kinds of things that you could also be coding for. So, there's a fine line between testing a prediction that you had at the outset versus just going about things strategically to find an effect. And I think people struggle with that.

Yet, because of the flexibility in the field, there were not clear standards. Different ideas of what qualified as smart, "strategic" expertise versus an abuse of trust created divisions between researchers.

For instance, I spoke with Nick about a project he had worked on for months with Dr. Church. Eventually, Dr. Church told him they should stop wasting their time since it did not look like it was going to produce anything. However, he then noted that,

> NICK: Different advisers have different styles in terms of the extent that they want you to continue to just see if anything is there.
> AUTHOR: Just fish for stuff?
> NICK: Yeah.

Because the vast majority of studies in these labs were coauthored with faculty advisers, those "styles" were communicated directly to students.

In other cases, advisers can foster flexible practices by leaving the work of analysis to the students and only engaging when strong results were produced. Daphne explained that she did not feel comfortable going to her adviser with questions about data analysis: "Whenever I've asked him detailed questions about anything he wants nothing to do with it. He's a big picture guy. Whatever the logistics and details are, he doesn't care." Later, she said, "I didn't know there were three different ways I could analyze this dataset. But when I go to my advisers, they can't tell me which one to use." In experimental science, learning to make these types of decisions is an important part of the training. However, in fields in which bench-building (and, thus, integrative replication) is rare, there is far wider latitude in analysis. Other labs will not necessarily depend upon Daphne's results to build their own research agenda. The robustness of the finding (or even the basic truth of it) will not be tested as other labs integrate her manipulations into their procedures. Even if they do, failures will be evaluated generously because, as Deng said, "People, man. You're just dealing with people [. . .] Stuff just doesn't work." Thus, the constraints on her analytic choices are almost entirely driven by her own internal sense of what constitutes "good research" rather than fear of professional embarrassment.

When these vague and weakly policed standards meet the practical pressure to publish, they may not provide much resistance. Thus, researchers engage in behaviors like "p-hacking," in which analytic choices are made with the goal of producing statistical significance.[3] They contribute to the file-drawer problem.[4] That is, they run many studies, only publish the ones that work, and bury the rest in their file drawers leading to a skewed perception of effects in a field.

As Mark argued, "There's a reason people are p-hacking. It's because their results aren't coming. I've analyzed plenty of data and things have gotten close, and I can analyze them in ways where they become significant. I could probably build a career out of doing that. I don't think I'd get caught." Similarly, Dr. Wright noted, "Very rarely is a paper published with a study that didn't work. So, what's going on? Are social psychologists just super brilliant at creating hypotheses that are bound to pan out? Or are their file drawers massive?" He later admitted,

> I do this. I've done this myself. I'm increasingly trying not to, but I've definitely been victim to this. You've got a study. It didn't perfectly work out the way that you thought it did. But, hey! There's this other thing that's happening. So, maybe that becomes what the study was actually designed to test. So, I end up writing a paper on that thing. Or, with coding, you know, you code a bunch of stuff and see what happens and then create your research program around that.

Even when initial ideas do not work out, it is possible to organize a research program around a finding that spontaneously emerges from the dataset. Yet when the data is designed to be rich with variables, it is likely that something *will* emerge. Because the conceptual side of the field is so fragmented and overlapping, it is nearly always possible to develop a compelling narrative around statistical significance.

THE PURSUIT OF THE INTERESTING

Flexibility in both the conceptual and empirical dimensions solves a set of problems for social psychologists who engage in this sort of pre-paradigmatic science. Conceptual flexibility allows social psychologists to define their research objects in ways that either places them within an ongoing lineage of or as a novel break from existing work. Empirical flexibility ensures that studies will produce enough statistically significant relationships with which to develop a narrative.

Yet the myriad possibilities in both conceptual and empirical dimensions create their own problems. How do researchers choose which literature to embrace? How do they select a framing within that literature? Which findings can they weave together? Which variables matter? As Dr. Church noted earlier, what ultimately constrains social psychologists is the "reality" of peer judgment, and, as such, the answer to these questions is found in the field. Yet because of interpretive flexibility, researchers are able to craft their literature reviews as "Whig histories" in which their study is the culmination of a research tradition.[5]

Although there are many reasons why ideas become ascendant in any context, one significant factor in the popularity of ideas is that they stand out in what Collins labeled the "attention space."[6] They become objects of collective focus and criticism and reshape the symbolic space of the field. In sciences that engage in ongoing bench-building, the attention space is largely occupied by the techniques and technologies that will enable new vistas of control and perception. Fields not organized around bench-building may choose different objects of attention. In Murray Davis's article "That's Interesting!," he argues that theories in social science do not rise and fall based upon their objective truth but upon how interesting they are. Careful, exacting theories are forgotten while bold, creative theories—even those that are sloppily conceived or incomplete—will find an audience.[7]

What makes a theory interesting? Succinctly, interesting theories undermine the assumptions of their audience. They are surprising in some way. Thus, in the context of sexually repressed European culture, Freud argued that sex was not some purely biological act that could be confined to the marital bedroom. Instead, his theory framed it as a primordial force, emerging in infancy, and affecting every part of the personality and even society. This was both shocking and intriguing.

Interesting theories surprise their audience, but they must do so in ways the audience is willing to entertain. Non-interesting theories either affirm audience assumptions or attempt to deny assumptions to such an extreme degree that the audience rejects them. Thus, had Freud written a theory supporting repressive views of sex, his work would have been uninspiring and little discussed. Alternatively, if he had argued that the primary motivating force was humor, he might have been dismissed as a crackpot. An important corollary to this second point is that an interesting theory can only emerge in relation to and in tension with the expectations of a specific reference group. Freud's theory would have had a different reception in a less repressive milieu.

This focus on interesting results is explicitly laid out in some writing guides for aspiring young psychologists. In these guides, the idea of "interesting" research plays a key role. It is of clear importance to Cornell psychologist Daryl Bem who advises young psychologists, "If you see dim traces of interesting patterns, try to reorganize the data to bring them into bolder relief. If there are participants you don't like, or trials, observers, or interviewers who gave you anomalous results, drop them (temporarily). Go on a fishing expedition for something— anything—interesting."[8] And Kurt Gray and Daniel Wegner, who title their article "Six Guidelines for Interesting Research," exhort young psychologists to "counter intuitions" and advise scholars to not be afraid to make their experiments "generally curious, bizarre, and outlandish."[9]

Although the dynamics of interest are at play in all fields, it is clear that social psychologists are being advised to be interesting not just to professional colleagues but also to the lay audiences. For instance, in explaining how to write up results, Bem argues that articles should be written for your "grandma" rather than professional psychologists. Bem suggests organizing your article like an hourglass with broad statements of significance at the beginning and end connected by a narrower discussion of the data and methods. He writes, "The hourglass shape of an article implies that your final words should be broad general statements of near-cosmic significance, not precious details of interest only to psychologists."[10] Thus, the goal is to present findings in ways that appeal to audiences beyond the narrow walls of the academy.

One practical outcome of this is a strategy of avoiding what Gray and Wegner call "intellectual crowding." Because dense intellectual environments tend to be structured around theoretical and experimental complexities that bore lay audiences, they advocate a continual search for fresh problems:

> As soon as you find yourself surrounded by others, consider seeking out the dangerous freedom of the unexamined. Usually—but not always—this risk is rewarded and can help lay the foundation for a new subfield. Like an architect, design and construct new buildings, but try not to dwell in them.[11]

Rather than continue to work on an idea, they advocate young researchers create ideas only to bequeath them to others. Good, ambitious researchers are expected to contribute fresh ideas, letting lesser psychologists grind out the implications.

The dynamics of interest play a special role in social psychology for two reasons. First, most sciences have evolved complex systems of meaning and technical terminology. This self-referential closure and monopolization of a domain is what defines a field. Like hearing an anecdote in a language that one does not understand, the public is in little position to evaluate what constitutes an interesting theory in most scientific fields. However, in psychology, and especially social psychology, theories are often enmeshed in the meanings of everyday life. Social psychological concepts like "implicit bias" and "grit" intersect with popular imagination in ways that "ion channels" and "glial cells" do not. Thus, there is an ongoing tension and exchange in the field between its technical/self-referential and lay/popular aspects.

Second, Davis's theory, while an insightful analysis of social scientific theories, is not adequate for understanding bench-building sciences. In these fields, interesting work need not merely subvert expectations. Rather, it may *fulfill* them. Interest is not only piqued because one is wrong about something. It can occur when something that one suspects, believes, or hopes is made real—for instance, a belief that directionally-selective retinal neurons can have their polarities flipped transforms from a mere possibility to an outcome that can be reliably produced. The relative paucity of bench-building in social psychology makes pursuing counterintuitive theories more important.

Interesting Research in Social Psychology

Several social psychologists told me that their field faced a unique problem because, unlike chemistry or physics, non-experts often feel qualified to weigh in on social psychological research. Dr. Wright explained that social psychology is in an odd position in the sciences (and even other psychological subfields like developmental psychology) because people "don't have intuitions about chemicals" and "don't have intuitions about a six-month old." However, because we do have intuitions about socialized adults and their behavior, it leads to a "constant struggle to come up with stuff that's new and creative, that's surprising to people." Supporting this point, Mary told me, "Part of the problem with psychology is that everyone is a lay psychologist. Everybody has ideas of how psychology works. So, if you find something that everyone says 'Well, of course!' [to] then nobody cares. So, everyone is trying to find something that will surprise people because that's the only way that you get people to actually care."

During a presentation by Allison, the lab was narrowing down an interpretation of the data she had presented. Dr. Church, however, was not happy with it and warned it was too expected. She worried that reviewers would claim "it's obvious and it's just saying what we already know." Allison replied, "Yeah, I get that criticism all the time. I hate it." The criticism was common enough that Dr. Church had internalized it. She told me that when her students presented her with non-surprising findings, she was often sarcastic in her response: "I'll say things, like, 'If you're nice to your partner, guess what? It's good for your relationship!' Are you kidding me? Oh! Show gratitude and it's good for your relationship! Show compassion and—Hey!—it's good for your relationship! You know, that kind of thing."

Although surprising findings were prized, the notion of "counterintuitive" raises an important question. Counterintuitive to whom? One of the problems with Collins' concept of "attention space," is that there are many nesting and overlapping attention spaces. Social psychology is a subfield within psychology. Within social psychology, there are crisscrossing specialties. Social psychologists are fighting for attention from cognitive and cultural psychologists when they publish in general psychology journals. They are fighting social psychologists when they publish in their subfield. Across these journals, they are competing with others in their specialty for the right to make the arguments that will drive their area of study forward. Finally, because social psychology intersects with lay imagination, they are fighting for attention in a public space that includes writers, artists, and public intellectuals. Because they are investigating concepts that we use in our everyday lives—things like power, kindness, generosity, validation, etc.—research communities in social psychology do not fully extricate themselves from it. Yet within the field, they develop their own expectations regarding what is considered novel or stale based upon the current state of the field.

Research that surprises the public can receive popular attention yet may be viewed within the field as shallow or sensationalist. Conversely, research of primarily academic interest might be respected, but is often dismissed as unimaginative. Several times, the distinction was framed as the difference between the two most prestigious journals in the field. *Psychological Science* had developed a reputation for publishing short, attention-grabbing studies that often received media attention while the *Journal for Personality and Social*

Psychology (*JPSP*) was known for producing longer, drier studies that were more respected.

In this context, researchers often tried to split the difference with studies that were intriguing, but not flashy. Rather than shock people, Allison argued the goal was to produce a finding that did not seem impossible yet was counterintuitive enough that it "makes someone raise their eyebrows a little bit. Makes them go, 'Huh. That's a new way of looking at it.'" She continued, "It doesn't have to be sexy. It doesn't have to be the [*Psychological Science*] model which is something short and snappy that the newspapers will pick up. But I think you shouldn't read and go, 'No duh.' It shouldn't be something that you've always known, and someone is finally bothering to document it." Separately, Dr. Church told me, "I'm not someone known for sexy findings. It's definitely not something that drives what I do. I think of it more as a more complicated, nuanced understanding [. . .] But, on the other hand, I'm not an idiot. I don't want to do totally boring stuff, because it's boring!"

Avoiding Crowds

Navigating between the public and expert attention spaces means understanding how to appeal to the public without alienating the field. This requires avoiding what Gray and Wegner call "intellectual crowding"—developing novel theories in new areas without getting bogged down in the details of a highly elaborated field.

For instance, Deng was beginning a project looking at the relationship between time pressure and the sense of beauty. He wondered if people with terminal illnesses developed a deeper appreciation for beauty because they were nearing the end of their lives. During a wide-ranging conversation during his presentation, questions were raised about how different types of "beautiful" objects are cognitively processed. "Beauty" might include such categories as dazzling, sublime, and appealing and time pressure might not have the same effect on all. Derick noted that previous research has already demonstrated that things that are merely "pretty" are more "fluent" and "easy to process." Because of this, Dr. Wagner argued that the study of things that are pretty was "a less interesting story because that ground's already been broken."

Yet the popular media and the academic literature are densely populated with claims. A lot of ground has been broken, and it can be hard to find an untrod patch of grass on which to build something new. When I asked about the challenge of coming up with something novel or surprising about human nature in a crowded market, Dr. Wright conceded, "It's totally crowded. And how do we set ourselves apart and find things that people didn't know? That's really hard to do. How do you uncover stuff that people didn't know?"

One answer to this is bench-building in which something genuinely novel is created. But, in the absence of bench-building, researchers manufactured novelty by exploiting the dynamics of interest in the attention space of their field. In one exchange, members of the Church lab were discussing "attachment theory," developed by John Bowlby and Mary Ainsworth, which argues that secure emotional attachment to a caregiver in childhood is key to emotional development. Dan had been speaking to a professor in the department who had conducted many studies on attachment but was leaving the area. Dan attributed her disinterest to the belief that the main findings were well-established, and there would be no more interesting findings: "Secure attachment is good. Insecure attachment is bad. It's getting to the point where nobody cares anymore." Dan wondered aloud if it was a "dead field," and Dr. Church agreed it was.

Mark, however, suggested that such consensus could be a "useful exercise" to subvert expectations and create a new interesting finding: "When can secure attachment be bad? Like in the context of an abusive relationship." Hannah agreed that the counterintuitive finding would be interesting but argued that, first, "it's important to establish basic phenomena." Mark replied, "Yeah, you can only say that when everyone is saying one thing, when everyone is saying that secure attachment is good. Then, when all that hard work has been laid down, then you can deconstruct it."

Here Mark explicitly laid out one of the strategies for exploiting the dynamics of attention in fields. An idea emerges that seems challenging and innovative. In this case, "Secure relationships in infancy and early childhood establish a relationship schema that benefits intimate relationships throughout the life course." The idea intrigues and excites other researchers who flock to it, embrace it, and begin to conduct research on it. This research produces a vague, general consensus ("Secure attachment is good"). This establishes a baseline intuition within the field that can then be undermined by studies which demonstrate conditions in which the expectation is proven wrong. The dynamics of interest produce a cycle of novelty-popularity-elaboration before either becoming "too crowded" and, thus, less beneficial or becoming disciplinary commonsense which can be caricatured and attacked.

Progress in Social Psychology

Exploiting the dynamics of interest is an unusual description of scientific progress. Yet when I asked social psychologists to define progress in their field, they did not offer anything like the technological development of bench-building. For instance, Lauren responded,

> I was actually just asking myself that same question and thinking I have no idea. It's tough because as a researcher you want to do things that not only progress the science but help people overall, like the application of research to the real world which I think gets lost a little bit. So, progress in social psychology? [Pause] I don't know. I'm having trouble thinking about it linearly where we're reaching for some sort of higher

goal. I would think about it more like a pool of knowledge and we're trying to expand outward and just try to understand more about the human mind, about our social relationships.

Nick was similarly conflicted when I asked him where he thought progress had been made in social psychology:

That's a good question. I don't know. I don't know if there is one theory that comes to mind. [. . .]. There [are] definitely theories within that field that have helped in terms of organizing research and moving it forward [. . .] I think that they're very useful for helping scientists talk to one another, for organizing the research that's already been done, and moving forward in the future. But I don't think they're sacrosanct or anything and wouldn't necessarily undergo revision in the future.

Both responses are notable for lacking a clear answer to what, one would assume, would be an easy question about a field to which they have dedicated themselves. Also, worth attending is they both understand how the current theories serve an important social function as a "pool of knowledge" useful for "organizing the research that's already been done."

Of course, social psychology has embraced certain innovations, and this can be viewed as a form of progress. The use of online research platforms has changed the field.[12] New methods like experience sampling, in which subjects use their smartphones to provide data during their daily lives, may prove useful.[13] Moreover, as new social phenomena emerge—for instance, the rise of social media—specialties develop to study them. As Ellie argued, "I think there are times where small pockets are new. So, in the way that society changes we can change."

Yet there was also a sense that, despite these changes, there is a timelessness to the problems of human nature. Ellie continued, "We're all people and were always doing the same thing. And we're also plagued by the same questions." Similarly, Lauren suggested that there might be some basic limits to progress inherent to the object of study: "How much more of the human condition can you actually expand outward on?"

At a basic level, few social psychologists I asked had a concept of scientific progress beyond "Find an interesting effect and explore its dynamics." In reply to the same question about how social psychology progresses, Dr. Mitchell admitted,

> In terms of thinking about new mediators or moderators, and maybe this is just my limited perspective, but what else would there be to create the type of fuller advances that you're thinking about? Maybe that just reflects how much I'm blinded by the low-depth norms of the field. That's just where you stop. But I'm not even sure where you'd go. I guess I don't even know how to think about the question. Where would you go next?

In a field characterized by bench-building, this sort of elaboration is just a means to further developments, not an end. When bench-building is uncommon in a field, the dynamics of interest can be used to define progress.

In fields without ongoing bench-building, one option is to organize around novelty. During our discussion about progress, Lauren explained that she felt that "if you just start looking at mediators of some relationship that has already been hammered over and over, that's just not interesting and people will not find that compelling enough to be published or to be presented." I ask if the work would be viewed as too technical and she corrects me: "Not novel enough. Like, you're not contributing enough unless it's very counterintuitive."

Avoiding crowds is a survival strategy when a field is governed by the dynamics of attention. Entire subfields will hollow out and die as researchers move to greener pastures. Dr. Wright told me about a moment of awakening he had shortly before going to graduate school. At the time, he had been studying behavioral analysis with animals and finally attended a conference to present his research. He was not impressed by the audience:

> There were about 40 other people there and they were all elderly. [laughter] I'm not exaggerating. I was definitely the youngest person there. To me, this was the first time where I saw what it looks like for there to be a paradigm shift. This is a paradigm shift. This was the cutting-edge shit 50 years ago. This is not the cutting-edge shit anymore.

Although he still had "a lot of respect for it," he did not believe he could make a career there. He contrasted that with his experience at the Society for Personality and Social Psychology conference: "Now, if you go to SPSP which is our area's main conference, there's house music playing. You've got 20,000 people walking around. Most of them are graduate students. You get a sense of 'this is what's in vogue now.' It's very hip. It's a very hip science."

7

CAN MERTON
DISCIPLINE PSYCHOLOGY?

Methodological Reform in Psychology

In the previous three chapters, I argued that fields that do psychological experiments on humans face both ethical and ontological problems that constrain their ability to engage in the practice of bench-building. There are different ways to address these issues within their field. I outlined how nativist developmental psychologists dealt with it by imposing a strong theoretical framework and adopting flexible empirical practice while the social psychologists I observed focused on exploiting the dynamics of attention. These strategies give the fields logics within which to operate. Like Feynman's cargo cults, they resemble other sciences with their experimentalism, quantitativeness, and theory-testing. Yet, the planes do not come.

Methodologist and firebrand Paul Meehl spent decades warning that the practices of experimental psychology were never going to produce science of lasting significance.[1] He noted ruefully that,

> . . . a zealous and clever investigator can slowly wend his way through a tenuous nomological network, performing a long series of related experiments which appear to the uncritical reader as a fine example of 'an integrated research program,' without ever once refuting or corroborating so much as a single strand of the network [. . .] In terms of his contribution to the enduring body of psychological knowledge, he has done hardly anything. His true position is that of a potent-but-sterile

intellectual rake, who leaves in his merry path a long train of ravished maidens but no viable scientific offspring.[2]

There is productivity without product.

This begs the question: can the situation be improved? I have thus far argued that the central problems are the ethical and ontological constraints that limit the possibilities for bench-building. Improvements come by either overcoming ethical limitations to produce more invasive and controlling experimental conditions or overcoming ontological limitations by selecting objects more amenable to measurement and/or manipulation. To some degree, psychological researchers have pursued both paths. Researchers from Facebook, for instance, manipulated what unwitting users saw on their feeds to demonstrate how they could alter their emotional states.[3] And the use of brain scans like fMRI and hormone tests such as cortisol measurements has become popular with psychologists looking for something more tangible than concepts.

Yet both strategies, should they be adopted widely, would fundamentally transform the field. Is there a way to continue to do lab-based studies of behavior but improve the science? For psychologists who do not want their field reduced to what one critic dubbed an "unaware branch of the entertainment industry,"[4] is there another path?

In the period I was observing psychology labs, a social movement within science was growing to address just this question.[5] Emboldened by a spate of publicized scandals in psychological science, psychologists long frustrated by what they perceived to be bad science began forcing this question into public view. However, rather than attempting to overcome the problems at the bench, these methodological activists have taken a different path. Framing the problem in cultural terms rather than one that has its roots in the material conditions of benchwork, they have embraced a vision of science that can aptly be called neo-Mertonian.

Robert K. Merton famously described a system in which a set of internalized scientific norms resulted in a social order that was beneficial to the field as a whole. It was a virtuous cycle of honest research and open critique all undergirded by transparency (Merton's "communalism"), valuing truth over personal gain ("disinterestedness"), and the incredulous replication of new claims ("organized skepticism"). Sloppy or fraudulent claims were said to be punished because sharing data and organized skepticism meant that findings were routinely tested for veracity. Frequent failed replications of one's work would harm one's reputation.

The Mertonian view of science was a central foil for the early field of science and technology studies, and it has been rightly criticized for its confusion of scientific rhetoric and scientific practice. To give a relevant example, as I mentioned in chapter 3, the replication-as-verification that Merton viewed as central to the scientific system is not at all common.[6] Fields that engage in ongoing bench-building tend to use integrative replication which has a different purpose, and, in fields that lack bench-building, replication is altogether rare (for instance, one study showed a 1 percent rate of replication in psychological research since the year 1900).[7]

As rhetoric, on the other hand, the Mertonian portrait of science continues to have influence.[8] Although modern science largely operates in a context of trusting networks, the public's conception of scientific practice is based largely on the image of surveillance and vigilance that one historian of science jokingly labeled the "great Panopticon of Truth."[9] In the current context of psychology, there is a movement to make this rhetoric a reality. Because this is simply a goal and not yet a reality, this chapter will be a bit more speculative than the previous ones. However, the movement raises significant questions for the future of experimental psychology and the theory of bench-building because it offers the promise of a path forward without overcoming the ethical and ontological limitations that have stymied the field.

REPLICATION PROBLEMS IN PSYCHOLOGY

When experimenters at the research frontier struggle to develop reliable manipulations and perceptive capacities, it gives all findings a permanently indeterminate quality. They may have been produced with good practices yet still not be replicable (or, at least, consistently replicable) because the randomness in the system cannot be fully controlled. In fields with unclear ontological categories and ethical rules limiting experimental control, replication problems are to be expected.

Yet how fields navigate replication issues can vary. In nativist developmental psychology, researchers slogged through the swamp, pursuing a strategy of normal science despite problems getting and replicating effects. Under this regime, replication failures could be forgiven as part of the unavoidable and insurmountable noise in the system. The social psychologists I observed, on the other hand, flitted from finding to finding, method to method enough that replication became marginalized. Since research rarely involved building directly on previous findings through the practical integration of experimental techniques and technologies, failed replications could be dismissed or ignored.

Despite these efforts, however, failed replications can take their toll in wasted time and mounting cynicism. As this section shows, these frustrations have been channeled into a coherent ideology at odds with dominant norms.

Replication failures are not uncommon at the cutting edge of all fields. Reproducing an effect may involve a specific technological setup or elaborated skill. Yet psychologists were often surprised to find themselves unable to replicate even highly regarded studies in their field. For instance, one of the graduate students in social psychology I interviewed had been conducting an experiment using a variation on the false consensus effect (the cognitive bias, first discovered in the 1970s, of assuming your attitudes and beliefs are the norm). Yet when the altered study design did not produce an effect, she went back and tried to directly replicate a previous study in the area to test her method. To her surprise, even though she attempted a time-consumingly faithful replication, the main effects would not replicate. When I asked her what she attributed it to, she replied "different samples, maybe. Maybe it was the way it was phrased or asked. I'm not sure."

Even an entire series of studies published by top journals may prove non-reproducible. One of the labs was concerned with issues of social power but had ongoing problems finding a reliable method of manipulating the subject's feeling of power. During a lab meeting, two social psychology graduate students, Allison and Hannah, were summarizing the findings from a major figure in the field but admitted being unable to actually use his methods:

> ALLISON: And he developed the prime which has never worked for any-
> body. [to Hannah] Does it work for you?
> HANNAH: No. It works for him.
> ALLISON: It always works for him.

Hannah then addressed the way that the increased focus on replication issues have affected her trust in the field: "It scares me that I go into all these things now, like, this data looks too perfect."

Later, I asked Dr. Church about her lab's difficulties using this well-known prime. The method itself involves asking subjects to write a short paragraph in which they recount an incident in which they were either in a position of power or powerlessness. She admitted that "We have not had great success with it. And I'm not sure what to attribute that to. We've had different hypotheses about that." She hypothesized that the undergraduate subjects at her university might have some unique features that makes this prime ineffective with them. For instance, maybe they had not been in positions of power yet. Yet she was not concerned about the veracity of the research using that method: "It's been used enough in the world where I don't attribute it to the people using it falsifying their data. Because it's not just being used in one lab."

Not everyone was so trusting, however. I asked Shan, who had been trying to conduct an experiment using a power measure, about the prime: "We pretty much all hate it because it just never works. Because if you ask them a manipulation check afterward— 'How powerful do you feel right now?'—it just flatlines across." Rather than attribute the replication problems to subtle differences in subject populations, she zeroed in on a different culprit:

> Researchers who are more powerful themselves or have a bigger lab or have more funding [. . .] they can afford to have that file drawer thing where they're running that study 10 times. Or if you have a small, underpowered study with 15 per cell, you can get the effect to work out. But everyone in our lab, we just don't get it to replicate, we don't get it to work. It's a hush-hush secret but [. . .] that's one of those things that we just know doesn't work.

Rather than attribute the failure to some yet undetected difference in subject population, Shan's faith in the prime—and, thus, all work produced using it—had eroded.

Similar to developmental psychologists, local knowledge regarding more and less robust manipulations evolved and was shared through social networks, and some felt this was sufficient. Dr. Church, for instance, expressed faith that, despite the recently publicized problems, the system was robust enough to make progress: "Part of me likes to still believe that there is the self-correcting process in our field [that] does work a lot of the time, that if a finding is important enough, that it will be found out because enough people will try to replicate it and extend it and it won't work. I know that's idealistic."

For those unwilling to embrace such optimism, the outcome was often disillusionment. Isolated incidents of fraud or failed replication can be compartmentalized, especially when, as Bourdieu has pointed out, there is strong social pressure to uphold the "collective hypocrisy capable of guaranteeing the minimum of common belief that is necessary for the functioning of social order."[10] This demands that participants approach the field with a level of credulity evinced by Dr. Church. Not all psychologists have maintained their trust in the self-correction of their field. Observations of the Shaw journal club, a weekly meeting dedicated to issues of psychological research methodology, reveal a group that has lost its faith in their field. Yet within this skepticism there is an emergent vision of a different psychology.

ORGANIZING SKEPTICISM
AT THE SHAW JOURNAL CLUB

Journal clubs are common features of experimental laboratories. Once a week, a group of like-minded psychologists will read a recent article and spend an hour or so discussing it. Graduate students, postdocs, and faculty sit in a circle, eat snacks, and talk about new research. Because they tend to be relatively informal, they are good opportunities for graduate students to interact with more advanced members of their field and, thus, become socialized while learning how to engage with cutting edge scholarship. In most journal clubs, articles are chosen by a faculty member who finds the article exciting. Because of this, discussions tend to be mostly positive, focusing on the article's contribution. Critique, in these groups, tends to be limited to discussing alternative interpretations for the pattern of data presented.

The Shaw journal club was typical in some ways. Every Friday, from three to four p.m., a group that ranged from ten to fifteen would meet to discuss a recently published article. Spearheaded by Dr. Larson, a social psychologist, the group included between three and five professors with the rest of the participants being a mix of postdocs and graduate students.

The main point of differentiation between Shaw and other journal clubs was the tone. Rather that trusting and supportive, the group was often hostile toward the articles, and rather than giving researchers the benefit of the doubt, they approached new research with skepticism. Because of this interrogative structure, the culture of the journal club was cynical and, at times, even depressing. Although the Shaw journal club could not be described as lighthearted, there was a lot of laughter. The humor tended to be either sarcastic or a variety of gallows humor. Studies, scholars, and analytical decisions were mocked. In other cases, despair at the state of the field was the object of humor. Yet the strong emotions—alternatively despondent and sardonic—that the group evinced produced strong cohesion. In private conversations, Dr. Larson's students expressed great affection for him and the journal club, and the meetings drew faculty and students from across the university and even visiting scholars.

Most members of the reading group had once been optimistic about the field and had trust in its findings. Dr. Whitman said, before engaging with the growing critical literature, "I thought, 'It's significant, it's true!'" Rachael, a graduate student, told me that before joining the group, "I used to think 'Oh, it's peer reviewed, it's totally true.'"

Yet, skepticism grew as more scandals emerged and pointed toward larger problems in the field. Rotten apples became sick trees, and sick trees became blighted orchards as skepticism swallowed more of the field. Dr. Larson explained how the Shaw reading group had been transformed:

> Over the years, it shifted from sort of a prototypical version of that where you're just, like, "I see two alternative explanations for this phenomenon" which is a standard critique. Like, "Aha! I think it could just be construal level theory that accounts for this" or whatever. But more and more of the discussion shifted from that. At some point, someone would say, "I don't know. This just doesn't seem possible. It just doesn't seem possible."

The "standard critique" Dr. Larson referred to meant accepting the facts that were presented while challenging the author's interpretation. As the group began to doubt the facts presented in the article, its attention moved away from the typical debates over its interpretation to the methodological details that purportedly supported its claims.[11]

Thus, rather than treat published claims as facts, the meetings were increasingly dominated by discussions about the nuts of bolts of psychological methodology. What was the sample size? What was the effect size? Does the latter make sense in light of the former? What were the p-values? Were too many just under .05 suggesting the researchers "p-hacked" (i.e., manipulated the data to achieve statistical significance)? How many conditions were run? Were they all reported? Did the researchers run multiple analyses and only report the one that worked? Was the "finding" the result of post hoc theorizing? All of these questions were ways to approach the most important question of all: Is this a real result that will replicate?

Yet having to address these questions—the joyless accounting of Mertonian science—was an often-deflating experience to the members of Shaw. Dr. Carter explained,

> I used to read more journals just for pleasure. I thought it was fun to read random articles from journals. Now, I like going to journal club, but I don't enjoy that as much because I just don't believe as much of what I'm reading. I used to feel like "Oh, there's this really interesting thing, and I'm going to learn something new about human psychology." And when I read academic articles, I no longer feel like that's a benefit I'm going to get from reading a paper.

This generalized skepticism led to problems regarding what to believe and how to evaluate claims. During an interview, Dr. Larson explained how he used to read articles uncritically. He would read a new article and conclude, "It's a nugget of information. Next time I work on my paper, I will know in the back of my mind that there is a fact about human behavior. It's easy to learn in that context." Skepticism of the literature meant "facts" were no longer trusted pieces of information. Instead, they were heavily loaded claims, weighted down and complicated by methodological details authors typically deemphasize. He confided, "I wonder sometimes if I've forgotten how to learn from papers."

Other faculty members expressed similar transformations. Early in his career, Dr. Whitman told me that he was willing to give articles the benefit of the doubt, even given evidence of problematic practice, believing that "The theories are true so helping the data along a little bit is a sin that everybody commits to some degree or other." However, in the last few years, he explained that he has been "stunned" to see how easy it is to exploit the analysis process to achieve statistical significance. Similarly, Dr. Carter explained that, before, he would "cordon off things" that did not replicate, telling himself that "Well, it's true in this circumstance but there are probably lots of boundary conditions, and that's why we don't notice this in the real world all the time [. . .] Whereas, now that I know that a lot of things are published that aren't in any sense replicable. Then that's a bad place to be in."

Dr. Myer described her own descent into this "bad place" when she tried to replicate a series of studies to extend them into an area she was interested in. She explained that the original studies were well-powered and had been replicated within the article four times. Despite seeing other favored studies fail to replicate, she felt confident that these would be reproducible, even betting another member of her lab a plate of nachos that they would.

DR. MYER: And Rachael ran it, and it was not even in the right direction. Nothing. That was a lot of it. That's when I started thinking journal club was so great. I mean, they replicate these studies, and they find nothing.

AUTHOR: That seems rough.

DR. MYER: Soul crushing.

AUTHOR: Okay. So, you get your soul crushed. How do you build yourself
back up again?

DR. MYER: Alcohol.

Later in the interview, she explained that journal club was deeply
ambivalent for her. Although she found herself interested in the critiques journal club members developed, the unrelenting bleakness
often left her feeling distraught and disillusioned. Dr. Myer was not
alone in her feelings. Jin recounted the emotional toll it took after
a particularly brutal stretch of journal clubs in which a series of
esteemed papers were savagely dismantled: "I feel that a lot of people
are getting burnt out. 'Oh my god, what's not true now?'" This same
burnout led Dan, another graduate student, to ask, "Do we really
believe anything anymore?"

Calling a Bluff

The meetings themselves felt like complete inversions from meetings in social psychology labs. Where the latter was freewheeling and
creative, the former was focused and critical. Where the latter was
focused on big picture ideas of concepts and literatures, the former
was concerned with the minutia of methodological details.

The first week I attended the journal club, they were meeting to
discuss an article that was not only published in one of the field's
flagship journals but also had received a bit of media attention. The
article purported to show evidence that the quality of poker players' hands could be inferred from the mechanics of their arm movements when betting. The psychological theory that motivated the
study was the idea that the same objective behavior (e.g., putting
chips into a pot) will belie mechanical differences when the inten-
tions differ (e.g., bluffing with the intention of trying to get players

to fold versus betting with the goal of trying to get players to stay in and wager more).

Empirically, the article was based on one-to-two second clips taken from the broadcast of the World Series of Poker. The segments were of professional poker players making wagers (20 clips were used in the first study, 22 in the second). After the clips were selected, a group of undergraduates coded the video for what they assumed to be the strength of the hand based solely on arm movements or, as the alternative condition, looking at faces. They were able to predict the quality of hand from the arm movements but not facial expressions. (There were three studies, several other variables and a complex analytic scheme, but this was the central finding of the article.)

According to the previous chapter, this study ticks many boxes of a successful social psychological study. It has a finding counterintuitive enough to satisfy both popular and expert audiences. For the public, if you want to know a new and surprising poker tell, they found it. Look to the arms! For the professional psychologist looking for a theoretical contribution, it argued that emotional states leak out and become perceptible to those with the right eyes. Even professional poker players, whose livelihood depends on managing impressions, cannot avoid detection. Additionally, the study has a compelling source of data. Rather than have undergraduate subjects participate in some artificial experiment, the data is drawn from a high-stakes, real-world context.

Yet the very things that made the article successful in getting both professional and public attention made it suspect in the eyes of the Shaw group. The striking finding, the novel data source, and even the framing came under a degree of scrutiny rare in their field.

Dr. Larson began the meeting with a broad question about the data used in the study—How does one randomly select videos? The logic of random selection, key for statistical interpretation, states that any item in a population has an equal chance of being included in the study. Yet, it was unclear what "random" meant in this context. Dr. Lee suggested that the authors probably collected hours of video and then sampled the relevant clips. This did not satisfy Dr. Larson. How does one get that video? Did they call ESPN and ask for every inch of footage? Renee noted that the supplemental materials explained that the broadcast videos from the poker tournament had been posted online. The clips were drawn from that. Again, Dr. Larson pressed: Does the broadcast video show every single hand? Renee did not think so. Rachael said the supplemental materials were frustratingly vague regarding how they selected their clips.

Dr. Andrews suggested that a better method would be to have a continuous video feed of every player for every hand. When Liam, a graduate student, thought the critique was getting too nit-picky he suggested the expectation of randomness would only be violated if there were some clear biases to the clips shown. Otherwise, they could assume that errors would be randomly distributed. Dr. Larson agreed that the point was important but disagreed with Liam's interpretation. Although it was not clear what the bias would be, there were reasons for thinking that having your data source essentially decided by camera operators and television editors would have some biasing effect.

To support Dr. Larson's argument, Renee noted that the authors used the word "push" to describe the betting movement. She admitted to watching poker broadcasts for fun and said that players usually only "pushed" their chips when they were going "all in" (i.e., betting everything they have). Otherwise, they tended to toss chips into the pot which is a very different type of movement. Dr. Andrews pointed out that this might be where the selection bias is problematic. Perhaps the clips of "all in" bets were overrepresented because the editors felt these were the most dramatic. Dr. Larson agreed and told the room that because of these issues, the authors should not be able to claim to have randomly sampled the world of poker. Although he admitted that this critique did not necessarily disprove their effect, Dr. Larson said it should serve as a warning sign that the effect could have been attained "artificially [. . .] through selection bias."

By beginning the meeting focused on a technical issue like selection bias rather than addressing the substantive argument in the article, the group set up a basic test of veracity. Not, "Do we believe the way this finding is interpreted given the facts presented?" But, rather, "Is this evidence for *anything*? Are there any facts here?" If the clips were not randomly sampled, then the article can be little more than suggestive. Thus, as the group moved on to discuss the theoretical points made in the article, it was already being treated with skepticism.

The very detectability of the effect increased this suspicion. An accurate poker tell would provide players with an incredibly valuable advantage. Dr. Larson argued that if it were real and observable, pokers players would already know about it and have developed countermeasures:

> If it's a large effect, then poker players would notice it and correct for it. If I want to fake smooth arm movements, no doubt that I can. I may not be perfect at it, but I can make my arms smooth. I should be able to add enough noise to the system so that arm movements are going to be a catastrophe for people to look at.

Dr. Larson then took out a book recommended to him independently by two friends who played poker—*Mike Carrow's Book of Poker Tells*. Carrow, he explained, has no discussion specifically on "arm movement" among his list which included things like "double checking," "instant reaction," and "glancing at chips." Dr. Lee asked if the variables had been validated, and Dr. Larson laughed and said, "Oh, god no!" He continued, "Maybe Mike Carrow is amazing, but I assume it's total nonsense. But, on the other hand, what he's diagnosing are variables that one could look at. It's not as quite as impoverished as 'we can see the face or we can see the arms'" (how the authors had framed their contribution).

Dr. Larson asked Dr. Lee, who had previously done research using nonverbal behavioral measures, what other variables might have been chosen: "How far down the list before you get to stuff on arm smooth-ness?" She joked, "Probably pretty far!" and explained that just using the face, the authors could have looked at dozens of variables includ-ing things like blink rate, emotional expression, and the specific posi-tion of facial muscles using the Facial Action Coding System (FACS). And, regarding non-facial variables, "there's an infinite number of things you could code, like postural shift or leaning."

Although she "wanted to believe" the study, Dr. Lee was irritated that the authors did not reference any of the literature on deception which would have demanded the authors consider at least some of these other variables. Dr. Larson pointed out the main study the arti-cle uses to frame its contribution was an obscure article from the 1980s. Renee hypothesized that maybe the authors choose arm movements because it seemed like a "novel" variable. If they had chosen some facial variable, it would not have been interesting. Dr. Larson agreed, add-ing "Arms puts them in this unusual space where they get to write a paper with no introduction. We don't know anything about arms! What happens with arms? They're crazy!"

The empirical and theoretical flexibility that likely allowed this article to be published and make a splash was also what weakened it in the eyes of the Shaw group. The novel data source was criticized because it was unclear how the authors sampled it. The choice to look at arm movement was criticized because it seemed strategically designed to avoid the already dense literature concerned with decep-tion. Finally, the very finding of the article was criticized for being too significant and too interesting to be true.

The Spiral of Skepticism

The level of skepticism expressed by the Shaw group has a pernicious effect. Like an immune response, labs typically isolate and reject such dangerous doubts. For instance, when Dr. Church held a journal club in her lab, she was frustrated when her graduate students (some of whom attended the Shaw journal club) focused on technical details they found problematic. However, rather than debate the specific methodological critiques offered by her students, Dr. Church replied, "Well, it got into *JPSP*, guys." The article was published in the field's top journal (the *Journal of Personality and Social Psychology*) and would likely be influential. According to the statement of Dr. Church's I recounted earlier, the article now comprised an aspect of "shared knowledge" that served to "constrain" new research. Thus, it needed to be confronted on its own terms. Yet her students were addressing a more fundamental question—what if it was untrue?

When skepticism grows, researchers lose confidence in traditional signals of research quality like publication in top journals. A cycle of cynicism undermines these signals of value and, in doing so, forces researchers to perform laborious study-by-study evaluations for every article they read. A Mertonian condition of generalized skepticism demands that researchers evaluate each item individually rather than rely on trusted proxies. Scientific researchers are already tasked with the evaluation of heterogeneous products: knowledge at the cutting edge. A lack of trust in the basic functions of quality assurance makes the task of evaluating studies even more complex. As Dr. Larson told me, "If you start doubting papers, then you have to selectively learn. So, I obviously do that. I try to selectively learn."

Opening the black box of "facts" presented in articles makes engaging with the literature far more challenging. During a journal club, Renee explained that she and Jin had scoured the literature on interpersonal power dynamics, looking for research that they felt confident with and had come up empty. Later, I asked Jin about it, she told me that Renee had been slightly exaggerating. Instead, she described her more nuanced way of evaluating studies.

> I think in most papers, at least one or two of the studies, there's something there. Or I might take a more lenient view. If they didn't

do any explicit p-hacking, if their values are too terrible—p = .o6 or something!—it's marginal and I'm thinking that still makes it potentially more true that something that is p = .9. There's still something there. In that case, if they make a compelling theoretical argument for why something could be and things are set up along the way so that some manipulations work, they show a manipulation check, show those steps along the way, I think I can still buy the general idea.

Rather than a true/false dichotomy resting on either side of a .05 alpha value, claims were given shadings of trust.

Although the belief that there might be degrees of truth may be a useful way to work with another author's claims, it presented a challenge to incorporating those ideas into one's own research practice. Jin said that even though she might cite an article and use it to frame her work, she would not necessarily try to expand upon it because "when the original is shaky, that's just too risky. I want to work on something that, if it doesn't work, it's because my idea failed and not because there [are] inadequate measures that can't truly capture things."

Dr. Whitman described how, when he confronted results that seemed dubious, he looked for alternative signals of quality in the articles beyond mere publication. For instance, he would look to see if they had used the twenty-one-word disclaimer which had been proposed by some critical psychologists: "We report how we determined our sample size, all data exclusions (if any), all manipulations, and all measures in the study."[12] Did they explain how they determined sample size? Did they publicly post materials so others can try to replicate? Did they post their data so others can do analysis? Did they pre-register their study to limit their ability to develop post hoc theories? He concluded, "So, all these things can give me confidence that the thing is actually true even if I find the theory implausible or the results so surprising as to strain credibility."

Disinterestedness and Competition

In scientific fields, powerful, central researchers attempt to win resources by publishing high status articles and populating the field with their students. However, in most accounts of science, success is supposed to be governed, at least in part, by nature. Social networks and apprenticeship may provide access to equipment and knowledge, but, ultimately, success requires the production of "true" findings rather than brute cronyism. Moreover, because the value of "disinterestedness" underpins the rhetorical power of science,[13] behavior that seems motivated by naked self-interest is discouraged because of its threat to the objectivity of the field. Members of the Shaw reading group were frustrated by what they deemed to be inappropriately competitive behavior in regard to both publication practice and, relatedly, student placement.

In scientific fields, peer review and methodology, in addition to signaling value, are supposed to be mechanisms that promote fairness. However, when researchers believe these mechanisms are failing, it fuels skepticism about the fairness of publication. The central problem, reiterated by several members of Shaw, is how academia rewards researchers who publish many flashy studies rather than a few robust and replicable studies. Rachael explained, "So, that's why the overall message with the false positive psychology stuff is that there should be fewer papers." Rather than rush to publish every significant finding, they advocated a far slower process that included internal replications with large sample sizes. Rachael continued, arguing that, rather than running many underpowered studies,

> Run the one. Take time to think about it. And make it good. The result of that is that they'll be fewer papers published. They say, "That's great. I want to read fewer papers. I want to write fewer papers. And I want the papers I do read and write to be good, to be worthwhile and actual science with a capital S."

However, in putting their money where their mouth is, they have vastly reduced their productivity. When I asked Dr. Whitman how the more rigorous practices affected his rate of successful studies, he replied, "I would say that, in grad school, I got about—and these are really rough guesses—I got about 80 percent of the studies I ran into a paper that got published eventually. And now, I think that's probably closer to 50 percent. Maybe lower." However, Dr. Larson suggested the reduction was even more dramatic. He explained that early in his career, he achieved significant and publishable findings of 80–85 percent. Now, "that number is massively lower. A tenth."

Moreover, the introduction of rigor introduced other changes to his work. Because Dr. Larson has become especially skeptical of counter-intuitive findings (largely due to ongoing failures to replicate), his own research has stayed closer to intuition: "My hypotheses have gotten way less exciting. I'm much more, like, 'Let's go with this really easy one now.'" In addition, he collects samples sizes five to ten times larger so, "if there's a little bit of truth lurking in the world, I'm much more likely to detect it than I used to be."

Of course, because publications are the currency of academia, they affect all aspects of a researcher's career. This includes getting tenure, promotions, grants, and popular media attention. However, one of the most important benefits of publication is being able to join the ranks of professional scientists. This is a material concern to graduate students and postdocs who desire financial security and recognition and advisers who want to populate the field with researchers who share their interests. However, when the social mechanisms regulating competition break down, the job market becomes a political struggle over the future of the field.

The result of publishing less, and of publishing more modest studies, is a less impressive, at least at a surface level, body of work. During an interview with Liam, he expressed worry that his high methodological standards would have a negative effect on his career. He was going on the market the following year and had no top-tier publications: "I'm supposed to have three 'A' publications. As it is, I have zero. That's because fully two-thirds of my studies fail. They don't replicate."

Similarly, after expressing doubts about her chances on the job market, Rachael said, "So, the places that might hire me do, at least conceptually, have an altered incentive structure where it's not 'Okay, how many papers did you publish and where did you publish them?' It's 'What's your best paper?'" However, she admitted that this perspective was unusual and argued that most prospective psychologists were unwilling to limit their search to the small set of departments with higher standards. Instead, she argued, they "will say, 'I need to publish, like, six papers to get a job, and what you're telling me is I won't be able to publish six papers. You're basically telling me I won't be able to get a job. So, forget that! I want to get a job and [so I'll] p-hack my way through five papers.'"

Dr. Whitman expressed sympathy for his graduate students, suggesting their dedication to producing good science would cost them: "Especially when it's just us, and the rest of the world is still playing by the old rules where there's no chance of you getting a job unless you have six papers in print by the time you're coming out of grad school."

In response, the faculty involved with the Shaw reading group did what they could to support their values. For instance, Jin explained that Dr. Larson "hates it when students with thirty publications get the top jobs. And that always happens every year. Meanwhile, his students only have one paper. [The finding is] true, but it took forever to find it. It makes him upset. He whacks those peoples' papers in journal club."

In our interview, Dr. Larson explained that he has learned to distrust research in which too many things appeared to go right. He argued it was "diagnostic of extreme danger" and suggested that, because good psychology was extremely challenging, "studies should fail." However, he acknowledged the ramifications of this belief on his students: "So, Jin is my student, you know. She is going to try to get a job this year.

She's going to have fewer papers than if she had worked in nearly any other lab in the country." This was an emotional issue for him:

> It's right there where things feel most painful and stressful. I really want to believe that the field does value quality in some way. I mean, I think the world of Jin, but it's not even that she's higher quality but that what she has has quality to it. It's not just a bunch of accidents of p-hackery that have built it up. It is what it is. And I think the field does care. There are so many variables pushing the other direction. More papers always look better. It's pretty identity challenging for me, honestly. If she fails to get a job, I will more or less stop taking students.

MERTONIAN SKEPTICISM MEETS A TRUSTING FIELD

It might be argued that the methodological critique at Shaw merely represented a call for the improvement of scientific culture and a return to principles that have been eroded. Whether methodological activism represents the true heir to the founding principles of scientific psychology or whether it is a break from that tradition is largely a rhetorical matter.

My point is not to suggest that this methodological activism is a superior alternative to the current state of practice in experimental psychology labs. What I want to make clear, however, is that the explicit organization around Mertonian norms has created clear fractures in the current field. This represents both challenges and opportunities for researchers. This can be seen through the strained social relationships such a vision produces, the belief within such communities that this movement represented a challenge to the dominant culture of the field, and the sense, especially amongst younger participants, that they had to "play along" with the existing culture despite harboring deep skepticism.

Broken Social Ties

The clearest indication of a social fissure is the severing of ties. The challenge brought up by the methodological critique of the field had become particularly contentious because, rather than a challenge to some established fact or theory, it posed a threat to the accepted culture of the group. This had prompted strong reactions. When asked if he has received blowback from other psychologists about his criticisms of the field, Dr. Larson replied, "Tons, yeah." He remembered one interaction:

> In the month after we published [an influential critique of the field] we got a handful of emails—I thinking of one right now from a very prominent researcher who's also a friend. It was the kind of email where my response to him was saying, "I'm pretty sure this means that we can't be friends anymore." He was basically saying that we were being needlessly destructive.

When I interviewed Dr. Myer, I asked her if she was worried that her association with the Shaw group might cause professional problems. She replied, "Actually, my adviser . . . I'm suddenly aware of being recorded. Actually, my adviser was, like, 'You know, very important people are concerned that things are getting taken too far.'" When I asked Rachael the same question, she answered, "Oh yeah! There are definitely places that wouldn't hire me having been tainted by Dr. Larson."

Although severing relationships is one of the more acute reactions to a breach in trust, a more common—but just as socially devastating—outcome is making routine interactions awkward. Jin explained that she no longer holds back her critiques in public: "I go to conferences, and I tell them, 'This is ridiculous.' [. . .] People are horrified."

During the journal club, Dr. Myer told a story about a recent conference she attended where people were talking about a recent psychology article in the journal *Science*: "I was, like, 'Oh, wasn't that paper retracted?' And, literally, everyone around me gasped. [Laughter] When people think that findings are cool and you bring up that they're probably not true it's just not a good way to make friends or find a job." When asked about the story later, Dr. Myer told me it was embarrassing because it created a distance between her beliefs and those of her colleagues.

> DR. MYER: People love this article. It was an article about how to close the racial GPA gap in children. When I first heard about that study, I thought it was awesome. I was super on board, and I loved it. And then I remember talking to Dr. Larson about it and he was, like, "Have you looked at the p-values?" That kind of thing. And from there, I was so crushed—I mean, this was early on when I just started going to journal club—I was so crushed that this article was probably not great evidence for whatever it was claiming to me that, in mind, it felt like a retraction. So, I coded it as such.
>
> AUTHOR: Oh, so it wasn't actually retracted!
>
> DR. MYER: No! [Laughter] And that was a group of people who loved that study like I used to, and I say "Oh, wasn't that study retracted?" Then, it was just . . . [makes the record scratch sound]

By subconsciously "coding" the highly esteemed article as retracted, Dr. Myer was living in a separate world of facts from her colleagues.

The friction caused by skepticism was evident when students who attended the journal club returned to labs which were trying to conduct business as usual. For instance, I observed Dan, a frequent attendee at the journal club clash with his advisor. During a lab meeting in which the Church lab was discussing hiring a psychologist who specialized in social cognition, Dan noted cynically that "most of that stuff is turning out not to work out anyway." After some uncomfortable laughter, Dr. Church shot back, "I disagree. I totally disagree. That's a crazy statement really. Most of that stuff? Really?" Dr. Church admitted that there have been three fraud cases but dismissed the idea that the field of social cognition was inherently problematic as "ridiculous."

For Dr. Church, a researcher who was critical of the growing skepticism in the field, dubious research in the field of social cognition was limited to the researchers who had been explicitly outed for producing fraudulent data. Dan, on the other hand, had been attending the Shaw reading group and had generalized his distrust to larger areas of the field. Rather than engage with Dan, Dr. Church signaled her moral and cognitive distance by calling his statements "crazy" and "ridiculous."

Having different methodological standards can create tension in existing social networks. When I asked Dr. Carter how he feels when the journal club trashes the work of a researcher he knows, he admitted, "It is weird or disappointing when you read something from someone you like or respect and you're, like, 'This seems kind of dumb. This is bad science.'"

Problems in cooperation become most visible when researchers who have divergent values were working together on projects. Tension arose when one partner supported publicly posting his data which made some colleagues "uncomfortable." When asked to elaborate, he explained that his coauthors worried that would make themselves targets "for all the haters out there who are going to go trawling for flaws." He went on to say that he always posted his failed experiments on his website so the data would not "disappear into my file drawer." However, he admitted that collaborators were concerned that showing a record of failure would make the article appear weaker: "I've had coauthors who have said, 'You're crazy. You're just going to torpedo our chances of ever getting it published.'"

Significantly, the embrace of Mertonian skepticism created its own problems with the Shaw group. Because doubt had encompassed so much of the literature, members of the Shaw reading group were nervous to admit that they liked articles or believed any findings. One day in journal club, Dr. Larson asked Rachael, who had summarized the article at the start of the meeting, if she found the evidence persuasive. She replied, "I thought it was okay. The critical p-value is, I just discovered, .02 which is okay. I never know. I never know with you. Sometimes, it's, like, .001 and you're, like, 'It's nonsense!'" Even though Rachael had no specific argument with the article, she did not feel like she could admit to liking the article or finding it convincing. When I asked her about this during an interview, she detailed her dilemma. Every person she works with attends that meeting so she does not want to embarrass herself. And, given the group's tenor, they are much more likely to let a vague critique slide than an endorsement. Because of this, she conceded that, "'I really liked study two' is a very dangerous thing to say."

Opportunities in Debunking

Although it caused strain in existing relationships, for some, embracing Mertonian skepticism had provided new career opportunities. Like investors shorting a stock they believe to be artificially inflated, when academic criticism meets a wave of discontentment within the field it can be career-making. Dr. Larson's most highly cited research was his critiques of the field. And Dr. Whitman described the sense of opportunity that criticism provided:

> I would characterize it as more of an empowering feeling. Like, "Wow! I'm smarter than the reviewers on these things!" There's a new role for a kind of clever cynic who can spot the bullshit that has made it into the published record. Reading the literature, it added this whole new level of intrigue. Like, [whispers] 'Do you think this stuff could possibly be complete bullshit?'

However, when I brought up that the production of critiques and methodological articles probably would not be enough to make up for the loss in productivity incurred by following the new methods, he admitted it was true.

Opportunities for skeptical takes are especially likely to emerge in fields that have endemic problems settling controversies and arriving at consensus. In psychology, there is a history of works claiming the field is in crisis that extends to the 1920s.[14] Similarly, in behavior genetics, a thriving market for skeptical work has existed since the field's inception.[15] More troublingly, Naomi Oreskes and Erik Conway have shown how the opportunities in skepticism can be artificially created when powerful outsiders dislike the consensus a field has achieved (e.g., the smoking/cancer link or human contributions to climate change).[16]

Yet several points should be made regarding the opportunities in publishing criticisms. First, contrary to Merton, skepticism itself is primarily beneficial in reference to a group that is not skeptical. Thus, although it may serve as a corrective, it seems unlikely that skepticism could become the organizing principle of an academic field. Instead, it can only be parasitic on a trusting system. In most fields, then, the benefits for embracing skepticism are small and will not entice a large number of scholars.

Of course, because skeptical writings are taken seriously, they represent a challenge to the dominant structure of the field. Although some psychologists have benefited from the small market for skeptical articles, it is a means to another end—a revolution. In this sense, skepticism is a strategy for challenging the prevailing structure of a field. Bourdieu has noted how fields are structured as much by attempts to reshape what counts as cultural capital than the accumulation of such capital.[17] Similarly, Neil Fligstein has argued that markets involve profoundly political processes and that struggles over the rules of exchange are as important to actors as the objects of exchange.[18] Thus, debates over "proper" scientific behavior are as much about the structure of the scientific field—who is trusted and esteemed, and who is not—as they are about philosophical ideals of truth. Under periods of normal science, skepticism can be used to socialize new members to these ideals.[19]

Directly challenging the norms of a field through skepticism may yield greater possible benefit than simply appealing to the small audience for skeptical takes since, through a revolution, challengers may find themselves in a newly powerful place. Yet mounting a coherent challenge to the structure of a field means escaping total skepticism and making some positive statement regarding what the field should look like. This risks the unity of the group as members who were joined in their mutual skepticism find that unity evaporate as they articulate different visions for the future.

Challenging the field also carries risks for individuals. If the challenge does not result in a change in the structure of the market, those in less secure situations may find themselves forced out of the field. Such decisions were especially difficult for graduate students. When I asked advanced graduate student Nicole what she thought about the challenge posed by skeptics, she told me it was good for the field. However, she cautioned that, despite the new attention on replication and methodological rigor, "there's still a tendency for people to talk out of both sides of their mouths. People are actually more interested in novel findings. You're still going to get more respect and acknowledgment for those kinds of findings." Thus, because most young scholars were not in a position to benefit from the potential fallout of academic critique, many chose to swallow their skepticism and engage with the field on its own terms.

The Stubbornness of the Thomas Theorem

For those in precarious positions, the field—as full of untrusted science as it may be—still represented a reality for them. An exchange between Liam and Dr. Larson illustrated this tension. During an attempt to justify an interpretation of a study, Liam referenced some existent literature: "I've read research that says dishonesty causes you to start thinking cognitively differently." Rather than treat the statement as factual—the sort of "civil inattention"[20] we routinely give to questionable statements in polite conversation—Dr. Larson undermined Liam's statement by reminding him of published research the journal club had deemed illegitimate: "I've read papers suggesting that if you hold a gritty rock, you will defect more in prisoner's dilemma games." This generated laughter. Rather than concede the point, however, Liam retorted, "Yeah, but we have to work on the basis that some of the research out there may be true."

Although members of the Shaw reading group shared a frustration with accepted behavior in their field, they were also aware of the pragmatics of the scientific profession. Thus, rather than engage in explicit acts of skepticism, they engaged in a form of cynicism in which they acted as though they still trusted the literature. When I asked Shan how she approached the literature, she told me that there were two questions. First, is it true? Her second question was more practical: "And, two, would it even matter at this point? It's come so far along that you just have to play the game at this point. If you're trying to publish you have to make it fit within this framework." Likewise, Jin told me that her doubt had reached some of the fundamental works in the field. Yet, like Shan, she argued that the issue of truth was somewhat irrelevant:

> I don't know if it's true but it's highly cited. It's considered the truth, right? You should always be careful. But it's hard because it's how they built this field. These articles are highly cited, and people take it as truth. That's our field. It's hard to doubt all of that and try to write your paper. You won't have any citations!

In addition to simply citing research that was disbelieved, several members of Shaw told me the strategy they used to deal with the cognitive dissonance: they separated the evidence presented in the article from its "ideas." Although they might have foundational criticisms of an article's methodology, if they found its ideas reasonable, they would still use them.

In one exchange during the journal club, Renee complained about the lack of articles in a subfield she felt were trustworthy. Dr. Myer responded, "Just use the ideas as though they're real. This is what I do. You treat the ideas as though they're real, and you cite them when you need them when you're doing your own work." Although Dr. Larson criticized this compromise, during interviews, several students told me they did just this. For instance, when asked about this exchange, Dr. Myer argued that a bad study does not necessarily mean an idea is wrong:

> DR. MYER: If I don't believe a study, it just means there's not great evidence.
> AUTHOR: So, you just work with the ideas?
> DR. MYER: I work with the ideas.
> AUTHOR: So, you read the intro, discussion, and conclusion and the rest of the article you ignore?
> DR. MYER: You can always find contradictory studies anyway. So, at some level, you were always working with the ideas.

When I asked Jin if she cited work that she doubted, she replied, "Yeah. I have to. You have to have a logic. I'm not saying that it's true or false. It may sound like it's true, but the sample size is too small for me to say it is. But that doesn't mean that it's not true." Thus, despite her methodological critiques, she was unwilling to completely reject the author's claim. Jin made an almost identical statement: "Just because I couldn't believe in the empiricism in the papers doesn't mean I couldn't believe in a lot of the ideas."

THE PROSPECTS OF
MERTONIAN PSYCHOLOGY

Methodological activists in psychology have channeled the frustration over recent embarrassments into a theoretical and practical program to challenge existing orthodoxy in the field. Theoretically, they have embraced a vision of science in which individual incentives should be aligned with the field's interests in producing robust science. Demanding transparency in data and methods makes replication easier. Common replication reduces incentives to publish weak or fake studies. It is a reinforcing logic that is vintage Merton infused with emergent arguments about "open science."[21] Practically, they have pushed for institutional changes in furtherance of these goals. For instance, some journals have begun offering "badges" for articles that engage in certain virtuous practices like publicly posting data.[22]

This movement is aided by several factors. First, it has positioned itself as a science-wide reform movement rather than one narrowly focused on psychology. For instance, the Center for Open Science, which raised more than $25 million in funding in its first four years, is an outcrop of a listserv primarily active among psychologists. By framing itself catholicly, these activists have been able to draw together replication problems in disparate fields into a single issue. Second, they have aligned themselves with "transparency" which is a core value in the rhetoric of science. When a fraud is discovered or replication problems are encountered, the demand for more transparency is an appealing panacea. Third, it aligns with the emergent movement around big data and machine learning which suggests that problems can be solved with a combination of more information and increased computing power.

Yet, returning to the central themes of this book, these changes are not about bench practice. They are concerned with *reporting* bench practice and analytic decisions, but they do not attempt to alter the conditions of data collection. Thus, the reforms are oriented away from the bench and toward the field and do not address neither the ontological nor the ethical constraints in bench-building in psychology.

Could this be a way around these problems? And what would a Mertonian psychology look like?

These activists are not making the swamp any less swampy. Nothing these neo-Mertonians are doing is changing the fact that, as

Erving Goffman noted, "From the perspective of the physical and biological sciences, human social life is only a small irregular scab on the face of nature, not particularly amenable to deep systematic analysis."[23] They are not giving psychologists better purchase on their research object. Rather, they are getting a better, more accurate survey of the swamp. This is not nothing. Knowing which areas are the firmest, and support research, and which are sinkholes that swallow time is valuable information. Yet the research domain is not made any more amenable to research than before. The upside is a much more modest but, potentially, much more trustworthy science. Judging from the changes members of the Shaw group described in their own practice, Mertonian psychology would be a less productive, less adventurous field but one less prone to embarrassing frauds and replication failures.

The focus on method serves as a type of boundary work that is meant to leave much of the field on the outside of the circle of trust.[24] This may be one significant reason why some powerful psychologists have lashed out against methodological activists. During different incidents, Princeton's Susan Fiske used the term "methodological terrorists" and Harvard's Daniel Gilbert used "shameless little bullies" to describe these activists. As senior scholars in their field, it is not surprising to see them react strongly to perceived threats to the fabric of the field.

More soberly, one set of social psychologists has argued that the fear of false positives propagated by activists was going to drive the field into narrower questions and lead to an equally problematic increase in false negatives.[25] And Roy Baumeister, whose work on the effect of "ego-depletion" has been a target of criticism, decries the "sad commentary [. . .] that social psychologists need to assert that the field has in fact made progress and accumulated some valid knowledge."[26] He goes on to criticize the proposed reforms for transforming the field into one reduced to searching for tiny, robust effects that will be uninteresting to outsiders.

It is not clear where these debates will settle.

8

PROGRESS IN PSYCHOLOGY, REAL AND IMAGINED

Voltaire once wrote, "If God did not exist, it would be necessary to invent him." The same can be said for psychology. Psychology has been the target of numerous attacks over the years from both within the field and from outsiders. Yet even the most vicious and dismissive criticisms do not argue that psychological science is undesirable. Governments want psychological science to make their constituents more legible. Businesses want it to make their organizations more responsive and efficient. Individuals want it to make sense of and provide meaning to their experience. Of all the uses of modern science, none could be more significant than solving our organizational and existential problems.

Yet psychology's track record solving these problems has been, at best, mixed. I have argued that the practice of experimental psychology differs in significant ways from the way experimental science is practiced in molecular biology. All experimental science shares an abstract set of phases. From the field (and, in some fields, the wider cultural milieu) they draw on the current state of knowledge to develop questions deemed worth asking. They either invent experimental methods or adapt previous used ones to address these questions. They then gather data at the "bench" of their field. These data are then coded, processed, and analyzed. Conclusions are made and a narrative crafted which are then presented to the field. Although they share a general adherence to the broad temporal structure of laboratory research, with its phases that move from the field to the lab to the bench and back again, constraints in data collection shape epistemic cultures.

Molecular biology is organized around the cycle of improving perception and manipulation that is characteristic of bench-building. This process organizes work at the bench but also plays a guiding role for the field to integrate new techniques and technologies that help harmonize a rapidly transforming field. Molecular biology progresses by an inchworm process in which technological advances create discontinuities in the field which are then bridged as labs seek to maintain their place at the cutting edge.

When bench-building is difficult, if not impossible, different aspects of scientific progress are emphasized. The focus of the field shifts from the bench to other areas. In the nativist developmental psychology labs I observed, difficulties at the site of data collection were due to the problems inherent in trying to get good data out of infants and toddlers. Their subjects were as unaware and uncooperative as laboratory mice. Yet, unlike mice, experimenters were prevented from physically controlling them in any way. Thus, at the point of data collection, they took no direct, physical control over their object of research. Given these constraints, there were few opportunities for the increased control and perceptual acuity that bench-building provides. Instead, the field was disciplined around a circumscribed set of theoretical questions. Nativism gave them a structure to work within, a set of doable questions, and a way to evaluate progress. In this way, a chaotic research object was, at least partly, tamed by an orderly theory.

A different set of issues emerged with social psychologists. Rather than address a set of abstract questions about the universal structures of human cognition, they were interested in the objects of everyday life. Romantic relationships. Power. Awe. Empathy. Unlike the concepts of cognitive philosophy, these ideas are less amenable to scientific analysis. They are the fruits of a living language that evolves and transforms. Thus, much effort was expended trying to transform these everyday concepts into technical ones that could be operationalized and analyzed. The myriads of options available was often overwhelming. Yet they too were disciplined. Rather than make incremental advances along existing theoretical lines, however, they were disciplined by the marketplace of ideas in the field. The dynamics of "interesting science" rewarded researchers with novel and exciting topics, methods, and findings.

An animating question for this book has been: Are psychologists engaged in a different type of epistemic activity than experimentalists in natural science? The preceding chapters make the case that they are. Despite their participation in the broad phases of experimental research, their focus is different. While life in the molecular biology lab was organized around the bench, this was a diminished focus in the psychology labs.

A second question springs from this conclusion. So what? I have made the case that improvements in technique and advances in technology are key aspects of the technological development that legitimates and justifies investments in science. But should bench-building (and technological progress, more broadly) be the standards upon which the reputation of a science rests? Is science simply too complex and diverse an enterprise to be measured along such a simple dimension?

Science studies scholars have long avoided making value judgments. In the face of the empirically demonstrable diversity of real scientific work, it is not clear what fundamental logic fields share and, thus what yardstick should be used. If fields differ in how they develop questions, gather and analyze data, craft reports, communicate findings, and decide what's worth publishing, who can claim to have the key to understanding what theoretical unity underlies this riot of practice?

Yet this decision to avoid evaluation as an operating principle has sometimes placed science studies in uncomfortable positions. If there is no way to cleave science from nonscience, how can we justify not teaching intelligent design next to Darwin?[1] From where can we launch a critique of baldly self-interested efforts to undermine climate change research by fossil fuel companies? The spread of conspiracy theories and the fragmentation of our information spheres has only increased the pressure to develop some way of evaluating scientific truth.

Recent discussions about a "replication crisis" in both psychology and in science more broadly has taken a different tact. Rather than avoid evaluation, they have embraced it, developing tools to make science more legible and open to evaluation. Yet, these moves have largely been driven by activists and institutions like funders and journals rather than the fields themselves. The absence of any theoretical discussions about the nature of science suggests that reformers, aware or not, are pursuing a very specific ideal of scientific practice.[2]

Neither of the two binaries offered are satisfying. Science cannot be fully understood as a practice that is either "good" or "bad" depending upon its relation to an explicated Method. Nor, however, is science a mix of idealized rhetoric and an unfathomable reality that cannot be in any way thematized or evaluated from an objective perspective.

To highlight the difference, consider two examples where researchers make decisions about data exclusion. In the first, a molecular biologist attempts to measure the electrical signal from a cell. However, over the course of the first few minutes, the waveform swings wildly. After a few minutes of attaching and reattaching the electrode to the cell, the researcher determines that the cells are dying and will not produce usable data. The researcher disposes of the tissue, deletes the data already collected, and begins with a new dissection.

In the second example, a social psychologist receives data from a study posted through Amazon's Mechanical Turk service. One of the respondents—who gets paid per study and, thus, has an incentive to move through them quickly—appears to have filled out their survey randomly. In several instances, they provided contradictory responses to multiple questions on the same topic (e.g., reporting "strongly agree" to both "I feel confident in social situations" and "I'm often nervous and afraid to talk in social situations"). However, the respondent correctly answered both explicit attention checks in the survey. The social psychologist decides to analyze their data both with and without the respondent and decides if to include or exclude them depending on whether it strengthens the finding.

I suspect most people would find the first case of data exclusion an acceptable use of expert discretion and the second to be a case of research misconduct. However, between these exists many other situations that are greyer. In place of unfruitful dichotomies, we need to approach the evaluation of science with an eye toward both epistemic difference and how fields comport with norms we broadly associate with science. Rather than simply good/bad or rhetorical/actual, we can seek to understand science as existing between three ideal typical forms of scientific behavior (Figure 8.1).[3]

Rhetorically ideal science occurs when practice aligns neatly with the rhetoric of science. Hypotheses are defined at the outset. Research attempts to adhere to a predefined plan, and any deviation is noted.

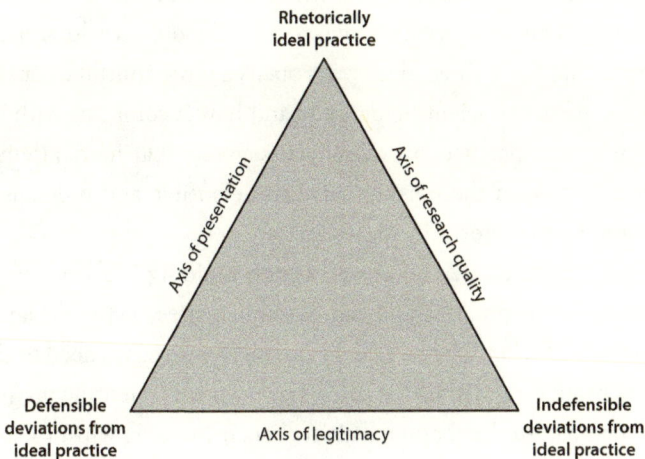

FIGURE 8.1 Triangle of Scientific Evaluation

Data and methods are fully transparent. Expert judgments are rule-based, or such choices are made clear to audiences.

The second are conditions where researchers engage in practices that are clearly bad or unethical. Data is fabricated or altered. Hypotheses are developed after data has been collected and presented as though they preceded it. Analytic choices are made with an eye toward achieving results that are publishable.

The last type of behavior encompasses situations in which scientific behavior deviates from the popular rhetoric of the Scientific Method but is, in some way, justifiable. This encompasses much of the ethnographic literature in science studies which has shown how science often deviates from the "Legend" we tell of the Scientific Method.[4]

Much of the debate about research reform in psychology (and science more broadly) has focused on the contrast between the rhetorically ideal and indefensible forms of practice. Meanwhile, the history of STS has focused on the contrast between the rhetorical ideal and the scientific practice which often involves defensible deviations from this ideal.

By themselves, both views are limited. Contrary to the reformer's rhetoric, good science can deviate from Method, and, contrary to STS scholars, some forms of scientific practice are bad and need to be called out. Rather than foreclose dialogue, as both dichotomies do, situating practice along these three ideal types opens a more fruitful discussion about the nature of scientific progress and how it comports with idealized scientific practice. Specifically, it suggests that more attention be directed toward the tension between defensible and indefensible deviations from rhetorically ideal science.

I have suggested that successful bench-building is a key component to scientific progress and can, to some degree, justify deviations from idealized scientific practice. To do this, however, we need to situate bench-building within the larger framework of scientific progress. In the first half of the chapter, I situate bench-building within a larger framework of scientific progress which also considers progress in both theoretical advancement and the spread of ideas.

The second half of the chapter returns to some of the overarching questions from the beginning of the book: What would a technologically successful psychology look like? Although psychological knowledge is an undeniable necessity of modernity and the past fifteen years have seen ongoing debates about improving psychological science, there is virtually no discussion about the social and political ramifications of a technologically-mature psychology.

DIMENSIONS OF SCIENTIFIC PROGRESS

I have argued that experimental psychologists struggle with bench-building and have found alternative strategies to discipline their field. However, the technological progress of bench-building is only one dimension of scientific progress. The expansion of perception and manipulation means little if others in a field fail to see their benefit. And, even if those in the field get on board, such developments can still be dismissed by those outside the field if they fail to yield products that are of interest to those outside the small cabal of scientific experts. Thus, providing a fuller picture of progress in both science, broadly, and psychology, specifically, means considering the multiple dimensions along which scientific progress can occur.

Bench-Building

The features of bench-building were outlined in the first half of this book. To briefly summarize, bench-building is concerned with transforming the possibilities of human perception and action. This includes notable technoscientific innovations that have transformed the world. But, significantly, it also includes the mundane accomplishments that would mean little outside a narrowly specified subfield or even an individual lab. Unique among the dimensions of progress, bench-building requires an intimate knowledge of both the objects and technologies involved. This form of "tacit" or "craft" knowledge can only be learned through extended periods of direct engagement. The biologist who learns how to keep her cells alive for long enough to conduct experiments has changed the conditions of data collection in a way that will ramify across her practice. Eventually, the techniques and technologies developed may extend beyond her practice to others in her lab, her subfield, and, perhaps, other fields entirely. Because bench-building is concerned with concrete developments that occur at the benches themselves, it inevitably begins as a local, piecemeal process. Over time, however, techniques that were once fledgling and unpredictable can transform into mature and stable practices that can be diffused through the field via networks.

I have argued that psychologists engage in relatively little bench-building. However, although these technological developments play a central role in disciplining fields like molecular biology, it is not a complete picture of scientific progress. Although bench-building is rare in psychology, the field has been successful in other ways. Thus, a fuller picture of progress in psychology, and the broader conceptualization of progress in science, demands an analysis of both theory- and market-building.

Theory-Building

Early research in both the history and philosophy of science have largely been concerned with theory-building. This was likely a product of the general intellectualist bias that privileges knowledge that is universal, communicable, and abstract over knowledge that is local, tacit, and concrete. For instance, despite fundamental disagreements regarding the nature of scientific progress, both the logical positivists and Karl Popper were oriented primarily at theoretical development. Their questions, at root, were not about technological advancement.

Rather, they were fundamentally about belief. What justifies belief? When should a belief be updated? What should count as valid evidence? Although science studies scholars have largely moved away from questions of the correct justification of belief, the focus on theory-building remains a central focus in the philosophy of science. Thus, even Philip Kitcher who sells his work as a corrective to both simple positivist accounts of scientific progress and the critical counterarguments which have rejected any notion of progress, still manages to offer a categorization of "varieties of scientific progress" that are entirely defined by their impacts to scientific theory.[5]

I take a more sociological stance on theory-building. Following Harry Collins and Robert Evans, I conceive of a theory as the internal communication framework of a "core-set."[6] The core-set is the small group of scientists who represent the universe of experts that have "contributory expertise" to a scientific field. That is, they are the ones who can legitimately contribute to the theory. These researchers are the judges for new theoretical developments and the promulgators of theoretical orthodoxy.

Because so much of the early philosophy and history of science focused on advancements in the theoretical development of science, there are many paradigmatic examples of theory-building. For instance, the theory of natural selection and its many refinements. Based upon observations of the natural world, this theory resulted in major changes to how members of the core-set understood and discussed the heritability of traits. Although nothing in the world had changed—no new power to alter the world in a concrete sense was immediately granted to scientists and, thus, no bench-building—the theory provided a new, fertile ground on which new theories could be developed. Other examples of theory-building that set research agendas on new paths include the theory of relativity and game theory. In psychology, large-scale theoretical movements like cognitivism and more limited developments like attachment theory demonstrate the fertile fields of psychological theorizing.[7]

Theory-building is characterized by conceptual or explanatory progress.[8] However, this begs the question, how does a scientist demonstrate "progress" in the realm of ideas? For bench-building, progress is always reflected in some change in our manipulative or perceptive powers that transforms what we can do with objects. Thus, the progress is objective in a literal sense. In the intersubjective domain of scientific theory, progress is trickier to measure. Research on the disunity of science suggests that the search for some objective characteristic of theoretical progress is fundamentally misguided since different fields have different standards for evidence.[9] Perhaps all we can say with generality is that theory-building is evidenced by the use of a theory by members of the core-set. Thus, theory-building does not require the theory to be correct or true in any ultimate sense, only to be accepted and used by the core-set. Conversely, a theory becomes a failure if is either rejected or ignored by those same scientists. Again, this says nothing about the ultimate veracity of the theory. Good theories may be rejected because they present too radical a break from accepted knowledge. A careful, accurate theory may be ignored because it represents too incremental an improvement on previous work.

Successful theory-building requires acceptance of a theory by the core-set of scientists most intimately associated with the topic. These researchers tend to be connected through social networks and— through schooling, training, and socialization—share a base of knowledge. Theory-building requires engaging both with the social network and with the knowledge the group shares. For theories to become adopted in the field, they must entice colleagues with their usefulness while being familiar within an accepted universe of discourse. Described by Kuhn as the "essential tension" within science,[10] the "normal" practice of science as it occurs within a stable and shared package of theory and methods is the necessary backdrop of scientific creativity and radical leaps forward. It is only by developing an intimate familiarity with an established theory that its limitations become manifest.

A mix of explicit knowledge about the field and unspoken knowledge regarding the rules of interaction in the group are prerequisites for theory-building. For the former, theory-building must demonstrate a working knowledge of the current state of the field. This includes previous research and current open questions. As for the latter, theory-building will only be successful if it abides by the standards of scientific exchange in the group. These skills include the style of argumentation that is accepted. Should new theories be presented polemically or diplomatically? Should old theories be framed as woefully misguided or as solid bases for new developments? Should new theories be represented as revolutionary reformulations or as corrective contributions? Thus, theory-building occurs within a matrix of conceptual expertise and rhetorical persuasion.

Market-Building

Theory-building and market-building share a focus on the opinion of others. The difference between the two is that, while theory-building is concerned with the judgments of colleagues within a limited professional network, market-building is based on the judgments of those external to the core-set of expert scientists. This external audience may be comprised of scientists outside the core-set, non-scientific institutions, or even the general public. Some research in the constructivist tradition has sought to eliminate the distinction between market- and theory-building, attempting to replace the internal/external dichotomy with a general theory of "recruitment."[11] However, the distinction between theory- and market-building is especially significant for psychological sciences which have thriving external markets both for novel, interesting theories and policy expertise.

Where theory-building changes meanings within the bounds of a small group of scientists, market-building seeks to extend into new domains. This can occur in a few ways. Theories or tools developed in a science may be imported by neighboring sciences. When this happens, those who can claim ownership of the theory of tools can extend their authority into these other fields. Psychology has been notoriously "generous"[12] with its tools and methods, offering its expertise in all areas where people seek human-engineering solutions.

Market-building occurs when outsiders either integrate a field's technologies or theories into their own practice or consume them. The importation of fMRI experiments into fields like political science and behavioral economics is an example of market-building by cognitive neuroscience. Intra-scientific examples of market-building are highlighted in patterns of asymmetric citations.[13] Low status fields tend to borrow tools and theories from higher status fields. When importing tools or theories, the recipient field tends to be in a weaker position to engage critically and, thus, become somewhat passive consumers.

Market-building also occurs with non-scientific audiences. Some scientists can become experts in policy domains or recruited by businesses to provide expert analysis. There are other cases of market-building among non-expert audiences that are less tangible but still important for the fields involved. For instance, psychological findings are often the topic of popular press accounts, especially when the work relates directly to a matter of social interest.

Market-building succeeds when external audiences find research either helpful for their own ends or as an interesting end-in-itself (e.g., popular science books). When neither of these occurs, the ideas will not escape the parochial bounds of the small group of researchers who are fully devoted to them. The central challenge to market-building is convincing audiences outside the narrow bounds of the core-set of one's authority. This challenge is met in several ways. Fields with high status may be endowed with a sort of mobile expert status which allows them to extend their authority outside the core-set.[14] Similarly, scholars from high status institutions may gain some reflected authority. Even with these advantages, however, scientists often work to market-build by translating their findings into terms that are meaningful outside of their narrow niche. To appeal to other scientists, tools or theories must be packaged in a way that can be integrated into their practice without forcing them to engage in the complexities of their field. Psychologists, in particular, have been adept at translating their science into popular books and articles.

Harmony and Tension

Bench-, theory-, and market-building are related, but analytically distinct, forms of progress in science. At times, they occur together or, at least in a lumbering, loosely coupled approximation of togetherness. A new theory can suggest a novel piece of technology which can generate interest from outside audiences. A newly achieved intervention may provide the data that can spur new theories. External interest and investment can drive theoretical and technological innovation.

However, these three goals are rarely met at the same time. In fields organized around ongoing bench-building, it can be unclear what value a new manipulation has for either the field's theories or to external consumers. When Blake explained that molecular biology "pushes hard even if we don't know where we're going," he indicated a commitment to a blind extension of power under the assumption that theory- and market-building would result as a byproduct of bench-building. They may not know where they're going, but they have faith that, along the way, they will discover places that others will want to visit. Conversely, theoretical claims can run far ahead of experimental refinement.[15] Gravitational waves were theorized long before instruments were sensitive enough to measure them.[16]

In the areas of psychology I observed, struggles with bench-building lead to a focus on theory- and market-building. To simplify two of my case studies, we can say that the developmental psychologists

I observed were broadly concerned with theory-building while the social psychologists I observed were mostly pursuing market-building.

For developmental psychologists, adherence to a set of philosophical beliefs regarding the nativism of basic forms of knowledge and the use of specific experimental technologies led to a clear trajectory for theory. Theory-building occurred when one could show the evidence for some ability (e.g., awareness of the physics of objects) in younger and younger children or when they could show evidence of some new potentially "innate" category (e.g., moral judgments). To a limited degree, this was accomplished through bench-building. New experiments were designed and tested. Yet the limitations of working with children resulted in restrictions regarding the types of manipulations that could be used.

Social psychologists, on the other hand, were mainly interested in market-building. The methodical work of extending theories was critiqued for being less creative and less important than developing fresh ideas. Instead, the goal was to produce findings that would generate attention. This, too, provided a predictable trajectory for social psychological research in which researchers attempted to undermine expectations through surprising findings that would eventually become accepted, expected, and could then be undermined by new, and now surprising, findings. These inversions are supported by the unavoidable interpretive flexibility of science concerned with research objects composed of natural language.

Is this enough?

THE POSSIBILITIES FOR PROGRESS IN EXPERIMENTAL PSYCHOLOGY

No one denies that psychology is an experimental science. Even Feynman's brutal charge that the field amounted to little more than "cargo cult science" was an admission that psychology was, in fact, closely emulating the form and practice of more established experimental sciences. The problem, according to Feynman, was the field's unwillingness to embrace the type of unflinching self-critique that gives the experimental method its power. This is the position taken by the epistemic activism detailed in the previous chapter. The critiques that have swept like a grassfire through the field were attempts to overcome the supposed delusion that scientific progress is possible without disciplining self-correction mechanisms.

Yet if the technological development of psychology is limited by ethical and ontological constraints, the next question is, are these permanent? Could they be overcome?

It is clear that at least the ethical strictures are relatively recent. Ethical rules on human experimentation have only been codified in the last half of the last century. Early behaviorists conducted experiments on young children that would be unthinkable today.[17] Continuing interest in the Stanford Prison Experiment, the Milgram Experiment, and others which used currently verboten methods reflects our fascination with a psychological science that did not have to play by these modern rules. They offer a glimpse into a different science, a bench-building science. If we could truly conduct *any* experiment, *what could we learn?* How much knowledge is simply inaccessible to psychologists because of human subjects' protection?[18]

The historical contingency of ethical constraints is clear. They did not always exist, and it is no law of nature that they continue to exist. Yet it is not universally accepted that lowering these ethical standards would yield significant advances because some argue that the material of interest—whether it be human consciousness or cultural meaning—does not operate by the same laws as natural objects. Lax ethics may allow you to intervene more aggressively on the body but may tell you little about the soul.

This is a comforting, humanistic vision. Yet the more intriguing and troubling issue concerns the possibility that the ontological problem could be surmounted. If the ontological problem could be made tractable, it would have the profoundest implications for both science and society.

THE PARADOX OF PROGRESS IN PSYCHOLOGY

What would bench-building in psychology look like? On one hand, it would imply a sophistication of the researcher's perceptive capacities. Through tools or training, they would be able to better detect and distinguish cognitive, emotional, or behavioral variables. On the other hand, the researcher's ability to manipulate and control these variables would be extended. For ongoing bench-building to occur, these two processes—refinements of perception and extensions of manipulation—would become alternating phases of a continual process in which improved perception leads to new manipulative possibilities which leads to new opportunities for improving perception and so on.

As a hypothetical, take the example of "power" manipulations. The social psychologists I observed were constantly frustrated by the lack of an effective way to manipulate subject's sense of power. Widely used methods like asking subjects to recount a time they were either powerful or powerless were unreliable, if not completely useless. But rather than rely on a non-invasive manipulation, if the social psychologists could give subjects a cocaine-like Substance X to manipulate their sense of power, they would have a robust manipulation that would cause an effect in every subject. The reliability of the manipulation would then provide new opportunities for research questions that promise more definitive answers. For instance, do increased feelings of power change a subject's answers on a Big Five personality test? Let us go one step further and hypothesize that subjects who normally score high on neuroticism become more confident when given Substance X. This could spark new questions like, does newfound confidence change the strategies subjects use in a prisoner's dilemma game? And do subjects with artificially-induced confidence use the same strategies as those with a natural inclination toward confidence?

Or, as a second example, say nativist developmental psychologists found a way to use an electroencephalogram (EEG) to distinguish different forms of an infant's "looking." Perhaps, some looking results in activation of the frontal lobe. We could hypothetically label this as "visual interrogation" because of the frontal lobe's association with problem-solving and looking that does not result in this activation they call "passive observation." This improves the perception of the researcher by allowing them to make novel distinctions which, in turn, provides a path to answering new research question: What sort of stimuli induces infants to engage in visual interrogation over mere passive observation? Again, let us extend the hypothetical one more step and assume that merely "interesting" stimuli result in observation while scenes that seem impossible—e.g., scenes that show a mathematically impossible event or one in which objects act in impossible ways—result in visual interrogation. This could give rise to new distinctions between stimuli that are interrogation-inducing and those that are not.

Both hypotheticals represent paradigmatic examples of bench-building. An improved manipulation in the first case leads to better perception which, in turn, leads to more manipulative possibilities. In the second case, improved perception creates new opportunities for interventions which lead to the ability to distinguish new variables. The cycle of perception and manipulation leads to a course of progress recognizable as bench-building science.

Yet what would either of these *mean*? The path of technological science leads to a withdrawal from the world of common meanings. All science begins with lay concepts. Science that begins enmeshed in the "thick" meaning of the social world becomes thinned (Figure 8.2).[19]

Science emerges from the social world. But as the field continues to evolve, its developments depend less and less on the social world

Social world₁   Social world₂   Social world₃   Social world₄

Technologically
evolving
science₁

Technologically
evolving
science₂

Technologically
evolving
science₃

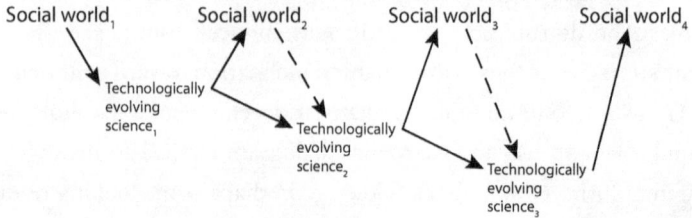

FIGURE 8.2 The Withdrawal of Technologically Evolving Science
from the Social World

and increasingly on its previous state. It moves further and further
away from lay meaning as new conceptual tools are created to address
the specialized problem environments of lab science.

The same is true for both examples above. Questions begin within
or nearly adjacent to everyday knowledge. "Power" and "looking" are
common terms. However, "Substance X-induced confidence" and
"visual interrogation-inducing stimuli" are not. In a technological
psychology, such developments would continue until their concepts
bore no resemblance to the common objects of our phenomenological experience. In technological science, this divorce is part and parcel of a process of the bench-building process and is essential to the
eventual development of technologies which are eventually absorbed
by social worlds.

However, as Bruno Latour famously argued, this uptake of technology is only possible to the degree that the target of the technology
is made to look like its source (e.g., the lab).[20] For technological sciences that are concerned with, for instance, treating dairy products to
eliminate pathogens, such transformation demands that dairy farmers
alter their practice. When the topic is human cognition, behavior, and
emotion, the success and failure of the science is subject to the design
of domains of human activity. The ethical and ontological constraints
on the technological development of science are not mere obstacles
to be overcome in the lab but a result of resistance to the growth of

technocratic power over political and cultural domains that has its roots in philosophical debates regarding the ultimate unity of knowledge.

The Assumption of a Unifield Social Reality

Philosophers currently disagree about whether science is unified or not. Scholars from the so-called "Stanford School" including Ian Hacking, Nancy Cartwright, and John Dupré have criticized the notion that science is a unified project that will achieve univocal knowledge about the world.[21] This line of philosophy offers a picture of science in which progress occurs. Yet this image differs dramatically from theories which would equate progress with Truth. It is *related* to questions of truth but complexly and always through social practices of communication and evaluation. That form of progress—the development of systems of instruments which produce regular outcomes and support further developments—is what I have been referring to as bench-building. However, this progress is not leading to *the* truth because we do not know if there is one truth. Progress can occur within a particular theoretical-material matrix, as an elaboration or extension of that matrix, but there may be other matrices and little way to arbitrate between them.

However, this view is profoundly unsatisfying for many who feel it violates a central belief that undergirds science: the belief that reality has a unitary, discoverable structure. As Isaiah Berlin once argued, a central tenet of the Enlightenment is the belief that "true answers, when found, must necessarily be compatible with one another and form a single whole, for one truth cannot be incompatible with another."[22] Yet "nomological pluralism" and "promiscuous realism" seem to imply just that—the possibility that reality could have multiple, overlapping ontologies and systems of laws.

Ronald Giere, whose positions are largely sympathetic with those of the pluralism of Stanford School, has offered a solution to this problem. In place of pluralism, Giere offers "perspectival realism." Similar to Cartwright and Dupré, Giere argues that theories do not and need not contribute to the project of unifying science. The diversity of scientific fields and theories is not only unavoidable but also productive. Yet while Cartwright and Dupré see this diversity extending into the very fabric of reality, Giere views these differences as the result of cognitive limitations. Scientists necessarily adopt narrowing theories on their objects of investigation because they lack the ability to have a "perspective from nowhere or from everywhere at once,"[23] but reality itself is perfectly unified. He calls this the "one world" hypothesis.

In the same vein, Kitcher has suggested that the unification of the sciences is simply a "regulative ideal."[24] It may not be a provable hypothesis, but it remains a goal of scientists to harmonize apparently incommensurable findings in a single, coherent framework. Both Giere and Kitcher provide ways out of the incommensurability problem that seems to be implied in the work of scholars like Cartwright and Dupré. Although both admit that "science" contains heterogeneous communities pursuing practices that look distinct, scientists cannot develop insurmountably incompatible theories that are both true. There may appear to be a disconnect between, say, fMRI studies and neuron population studies regarding how learning occurs but, according to this position, this only illustrates that the two fields have not reached the denouement that would resolve the disagreement and reveal the underlying harmony.

It is clear given the hedging language ("hypothesis" and "ideal") that neither Giere nor Kitcher believe that unification of the sciences around a specific ontology is a goal achievable in the foreseeable future. Rather, it is akin to an orienting philosophy. Giere explains that "from a naturalistic perspective, one cannot offer transcendental arguments in favor of a 'one world' hypothesis. One can, however, take it as a methodological rule: Proceed as if the world has a single structure."[25]

The one world hypothesis is a debatable position in its place of origin, the natural sciences. My goal is not to wade into these debates.

However, I do want to note that the same hypothesis transforms into something very different when applied to sciences concerned with human cognition, behavior, and emotion.

As Berlin wrote, when the hypothesis that all knowledge is singular is applied to the social realm, it has profound political implications: "The implication of this position is that the world is a single system which can be described and explained by the use of rational methods; with the practical corollary that if man's life is to be organized at all, and not left to chaos and the play of uncontrolled nature and chance, then it can be organized only in the light of such principles and laws."[26] The problem with this position, according to Berlin, is that, unlike natural objects, humans organize themselves around particular "forms of life." The Spartans may value strength and the Athenians beauty. Even if neither are our values, they are both understandable to us. The key point here is that many of our values are incompatible. A society cannot pursue, for instance, liberty and equality in equal measure. These opposing and crisscrossing values produce different worlds because they produce different possibilities and different goals.

The one world hypothesis only holds if we view humans as essentially passive, buffeted by forces they have no control over. If we simply respond to external stimuli then there is reason to believe, at least hypothetically, that a complete list of stimuli and responses would yield a singular image of humans that could be manipulated by some Laplacean demon-psychologist. However, if we grant humans the ability to act on the world, to have ideals and transform reality to meet them—if we suppose that we can pursue the "art of the possible" and not just tumble down a funnel of necessity—then the one world hypothesis fails. It fails because there are many ideals, many visions of the possible, and they are not all compatible. This is why Dupré suggests that "there might be large parts of the human sciences in which patterns do not exist to be discovered, but are rather created by our decisions to conceive of them in particular ways. This possibility would show that scientific theories in such an area could not be merely descriptive, but must be at least covertly normative."[27]

Under these conditions, the one world hypothesis, in fact, becomes a political stance used to smuggle a particular set of social values into science. For instance, lamenting the ability of the natural scientists to achieve the social closure and monopoly of knowledge implied in the technological scientific withdrawal from the lifeworld, Bourdieu writes,

> . . . the social sciences, and especially sociology, have difficulty in real-izing this ambition of monopoly, although it is inscribed in the fact that "the truth is one", because, in the name of, among other things, a contamination of the scientific order by principles of the political order and of democracy, people like to think that truth is "plural", as the cur-rent phrase goes, and that different powers, particularly with symbolic, political, religious and above all journalistic dimensions, are socially armed to claim, with some chance of success, the right to utter the truth about the social world.[28]

To Bourdieu, the democratic political order has "contaminated" the social sciences with its pluralism, and he derides the ability of other players to lay claim or to "utter the truth about the social world."[29] Hardly disguised in this passage is a desire that social sciences could withdraw from the hurly-burly and lay exclusive claim to statements of truth about the social world. Bench-building social science is the dream of technocracy.

The danger of applying the one world hypothesis to the human sciences, according to Berlin, is its insidious utopianism: "For if one really believes that such a solution is possible, then surely no cost would be too high to obtain it: to make mankind just and happy and creative and harmonious forever—what would be too high a price to pay for that?"[30] Social problems become technical problems with def-inite solutions. Political resistance to these solutions, itself, becomes a

mere impediment: another technical problem requiring a technological solution.

Relating this argument more directly to the logic of bench-building I laid out in chapter 2, the process of pragmatic problem-solving
takes on a different tenor when applied to social worlds. Our world is
replete with "unsettled situations." Taken as scientific problems means
that researchers need only discover their composite elements to begin
usefully intervening. Yet this most basic step cannot be accomplished
without smuggling in hugely significant value judgments. What are
the fundamental elements of the personality? Of families? Of romantic relationships? Of class? Of power? What is the correct classification
system for race? Gender? Age?

Bench-building results in the settlement of unsettled situations.
Experimental research traditions provide useful solutions so that
researchers are not confronting completely unsettled situations anew
with each study. Yet for this science to produce technological knowledge for use outside the laboratory, the target domain—that is, our
social, economic, political, and cultural worlds—would also need to
have these debates settled.

However, the "solutions" to these issues would be political as much
as scientific. Or, rather, they would involve the dissolution of that distinction. The result of inquiry, according to Dewey, is the emergence
of a settled and unified situation. Yet the goal of a settled and unified social world is the fever dream of the ideologue. Hannah Arendt
warned us that the problem with viewing human activity through the
cold theories of behavioral science "is not that they are wrong but
that they could become true, that they actually are the best possible
conceptualization of certain obvious trends in modern society."[31] We
become better, more tractable scientific objects as political diversity
wanes, as possibilities for expression are limited, as the categories of
experience harden and confront us with unalterable facts.

Throughout this work, I have argued that bench-building in psychology is constrained both ethically and ontologically. While this

categorization was suitable for my purposes in earlier chapters, this division itself is not a natural feature of the world. Rather it is the result of the political and cultural environment. Ontological and ethical problems are both products of a historical junction in which humans are somewhat free to develop their own opinions and beliefs.

If society contains multiple, overlapping social worlds organized around diverse and incompatible values, then any claim that one has uncovered *the* fundamental components and processes governing it will necessarily already be making implicit value judgments. Thus, the ontological and ethical problems can only be "solved" together. As Cartwright has argued regarding all experimental sciences, predictable manipulations depend upon the establishment and maintenance of nomological machines that can induce particular activity while shielding that activity from outside contaminants. Yet, in the case of a technological psychology, these "machines" would not be made of metal. They would be composed of definitions and norms of behavior, of rigid bureaucracies, and of systems of rewards and punishments. And the "shielding" they would do would prevent more than mere "complication" or "contamination." It would mislead, coerce, and suppress.

Like all technological sciences, a technological psychology would withdraw farther and farther from the social world as it evolved. And, like technological sciences, a technological psychology would introduce technological products into that same social world. Yet such products would only have power to the degree that the social world could come to take on the characteristics of the psychological technology itself. Foucault's "technologies of the self" is a descriptive phrase for the various currents of power that are internalized by individuals. Yet technologies of the self are diffuse and confusing, decentralized and contradictory. An actual psychological technology need not be.

Moreover, equating scientific progress with technological accomplishments is an impoverishment of science. The bench-building of technological science is seductive, but not a *sine non qua* of scientific practice. Just because a swamp frustrates our attempts to drive piles into it does not mean that we should end our effort. The things we care the most about are often wild and unsuitable to a narrowly scientific interpretation.[32] They tend to resist technological intrusions. But although I have argued that scientific practice is significantly about extending perception and enhancing manipulation, it is not *solely* about that. It is also about using evidence to develop theories and make arguments to convince others. Even in cases where the evidence cannot be refined, it may be the best we have.

AFTERWORD

Where Does Archimedes Stand?

The research and writing of this book have taken place between two debates. One arose in psychology and has been roiling the field as it attempts to overcome research misconduct and replication scandals. The other has caused researchers in science studies to question their commitment to maintaining neutrality regarding issues of truth. In an age where conspiracy theories and post-truth politics poison our culture, science studies scholars have debated whether they need to stand up for the sanctity of objectivity and truth.

This environment has, and I'm sure will continue to have, a large influence on how this work is received. Psychologists who have read articles based on this work or have seen me present this research have often treated this project as an exposé, a salacious account of terrible research practice that should shame those involved. Meanwhile, I have been criticized by scholars in science studies for not being more explicitly judgmental regarding the research practices I report. Shouldn't some of the obvious instances of research malfeasance be called out?

So is this book a brutal portrait of indefensible research practices or a milquetoast, mealymouthed justification for those practices? I hope neither.

I had two goals for this book. The first was to provide an unflinching anthropological look at research practice in psychology labs in an attempt to understand if psychologists are fundamentally engaged in a different type of practice than, say, molecular biologists. That is, could we explain the ongoing status issues in psychology and their problems producing behavioral technologies to something happening within the labs? The evidence strongly suggests there are significant differences between what these two groups of experimentalists are doing in their labs.

The second goal was to provide some conceptual tools for thinking about progress and evaluation in science. Toward this end, I offered a theory of progress in science as a mix of bench-, theory-, and market-building and suggested the triangle of scientific judgment to bridge the gap between the science reformers and science studies scholars.

That said, while I hope this work causes some reflection within psychology regarding their research practices, I do not feel this work justifies the condemnation of psychology as a whole or even the sub-fields I discuss. This is a piece of qualitative work, and, in line with the theory detailed in chapter 3, the goal of qualitative work is to discover the structure and dynamics of a situation we don't understand. From thousands of pages of fieldnotes and interviews, the examples chosen were selected to highlight particular features of these epistemic cultures that I feel are necessary to conceptualizing how these labs operate. In molecular biology, building out the lab's experimental capacities was completely integrated with the lab's intellectual goals. They simply could not do what they wanted to do or be who they wanted to be in the field without this evolving cybernetic integration of technique and technology. In contrast, the psychology labs were significantly less invested in advancing the possibilities of manipulation and perception. The lack of bench-building led them to pursue different notions of progress.

That said, there were certainly specific instances detailed in the preceding chapters which constitute bad practice that should be condemned. For instance, keeping subjects who fail attention checks to decide later whether the results look better with them included is textbook p-hacking. Yet, while I witnessed egregious examples, these existed on the fringe of a body of practice that often deviated from rhetorical ideals but not always in ways that were obviously problematic. That is, these labs were dealing with judgment calls in an ongoing way. Certainly, it can be argued that the labs were too permissive and began sliding into darker shades of grey until even plainly unjustifiable decisions were somehow made to seem legitimate. In his autobiography, Diederik Stapel, psychology's most famous data fabricator, explains his dissent into scientific misconduct in precisely these terms.[1] But it is also not clear to me that a complete transformation of experimental psychology would suddenly put psychology on the sure path to good science.

The righteous ascetic rigor of science reformers does not reflect how science has been done, and trying to self-consciously design psychology to mirror a freshman science course's version of the Scientific Method is a recipe for unintended outcomes. At the same time, science studies scholars have too often abdicated their responsibility to call out bad science even in the face of real dangers. Moving forward, then, I hope this book generates a productive debate around how to judge the quality of psychological science between experts within the field and those who study the practice of science more widely.

NOTES

FOREWORD

1. Ian Hacking, *Rewriting the Soul* (Princeton University Press, 1995).
2. Nikolas Rose, "Engineering the Human Soul: Analyzing Psychological Expertise," *Science in Context* 5, no. 2 (1992): 351–369, 351.
3. Nikolas Rose, *Inventing Our Selves* (Cambridge University Press, 1998), 60.
4. Richard Feynman, "Cargo Cult Science," Commencement speech, California Institute of Technology, Pasadena, CA, 1974. Retrieved April 18, 2024, from https://calteches.library.caltech.edu/51/2/CargoCult.htm
5. Karin Knorr Cetina, *Epistemic Cultures* (Cambridge, MA: Harvard University Press, 1999), 2.
6. See Morris, Charles. 1946. "The Significance of the Unity of Science Movement." *Philosophy and Phenomenological Research* 6(4):508–15.

    Oppenheim, Paul and Hilary Putnam. 1958. "Unity of Science as a Working Hypothesis." In H. Feigl, M. Scriven, and G. Maxwell (Eds.), *Minnesota studies in the philosophy of science* (Vol. 2), Pp. 3–36.
7. Hans-Jörg Rheinberger, *Toward a History of Epistemic Things* (Stanford University Press, 1997).

1. THE PROMISE OF EXPERIMENTAL PSYCHOLOGY

William James, *Psychology: The Briefer Course* (University of Notre Dame, 1892), 335.

1. Jana Winter and Cora Currier, "TSA's Secret Behavior Checklist to Spot Terrorists," *The Intercept*, March 27, 2015, https://theintercept.com/2015/03/27/revealed-tsas-closely-held-behavior-checklist-spot-terrorists/.

2. GAO, "Aviation Security: TSA Should Limit Future Funding for Behavioral Detection Activities," GAO-14-159. 2013.

3. Sharon Weinberger, "Airport Security: Intent to Deceive," *Nature* 465, (2010): 412-415.

4. Winter and Currier, "TSA's Secret Behavior."

5. Josh Hicks, "ACLU Sues for Details of TSA's Controversial 'Behavioral Detection' Program," *The Washington Post*, March 20, 2015, http://www .washingtonpost.com/blogs/federal-eye/wp/2015/03/20/aclu-sues-for-details -of-tsas-controversial-behavioral-detection-program/.

6. Ben Buchwalter, "Forget your 'Junk'—The TSA Wants to Feel Up Your Mind," *Mother Jones*, February 2, 2011, http://www.motherjones.com/politics/2011/02 /tsa-spot-scan-paul-ekman.

7. Weinberger, "Airport Security," 412-415.

8. Ken Alder, *The Lie Detectors: The History of an American Obsession*, (New York: Simon & Schuster, 2007).

9. The role that top officials in the American Psychological Association (APA) played in providing scientific support for the Bush administration's use of torture is just the most recent in a long line of possible examples. See James Risen, "American Psychological Association Bolstered C.I.A. Torture Program, Report Says" (*New York Times*, April 30, 2015), https://www.nytimes .com/2015/05/01/us/report-says-american-psychological-association-collaborated -on-torture-justification.html.

10. Ian Hacking has argued that the human sciences have achieved success using several "engines of discovery." For experimental psychologists, the most significant include counting and quantifying people, creating norms, and correlating. This type of work has significant effects, especially when it intersects with systems of institutional control. Yet, institutional processes of classification and accounting have power regardless of their origins. Moreover, I will demonstrate that these engines of discovery are only weakly related to technological progress. See Hacking, *Rewriting the Soul: Multiple Personality and the Sciences of Memory*, (Princeton University Press), 1995.

11. APAb, "About APA," 2018, http://www.apa.org/support/about-apa.aspx. James Capshew (1999:3) argues that the expansive mission of modern psychology is a direct project of its integration into the war effort during WWII. After the war, "psychology capitalized on its manifold identity as a natural science, a social science, and a mental health profession and took advantage of multiple sources of support."

Now, psychological expertise has become an unavoidable aspect of modern life. Thus, historian of psychology Ellen Herman (1995:1) notes that,

> It is taken for granted that they have a right to a central place in debates about the current state and future direction of American society. From families to governments, from abuse and recovery to war and urban violence, from the mysteries of individual subjectivity to the manifest problems of our collective social life, few institutions, issues, or spheres of existence remain untouched by the progress of psychology in American society.

12. James Scott, *Seeing Like a State: How Certain Schemes to Improve the Human Condition Have Failed* (New Haven: Yale University Press, 1999).

13. Nikolas Rose, *Inventing Our Selves: Psychology, Power, and Personhood* (Cambridge University Press, 1998), 59–60.

14. This is a modern debate, but it runs like a red thread through the history of the discipline. In one of the earliest works advocating empirical psychology, Franz Brentano (1874, 2) urged psychologists to follow the path of physics, chemistry, and other successful science in finding "a nucleus of generally recognized truth to which, through the combined efforts of many forces, new crystals will adhere on all sides. In place of psychologies we must seek to create a psychology." However, the nature of this "nucleus"—just what it is, how to achieve it, whether it exists, whether the field even needs it—has been an ongoing debate.

In fact, as long as psychologists have been experimenting, there has been disagreement regarding whether the field was moving toward unification or disintegrating. For instance, one of the first editorials in *Psychological Bulletin* fretted about the "rising tide of dissatisfaction threatening to engulf some of the 'older' (and almost consecrated) terms in psychology" (Buchner 1907, 1), while, in 1922, the behaviorist Jacob Kantor expressed relief that "Signs are many and important too that much general agreement is possible and in fact gradually being arrived at with respect to the data and fundamental principles of psychology" (482–83). Yet in the following five years, three books were published with "the crisis in psychology" in their titles (Bühler 1927; Driesch 1925; Vygotsky [1927]1997). In 1957, the APA president celebrated that "The tide of separation in psychology has already turned" (Cronbach 1957, 673) while, just a few years later, Sigmund Koch (1961) expressed mounting frustration with behaviorism and suggested it represented a chance for psychology to embrace a more pluralistic, theoretical orientation.

Koch is an illuminating character in this saga. An ardent experimental positivist, Koch was charged by the APA's Study of the Status and Development of Psychology to write a report on the "methodological, theoretical, and empirical status of psychological science" (Capshew 1999, 232). Koch began the project eager to establish a solid, unifying set of core principles. Instead, the project became a 10-year odyssey that resulted in Koch becoming a staunch advocate of humanistic psychology (Koch 1961; 1981; 1993). However, he believed the field was not designed for a fuller, more holistic approach to studying human beings. Rather, he wrote that the "suppression, starvation, and eventual atrophy" of humanist feeling was "a necessary condition for Guild membership" (Koch 1961, 629). Koch argued that this was a problem for psychologists because many of the most important questions in human experience are not fundamentally answerable in rational form. Instead of embracing this challenge, however, most of the field acts "as if uncertainty, mootness, ambiguity, cognitive finitude, were the most unbearable of the existential anguishes" (Koch 1981, 259). At the end of his long career, Koch went so far as to suggest that psychology be renamed "the psychological studies" to acknowledge the value in this diversity (Koch 1993). This suggestion did not gain any traction.

15. H. L. Mencken, "Psychologists in a Fog," *A Mencken Crestomathy* (New York: Vintage Books, 1927 [1982]), 317.

16. Quoted in Donald S. Napoli, *Architects of Adjustment: The History of the Psychological Profession in the United States*, (Port Washington: Kennikat Press, 1981), 42.

17. John B. Watson, "Psychology as the Behaviorist Views it," *Psychological Review* 20, 1913:158–177, 158.

18. Charles Taylor, *Philosophy and the Human Science: Philosophical Papers 2* (Cambridge University Press, 1985), 117.

19. Rebecca Lemov, *World as Laboratory: Experiments with Mice, Mazes, and Men* (New York: Hill and Wang, 2005), 33.

20. Kurt Danziger, *Naming the Mind: How Psychology Found its Language* (London: Sage Publications, 1997).

21. John D. Greenwood, "Understanding the 'Cognitive Revolution' in Psychology," *Journal of the History of the Behavioral Sciences* 35, no. 1 (April 1999): 1–22.

22. Danziger, *Naming the Mind*, 1997.

23. Theodore Porter, *The Rise of Statistical Thinking: 1820–1900* (Princeton University Press, 1986) and *Trust in Numbers: The Pursuit of Objectivity in Science and Public Life* (Princeton University Press).

24. Lemov, *World as Laboratory*, 2005; and Kurt Danziger, *Constructing the Subject: Historical Origins of Psychological Research* (Cambridge University Press, 1990).

25. Karl Popper, *The Poverty of Historicism* (New York: Routledge, 1957), 1.

26. Steven Shapin, *Never Pure: Historical Studies of Science as if it was Produced by People with Bodies, Situated in Time, Space, Culture, and Society, and Struggling for Credibility and Authority* (Baltimore: The Johns Hopkins University Press, 2010), 37.

27. Steve Fuller, "Disciplinary Boundaries and the Rhetoric of the Social Sciences," *Poetics Today* 12, no.2 (1991): 301–325: 316.

28. Howard Gardner, "Scientific Psychology: Should We Bury it or Praise It?" *New Ideas in Psychology* 10, no. 2 (1992): 179–190.

29. Although much of the focus of the recent "replication crisis" has focused on psychology, it is certainly not the only science wrestling with its legitimacy. Most famously, a mass replication of pre-clinical cancer studies found that only 11 percent of the studies could be replicated (Begley and Ellis 2012). Replication problems can originate in many ways. This study is not intended to be applicable to replication problems in all fields.

30. Jeremy Freese and David Peterson, "The Emergence of Statistical Objectivity: Changing Ideas of Epistemic Vice and Virtue in Science," *Sociological Theory* 36, no. 3 (2018): 289–313.

31. Open Science Collaboration, "Estimating the Reproducibility of Psychological Science," *Science* 349, no. 6251 (2015).

32. Unsurprisingly, when the replication study was released, another group of scholars reanalyzed the data and found that the replication actually showed a level of replication that was "statistically indistinguishable from 100 percent" (Gilbert et al. 2016: Appendix). Throughout the history of psychology, the crisis narrative has often been accompanied by a defensive counternarrative.

33. Paul Meehl, "Theoretical Risks and Tabular Asterisks: Sir Karl, Sir Ronald, and the Slow Progress of Soft Psychology," *Journal of Consulting and Clinical Psychology* 46, no. 4 (1978): 806–834.

34. Of course, not everyone sees the current state of psychology as a result of problematic practice. For some, it is simply the result of psychology's youth or its lack of funding. Both positions are problematic and must be dismissed.

  1. Psychology is a young science. It is not clear where to place the birth of a science. As one historian of psychology has argued, "Contrary to an all too common claim, [psychology] is not in any sense a 'young subject,' even if its extensive experimental programs are relatively recent" (Robinson 1995:4).

Topics still relevant to the study of psychology, like the organization of the self and the relationship between individuals and the social world, have been the topic of study since the Hellenic era. Wundt's experimental psychology lab was only founded in 1879, making modern, experimental psychology just a century and a half old. Yet, the first PhD in psychology, G. Stanley Hall, was just Harvard's 18th PhD awarded for any subject (Hilgard 1978).

Regardless, when thinking about collective endeavors like the accumulation of scientific knowledge, however, linear time is an inappropriate measure. A project that may take an individual many months to complete might take a large group only a few days. For the first several centuries of physics, there were only a few hundred active physicists, and, of those, most were amateurs (Shapin 1995). Despite this sparsity of scientific labor, physicists were able to develop knowledge about mechanics, electrodynamics, thermodynamics, and other areas that gave birth to technological developments that still shape our world.

Although experimental psychology was institutionalized later, since the explosion in secondary education after World War II, there have been tens of thousands of full-time experimental psychologists working on issues of mind and behavior. Over the last sixty years, psychology has been characterized by a density of scientific labor that was unheard of before the mid-twentieth century. Yet it is unclear what contributions can compete with even the early periods of modern physics, chemistry, or biology.

2. Psychology is underfunded. It is true that psychology receives much less funding than many natural sciences. However, attributing psychology's issues with this conflates cause for effect. Limiting the discussion to just military investment reveals significant returns of technological products from the natural sciences including radars, transistors, satellite navigation, and digital photography. The returns from investments in psychological science, on the other hand, have been ambiguous. If these had paid off more handsomely, the current funding regime in science might look very different.

To provide one example, during the cold war, the US government was extremely interested in weaponizing psychology. For instance, CIA researchers conducted several investigations into mind control in which they tested the effects of drugs and hypnosis on subjects, some of which were enrolled without their consent. Although the program had several arms, they shared a common goal of developing reliable behavioral manipulations that could force subjects to engage in certain behaviors against their will (e.g., telling the truth during interrogation, "reprogramming" personalities, etc.). This infamous research has been mythologized in pop culture in everything from the *Manchurian Candidate*, *Jacob's Ladder*, and the Bourne franchise.

My reason for referencing these programs is that, despite their ongoing cultural resonance as embodiments of the terrifying power of psychological expertise untethered by ethical norms, the history of these programs makes the opposite point. Setting aside the indefensible ethical breaches, they simply did not work. Despite their image as shadowy and powerful, these programs may have just been shadowy. The brainwashing program, for instance, was successful in using LSD in conjunction with emotional and physical torture to reduce people into blubbering shambles but was completely unsuccessful in building up new personalities (Lemov 2010). If these CIA programs had produced useful behavioral technologies, if mind control had been successful, if people were brainwashed and reprogrammed, psychology would have become viewed as a major new front in the Cold War and, thus, would have been well-funded. It is the lack of reliable, robust behavioral technologies that results in less funding for psychology, not the other way around.

35. James M. Cattell, "The Psychology Laboratory at Leipsic," *Mind* 13, no. 49 (1888): 37–51, 38.

36. This project is the first major study of psychology laboratories. In science and technology studies, there is a long history of laboratory ethnographies. Researchers have investigated physicists, biologists, neuroscientists, and other natural scientists in laboratories from NASA to CERN. In doing so, they have detailed the ways that data are extracted, interpreted, framed, and enshrined as facts. Early on, researchers reached a consensus. As told by Knorr Cetina, "It is perhaps the single most consistent result of laboratory studies to point to the indeterminacy inherent in scientific operations, and to demonstrate the locally situated, occasioned character of laboratory selections." Researchers devoted to outlining the "local" and "contingent" foundation of laboratory research have produced a body of theory which has come to treat all research environments as the same regarding their degree of locality and contingency. Yet, as Shapin noted, the focus on the local character of lab work has never been able to answer a very important question: "If, as empirical research securely establishes, science is a local product, how does it travel with what seems to be a unique efficiency?"

Although this is a large, rich literature, there are significant holes that allow Shapin's question to go unanswered. First, there is a relative dearth of empirical studies on the production of social science which does not travel with the same efficiency. Although a traditional blind spot in the social studies of science, investigations of "social knowledge making"—that is, empirical investigations of social science—have become more common in the last two decades. This work has highlighted the work that psychologists have put into establishing their authority by focusing on public demonstrations and appeals to self-evidence.

37. Shapin and Shaffer (2017) make it clear that these public displays are not as self-legitimizing as experimentalists would suggest. However, the important point at present is merely that experimentalists typically justify science using this argument.

38. Nicole Nelson, *Model Behavior: Animal Experiments, Complexity, and the Genetics of Psychiatric Disorders* (University of Chicago Press), 16.

39. Aaron Panofsky, *Misbehaving Science: Controversy and the Development of Behavior Genetics* (University of Chicago Press, 2014);

40. James Risen, "American Psychological Association Bolstered C.I.A. Torture Program, Report Says," *New York Times*, April 30, 2015, https://www.nytimes.com/2015/05/01/us/report-says-american-psychological-association-collaborated-on-torture-justification.html; and Michael Bailey, *The Boy Who Would be Queen: The Science of Gender-Bending and Transsexualism* (New York: Joseph Henry Press, 2003).

41. There is a lengthy history of laboratory ethnographies in science studies, but they (a) are based on observations of natural scientists and (b) mostly focus on a single site. The former obviously needs to be rectified if we are to discuss laboratory practice in psychology. However, the latter is at least as important. Without comparison, it will be impossible to understand where experimental psychology converges with other forms of experimental science and where it diverges.

42. Knorr Cetina (1999). Despite an early call for comparative case studies (Pinch 1985) and a highly cited theoretical comparison (Whitley 2000), empirical case study comparisons remain frustratingly rare. This is especially problematic because, as Whitley (2000:5) points out, "The possibility that these laboratories may be unusual in their pattern of working, or historically variable in their organization, does not seem to have been taken seriously by these authors." Thus, although deep, detailed ethnographies are important, their significance cannot become manifest in the absence of comparative studies which situate them in broader scientific and social context.

43. Karin Knorr Cetina, *Epistemic Cultures: How the Sciences Make Knowledge* (Cambridge: Harvard University Press, 1995).

44. Theodore Schatzki, Karin Knorr Cetina, and Eike von Savigny, *The Practice Turn in Contemporary Theory* (London: Routledge, 2001) and Léna Soler, Sjoerd Zwart, Michael Lynch, and Vincent Israel-Jost, *Science after the Practice Turn in the Philosophy, History, and Social Studies of Science* (London: Routledge, 2014).

45. See Price (1984); Rheinberger (1997); Hacking (1992); Hackett (2005)

46. The work that most closely mirrors my focus here is Rheinberger (1997). However, because his entire manuscript is concerned with molecular biology, his account of "experimental systems" is heavily skewed toward that science. As will be clear, his account is a valuable depiction of bench-building in molecular biology but does not describe how experimental systems operate in psychology.

47. See Cartwright (1999); Hacking (1983)

48. Bruno Latour, "Give Me a Laboratory and I Will Raise the World." In *Science Observed*, ed. Karin Knorr-Cetina and M. Mulkay, (Sage, 1983), 141–170.

2. BENCH-BUILDING AS THE MEANS AND ENDS OF TECHNOLOGICAL PROGRESS

1. Throughout the book, I will use the capitalized "Method" or "Scientific Method" to refer to the set of theories concerned with discovering the unitary logic that classical scholars believed unified the sciences.

2. Steven Shapin, *Never Pure: Historical Studies of Science as if it was Produced by People with Bodies, Situated in Time, Space, Culture, and Society, and Struggling for Credibility and Authority* (Baltimore: The Johns Hopkins University Press, 2010), 5.

3. The rejection of unified science by constructivists begs an important question; Why was so much attention paid to Scientific Method in the first place? As Kitcher (1993:4) argues, the most aggressive defense of Method has come "not by the practitioners but by their amanuenses in the history of science, philosophy of science, and sociology of science." Experimental scientists, on the other hand, only proclaim Method "on high days and holidays" while, in private, confessing that it does not describe their practice. And Shapin (2010:37) notes that "Few chemists, biologists, or physicists will have taken courses on Scientific Method."

   It is possible that scientists, while ignorant or disinterested in the articulations of Method, have still internalized the fundamental tenets of Method through apprenticeship into the culture. However, the opinions scientists have regarding Scientific Method do not reveal any hard-won consensus arrived at through practicing science. Scientists draw on different, sometimes contradictory formulations of Method (Mercer 2002) and hold a range of opinions on meta-scientific questions (Shapin 2010:35). Some are realists, some are not. Some argue for the unity of knowledge, others, pluralism. Some believe that science might have an end point, others do not. While there might be general agreement around vague values like "rigor" and "skepticism," observations of scientific practice reveal that this agreement is little more than rhetoric.

Ironically, scientists themselves deserve much of the blame for fetishizing Method. As Bourdieu (2004:77) has explained,

> The ruse of scientific reason consists in making necessity out of contingency and chance, and in making a scientific virtue of social necessity. The official vision of science is a collective hypocrisy capable of guaranteeing the minimum of common belief that is necessary for the functioning of social order; the other face of science is both universally known to all those to take part in the game and unanimously disguised, as a jealously guarded 'open secret' (economists would call it 'common knowledge'). Everyone knows the truth about scientific practices, which the new sociologists of science noisily discover and unveil, and everyone keeps pretending not to know and to believe that things do not happen that way.

Although appeals to Scientific Method may not have much practical effect on their behavior, they, nonetheless, play an important role. They provide an apparent logic to the field even in the face of persistent violations. Unofficially, of course, many scientists are willing to admit the divergence between what Gilbert and Mulkay (1984) called the "empiricist" and "contingent" repertoires (e.g., official accounts versus how scientists themselves talk about what they do). Yet, officially, the need to maintain appearances leads scientists to "present practices which may be in complete transgression of the rule as being performed in accordance with the rule, because the essential thing is to save the rule" (Bourdieu 2004:25).

Scientific Method has proved to be an important rhetorical weapon, wielded whenever scientists feel their autonomy threatened. For example, in Gieryn's (1999) summary of congressional hearings regarding the potential inclusion or exclusion of the social sciences into the National Science Foundation, the debates were dominated by questions about whether the social sciences properly used Scientific Method. Natural scientists sought to maintain their special status by arguing that the social sciences did not (or could not) follow their Method.

Yet, waving the banner of Method is clearly not the only defense to threats to their autonomy. Scientists, at times, have chosen to defend themselves, not on the basis of their process but by their products. Appealing to the ability to produce technological marvels, however, comes with its own dangers. Scientists have often resisted defining their enterprise by its outcomes, because to do so would put science in the same category of other modes of production (Shapin 2010). Unlike producing, say, furniture, producing novel insights about nature that can lead to useful technologies is an unpredictable enterprise, sometimes embarrassingly so. While it is undeniable that scientific research does, in fact, occasionally produce fantastic technological products, it often does not. Or, rather, often such technological products are at the end of a process that may take decades during which the technological possibilities are unclear. Demanding that scientific work focus on concrete ends is viewed by many scientists as an existential threat to the intellectual freedom that they deem to be necessary to actually produce important technological ends. What the non-scientist manager sees as an undisciplined, inefficient mode of production, the scientist recognizes as the necessarily flexible conditions that foster creativity and innovation. This can be seen in the resistance from the scientific community to threats to "pure research" and the related demands by funders for greater goal-orientation.

By grounding their value not on technologies but on the (supposed) process by which they work, they seek to counter the productivity argument with a plea for patience. It is an argument that certain strains of science may not actually produce anything of wider value for a frustratingly long time. The promise of science need only be that—promise. Expressed frustration over decades of failure can be met with the rejoinder that pure research hasn't yet gone far enough and that, just around the bend, might be scientific findings of epic significance.

However, this focus on method over product misrepresents how science actually functions and provides fuel to philosophical and social science critiques of Method. Yet, although the constructivist critiques of Method are persuasive, they have not made the necessary next step and explained how science produces technology at all. If not Method, what? In response, science studies scholars have offered many case studies but have by and large shied away from addressing the major question I took from Shapin (1995:308) in the introduction, "If, as empirical research securely establishes, science is a local product, how does it travel with what seems to be a unique efficiency?" But, understanding the difficulty psychologists have had in producing useful technologies requires an answer to this question.

4. In addition to the theoretical and methodological problems that a thorough-going embrace of epistemic diversity has for a project like this, it also results in some significant ethical issues for the field. Harry Collins and Robert Evans (2002) have warned that commitment to epistemic neutrality prevents researchers from making important distinctions regarding legitimacy. Adhering to the theories and methods that led to the successes of science studies meant there was no ground on which to make distinctions regarding veracity. In a world in which cynical actors fund scientists to produce beneficial "findings" about whether smoking is harmful, global warming is man-made, or if sugar is related to obesity, the inability to demarcate science done in bad faith from science done in good faith makes science studies scholars either irrelevant or dangerous.

Similarly, Bruno Latour (2004:227–230) has asked if the critical tools developed by science studies researchers to "emancipate the public from prematurely objectified facts" have been co-opted by conspiracy theorists and cynical operators who have used these tools to undermine science. Thus, the tools that allowed them to reframe scientific consensus as (at least partly) a product of social recruitment and political machinations, could be abused. He laments, "like weapons smuggled through a fuzzy border to the wrong party, these are our weapons nonetheless."

We have, thus, found ourselves in a place in which science studies scholars are unable to make determinations regarding scientific legitimacy. In an age where "merchants of doubt" (Oreskes and Conway 2010) have hijacked the imprimatur of science in order to undermine scientific consensus and advance the interests of the powerful, silence is unacceptable.

This project contributes to this ongoing project by attempting to better understand both the dimensions and nature of scientific progress.

5. Pierre Bourdieu, *Science of Science and Reflexivity* (Chicago: University of Chicago Press, 2004) and Aaron Panofsky, *Misbehaving Science: Controversy and the Development of Behavior Genetics*, 2014).

6. Bourdieu, *Science of Science and Reflexivity*.

7. Erin Leahey, "Overseeing Research Practice: The Case of Data Editing." *Science, Technology, & Human Values* 33, no. 5 (2008): 605–630.

8. Andrew Pickering, *The Mangle of Practice* (Chicago: University of Chicago Press, 1995).

9. See, Hickman (1990); Marres (2007); Salinas (2016); Timmermans (2017)

10. John Dewey, *Logic: The Theory of Inquiry* (Carbondale: Southern Illinois Press [1938]2008), 108.

11. Larry Hickman, *John Dewey's Pragmatic Technology* (Bloomington: Indiana University Press, 1990), 36.

12. Dewey, *Logic*, 111–112.

13. It is notable that Timmermans (2017) makes a similar move to pragmatism (although, to Peircean semiotics rather than Dewey) to provide more sensitive tools for analyzing the closure of controversies than he feels are offered by actor-network theory and constructivism.

14. Dewey, *Logic*, 121.

15. In Dewey's ([1938]2008:121)own words, "The pre-cognitive unsettled situation can be settled only by modification of its constituents. Experimental operations change existing conditions. Reasoning, as such, can provide means for effecting change of conditions but by itself cannot affect it."

16. Gross (2009) argues, "*Pragmatists would view social mechanisms as composed of chains or aggregations of actors confronting problem situations and mobilizing more or less habitual responses.*"

17. This is why Hacking (1983:167) has argued that, "Often, the experimental task, and the test of ingenuity or even greatness, is less to observe and report, than to get some bit of equipment to exhibit phenomenon in a reliable way." The pragmatics of simply getting a thing to work are typically the precondition for the conceptual ingenuity typically associated with scientific success.

18. John Dewey, *Experience and Nature*, (New York: Dover Publications, 1958) 66.

19. Dewey, *Experience and Nature*, 154

20. It is true that there are situations in which we seek out problems. Games and puzzles are self-contained projects where the joy comes from moving from the problem-solving. What separates science is its unending nature. Problems are never really "solved." Sequencing the genome may have seemed like an "end," but it produced vast new areas of unanswered questions.

21. Dewey, *Logic*, 119.

22. Hans-Jörg Rheinberger, *Toward a History of Epistemic Things: Synthesizing Proteins in the Test Tube* (Stanford: Stanford University Press, 1997).

23. Collins (1984); Freese & Peterson (2017)

24. Dewey's student, Sydney Hook (1927:22–23), pursued this line of thought, arguing that when the natural environment is amenable to intervention, technological instruments "stabilize and fasten for future purposes the probable direction and intent of natural forces and define for physical reference the reliable substantive aspects of natural events."

25. Michael Polanyi, *Personal Knowledge: Towards a Post-Critical Philosophy* (Chicago: University of Chicago Press, 1958).

26. For example, see Collins (1985; 2010), Doing (2004), Jordan & Lynch (1998), and Myers (2008).

27. Although the importance of "tacit" or "craft knowledge" in experimentation, STS scholars have increasingly highlighted the recursive relationship between embodied skill and perception (Alac 2008; Myers 2008; Vertesi 2008).

28. As Hacking (1983:230) has explained, "To experiment is to create, produce, refine and stabilize phenomena. If phenomena were plentiful in nature, summer blackberries there just for the picking, it would be remarkable if experiments didn't work. But phenomena are hard to produce in any stable way. That is why I spoke of creating and not merely discovering phenomena. That is a long hard task."

29. Rheinberger, *Toward a History of Epistemic Things*, 80.

30. Rheinberger, *Toward a History of Epistemic Things*, 135.

31. E.g., Callon (1986); Latour (1987)

32. Bruno Latour, *Pandora's Hope* (Cambridge: Harvard University Press, 1999), 304.

33. Bench-building also represents a challenge to the black-boxing concept insofar as it highlights why the notion of "invisibility" can be misleading. When scientists use technologies innovated by other fields—for instance, psychologists who collect saliva to measure cortisol levels—the relationship between researcher and technology take on the characteristic of consumer technology since these researchers lack the ability to engage with it more meaningfully. Yet, it is glib to equate technology in general with the invisibility and, thus, ignorance of black boxes.

   Black boxing is a borrowed term from engineering, yet it is also closely related to insights from phenomenology regarding attention. These two sources are not congruous. In engineering, black boxes are treated in schematic, idealistic terms as opaque devices that transform some input into some output. This is actually a rare outcome in technologically dynamic labs because it is the very limits of technology the lab is constantly pushing up against. Bench-building changes technology and, as such, is directly concerned with the inner workings of the "box."

In contrast, the phenomenological approach is more fruitful here. Phenomenological investigations have shown that techniques learned, absorbed, and embodied and technologies adopted, integrated, and relied upon retreat from focal awareness (Merleau-Ponty 1945; Polanyi 1958). The carpenter concentrates on the nail, not the hammer. The surgeon attends the flesh and not the scalpel. The blind man feels the street, not the cane. Technique and tool become a part of background knowledge that produces new horizons of possibility.

Yet, even the white cane is not blindly accepted. Learning a technique or adopting a new technology involves also developing an intimate understanding of its flaws and limits. This keeps users on edge and prevents the complete trust that black boxing assumes. When it is a matter of existential importance to us, we do not even fully believe our own eyes. We seek reassurance from another sense or another person. In science, this skepticism motivates researchers to triangulate methods when possible to overcome the limitations or biases of whatever "box" they are using.

Moreover, equipment failure—or, even more common, equipment "acting up" (that is, acting strangely while seemingly still working)—is a constant irritation in cutting edge laboratories. This demands that a technology that was, at one point, seamlessly integrated into practice become highly visible so it can be diagnosed and corrected. Knowledge about which devices are finicky or biased is essential to working in a lab. Thus, it is better to think about the various technologies in laboratories becoming "blacker" as they disappear into practice and more visible as challenges arise. To the degree that the task at hand is comfortably within their limits and they are functioning as expected, a technology can truly operate like a black box. However, when a task requires pushing a piece of machinery past its limits or when it requires attention to function at all, then the lab worker must keep it visible and hold it in attention.

Finally, bench-building often demands that black boxes get opened up. Jordan and Lynch (1998:795) described the standardization and diffusion of a molecular biological technique known as the polymerase chain reaction. Yet, it was not a simple, one-way evolution of progressive shrouding. Rather, they note that "The incentives to stabilize and standardize the technique are counteracted by other, locally prevalent, incentives to de-stabilize and

de-standardize it." Among the countervailing incentives are the new possibilities that materialize when the technique retreats to peripheral awareness.
On the other, however, are the potential benefits from maintaining the technique in focal awareness for the purpose of altering, improving, or refining it.
Nelson (2020) has suggested that the tensions between treating black boxes as
closed or open are often examples of sub-threshold controversies.

Thus, although black-boxing is a useful description of the way technological development in labs occurs, the blackness of these boxes is more like the
relative, phenomenological concept than the absolute, engineering concept
given that there are predictable pressures that lead to trusted technologies
being brought back into focal awareness.

34. Robert Weinberg, "The Molecules of Life." *Scientific American* 253, no. 4
(1985): 48–57.

35. Ian Hacking, *The Social Construction of What?* (Cambridge: Harvard University Press, 1999).

36. Sergio Sismondo, "Some Social Constructions." *Social Studies of Science* 23, no.
3 (1993): 515–53.

37. For Popper (1957), the unpredictability of scientific development was a necessary belief because it undermined what he viewed as dangerous historicist theories of human progress. For my purposes, the unpredictability of knowledge
helps decouple the instrumentalism of bench-building from any teleology.

38. See, Peterson & Panofsky (2021) and Freese & Peterson (2017).

39. In reference to the standardization molecular biology technique, Jordan and
Lynch (1998) note that "The incentives to stabilize and standardize the technique are counteracted by other, locally prevalent, incentives to de-stabilize
and de-standardize it" (795). Again, "black-boxing" is not a one-way, irrevers-
ible process but, rather, a temporary state in which scientists do not feel the
need to tinker with what is already working. Integrative replication is about
getting it "working" based upon the "locally prevalent" conditions of the lab
and, thus, represents both standardizing and destabilizing tendencies.

40. Randall Collins, *The Sociology of Philosophies: A Global Theory of Intellectual
Change*, 1999).

41. I believe this misinterpretation is clear when he suggests that fields in sociology that have embraced various forms of technology might turn into
high consensus, rapid discovery sciences. Simply adopting technology will
not transform a field. What is key—and this will be clearer in the coming
chapters—is whether the new technology gives the experimentalist additional purchase on their object of study.

42. Ian Hacking, *Representing and Intervening: Introductory Topics in the Philosophy of Natural Science*, (Cambridge: Cambridge University Press, 1983), 231.

43. Jeremy Freese and David Peterson, "Replication in Social Science." *Annual Review of Sociology* 43 (2017): 147–165.

3. BENCH-BUILDING IN MOLECULAR BIOLOGY

1. Stephen Cole (1992) suggests this is characteristic of all scientific fields.

2. G. Nigel Gilbert and Michael Mulkay, *Opening Pandora's Box: A Sociological Analysis of Scientists' Discourse*, (Cambridge University Press, 1984).

3. Theodore M. Porter, *Trust in Numbers: The Pursuit of Objectivity in Science and Social Life* (University of Princeton Press, 1995), 15–16.

4. See, Ryle (2009); Geertz's (1973).

5. Another strategy for getting thin data from a complex experimental situation is simply to use artificial gates meant to restrict the type of data provided. This is one appealing option in fields in which data are multiplex. In psychology, for instance, forced-choice questionnaires are a way to limit responses to data and make it more amenable to quantitative analysis. It forces potentially complex responses into narrow channels. Contention can arise, however, regarding decisions about what data to collect and what to exclude. This raises the possibility that evidence collected by making certain choices about what to restrict can be contradicted by researchers who chose to restrict data using a competing set of parameters. The contentions that can arise from this form of data thinning will be addressed in the chapters on psychology. For my present purpose, I want to focus on the second way to thin data which is to transform the moment of data collection not through fiat, but through intervening into the indeterminate situation itself.

6. One enlightening counterargument here is that molecular biology might be unusual in this respect and that other experimental fields do not require the same level of craft skill. The most obvious example is physics where much of the work is purely mathematical. Although this is true, theoretical physics largely depends upon the findings from experimental physics and this work still requires advanced craft skills (Doing 2004; Traweek 1988). Thus, it is not that the work is fundamentally different in a way that negates the materialist premise of bench-building. Rather, it shows that the cybernetic evolution of eye, hand, and object that occurs within the body of the molecular biologist has been socialized through a division of labor. This division, which tends to

elevate intellectual work while obscuring the physical aspects of experimentation, has been common since the age of Boyle (Shapin 1989).

7. Karin Knorr Cetina, *Epistemic Cultures: How the Sciences Make Knowledge*
   (Cambridge: Harvard University Press, 1999), 100.

8. Haraway (1991) has done much to transform the concept of the "cyborg"
   into a broad critique of essentialisms of all stripes. My general preference for
   "cybernetic evolution" is meant simply to draw focus far more narrowly than
   Haraway does.

9. Robert E. Kohler, *Lords of the Fly: Drosophila Genetics and the Experimental
   Life* (University of Chicago Press, 1994).

10. Michel Callon, "The Sociology of an Actor-Network: The Case of the Elec-
    tric Vehicle." In *Mapping the Dynamics of Science and Technology: Sociology of
    Science in the Real World*, edited by M. Callon, J. Law, and A. Rip, 19–34. Lon-
    don: The Macmillian Press., 1986.

11. Jacob Foster, Andrey Rzhetsky, and James A Evans, "Tradition and Innova-
    tion in Scientists' Research Strategies," *American Sociological Review* 80, no. 5
    (2015): 875–908.

4. UNBUILT BENCHES IN PSYCHOLOGY LABORATORIES

1. Joseph Ben-David & Randall Collins, "Social Factors in the Origins of a
   New Science: The Case of Psychology," *American Sociological Review* 31, no. 4
   (1966): 451–465.

2. Of course, this schema—dividing skills from technologies, ceilings from
   floors—implies that these categories are more distinct than they are in practice. For working scientists, these distinctions are blurry, and they can change.
   As is well known in the sociology of work, things that were once skills can
   be turned into technologies. Moreover, skills and technologies on the frontier
   can become "settled," while skills and technologies once considered "good
   enough" can suddenly become areas of growth and change. However, despite
   its limitations, this schema is a useful way to understand where bench-building
   happens. The somatic and material frontiers are where the opportunities for
   data collection are extended and refined.

3. Edward B. Titchener, "A Psychological Laboratory," *Mind* 7, no. 27 (1898):
   311–31, 311.

4. Titchener, "Psychological Laboratory," 324.

4. UNBUILT BENCHES IN PSYCHOLOGY LABORATORIES 271

5. Edward B. Titchener, *Experimental Psychology: A Manual of Laboratory Practice* (London: Macmillan and Co, 1915).

6. Karin Knorr Cetina, *Epistemic Cultures: How the Sciences Make Knowledge* (Cambridge: Harvard University Press, 1999), 35.

7. See, Buhrmester, Kwang, and Gosling (2011) and *The Economist* (2012).

8. Jacob Foster, Andrey Rzhetsky, and James Evans, "Tradition and Innovation in Scientists' Research Strategies," *American Sociological Review* 80, no. 5 (2015): 875–908.

9. Titchener, "Psychological Laboratory," 331.

10. See, Collins (1974, 2010)

11. Harry M. Collins, *Tacit and Explicit Knowledge* (University of Chicago Press, 2010).

12. Loïc Wacquant, *Body and Soul: Notebooks of an Apprentice Boxer* (New York: Oxford Univeristy Press, 2004), David Sudnow, *Ways of the Hand: The Organization of Improvised Conduct* (Cambridge: Harvard University Press, 1978), and Harry M. Collins, "The TEA Set: Tacit Knowledge and Scientific Networks." *Science Studies* 4, no. 2 (1974): 165–86.

13. Pierre Bourdieu, *Outline of a Theory of Practice* (Cambridge University Press, 1977).

14. See, Ekman & Friesen (1978); Ekman, Friesen, & Hager (2002)

15. See, Caeiro et al. (2013), Parr et al. (2010), Vick et al. (2007), Waller et al. (2012), and Waller et al. (2013).

16. For instance, see, Buhrmester et al. (2011), Mason and Suri (2012), Paolacci et al. (2010), and *The Economist* (2012).

17. Joseph Henrich, Steven Heine, and Ava Norezayan, "The Weirdest People in the World," *Behavioral and Brain Sciences* 33, nos. 2–3 (2010): 61–83.

18. Park Doing, "Give Me a Laboratory and I Will Raise a Discipline: The Past, Present, and Future Politics of Laboratory Studies," In *The Handbook of Science and Technology Studies*, edited by E. J. Hackett, O. Amsterdamska, M. Lynch, and J. Wajcman, 279–295. MIT Press, 2008.

19. Kahneman Daniel. 2012. "A Proposal to Deal with Questions about Priming Effects." Open letter hosted on *Nature.com*. (http://www.nature.com/polopoly _fs/7.6716.1349271308!/suppinfoFile/KahnemanLetter.pdf).

   Yong, Ed. 2012a. "Nobel Laureate Challenges Psychologists to Clean up Their Act." (http://www.nature.com/news/nobel-laureate-challenges-psychologists -to-clean-up-their-act-1.11535).

   Yong, Ed. 2012b. "A Failed Replication Draws a Scathing Personal Attack from a Psychology Professor." Discovermagazine.com. (http://blogs.discover

magazine.com/notrocketscience/2012/03/10/failed-replication-bargh-psychology
-study-doyen/#.UVMv9JMQZvl).

20. Doyen et al. (2012); Bargh et al. (1996)

21. John A. Bargh, "Nothing in Their Heads." *Psychology Today*. Originally pub-
    lished in a column for *Psychology Today* in 2012, it has been largely stripped
    from the internet. Luckily some replication activists archived a version. Last
    accessed April 21, 2024 from *https://replicationindex.com/wp-content/uploads/2020
    /07/bargh-nothingintheirheads.pdf*.

22. Sally Satel, "Primed for Controversy." *The New York Times*, February 24, 2013,
    SR8. Accessed February 26, 2013. *http://www.nytimes.com/2013/02/24/opinion
    /sunday/psychology-research-control.html?_r=1&*.

23. See, Arribas-Ayllon et al. (2019); Nelson (2018)

24. "Ontological" and "ethical constraints" are useful analytic constructs to adopt
    at this stage. However, I am not suggesting that these issues can be cleanly
    divided through some pre-theoretical decision regarding the proper domains
    of ontology and ethics. I agree with Lynch (2013:451) who notes that "STS
    research tends to pluralize, 'mundanize', and merge epistemology, ontology,
    ethics, and aesthetics" (451). That is, this tradition has often shown that claims
    about what exists cannot be distinguished from how we know, what we believe
    should be, and what is most pleasing to us.

    Recently, some have argued that science studies have taken an "ontological
    turn" in which the very categories of existence are treated as products of social
    practice. In the final chapter, I take this argument seriously to imagine a social
    world in which the ontological constraints did not exist.

    However, these constraints do, currently, exist. The accounts of ethical and
    ontological constraints emerged from observations rather than philosophical
    commitments. The present cultural, legal, and scientific milieu has produced
    these particular ontologies by supporting certain types of practice and mak-
    ing others verboten. Thus, although it is necessary not to attribute Platonic
    permanency to the current ontological order, we must acknowledge it.

25. Charles S. Peirce, *Philosophical Writings of Peirce* (Mineola: Dover Publica-
    tions, 1955), 376.

26. Robert K. Merton, "Science and the Social Order." *Philosophy of Science* 5, no.
    3 (1938): 321–37.

27. Ernest R. Hilgard, *American Psychology in Historical Perspective: Addresses of the
    Presents of the American Psychological Association* (Washington DC: APA Press,
    1978).

28. See, Brown et al. (2004) and Epstein (1996)

29. For instance, Habermas (1967) and Winch (1958)
30. Collins (2016) offers a useful argument regarding the possibility of replication in social science. Although he notes that the social sciences have "many obstacles to replicability" he argues that "these are often misplaced or can be circumvented" (75). He suggests that since social science aims at producing general principles, if it is correct, it can be replicated: "A scientific social science must stress the repeatability of observations" (78). He offers his own concept of experimenters' regress as an example of a theory that has been replicated. I believe there are two significant problems with this account. First, the focus on observations may be necessary for much of social science. Yet this is only one aspect of bench-building. In an email exchange with Collins, he suggested that improved observations occur when noise can be reduced and signal increased. However, in social science, both ethical and ontological constraints limit the degree to which observations can be improved. Ethically, there are limitations based on privacy. Ontologically, it is unclear how much better an observation can get regarding a behavior like "feeling awe." In most experimental fields, manipulation is key to the production of new forms of observation. Limits on manipulation, thus, also serve as a powerful limit to observation. Second, the very idea that the concept "experimenter's regress" (ER) is a scientific concept that can be replicated is deeply problematic and reveals a theoretical flexibility in how he views science. I in no way want to diminish the value of ER in understanding debates over replication. Although I think Collins' view of replication is one-sided, focusing too much on probative replication and ignoring integrative replication, as an account of probative replication, is hugely significant. That said, it is a social theory, useful for understanding but not for predicting nor controlling. As a schematic framework, it can be applied to different empirical contexts, but that is no more a replication than the application of a feminist interpretation to a case of employment discrimination. It is simply an interpretation. Useful, perhaps, but unable to become orthodoxy. Reasons for this will be made clear in the conclusion.

5. MAN AT POINT ZERO: DEVELOPMENTAL PSYCHOLOGY AND THE PRODUCTION OF NORMAL SCIENCE

1. Karl Popper, *The Logic of Scientific Discovery* (New York: Routledge, [1934] 2005), 94.

2. Joan Fujimura, "The Molecular Biological Bandwagon in Cancer Research: Where Social Worlds Meet," *Social* Problem 35, no. 3 (1988): 261–83.

3. Rebecca Lemov, *World as Laboratory: Experiments with Mice, Mazes, and Men* (New York: Hill and Wang, 2005).

4. John Greenwood, "Understanding the 'Cognitive Revolution' in Psychology," Journal of the History of the Behavioral Sciences 35, no. 1 (April 1999): 1–22.

5. Erica Burman, *Deconstructing Developmental Psychology* (London: Routledge, 2007), 14.

6. Aaron Panofsky, *Misbehaving Science: Controversy and the Development of Behavior Genetics* (University of Chicago Press, 2014).

7. Burman, *Deconstructing Developmental Psychology*, 41.

8. Sharon Traweek, *Beamtimes and Lifetimes: The World of High Energy Physicists* (Cambridge: Harvard University Press, 1988).

9. Harry Collins, "Lead into Gold: The Science of Finding Nothing," *Studies in History and Philosophy of Science Part A* 43, no. 4 (2003): 661–691.

10. Joseph Simmons, Leif Nelson, and Uri Simonsohn, "False-Positive Psychology: Undisclosed Flexibility in Data Collection and Analysis Allows Presenting Anything as Significant," *Psychological Science* 22, no. 11 (2011): 1359–66.

11. Panofsky, *Misbehaving Science*.

12. Lorraine Daston & Peter Galison, "The Image of Objectivity," *Representations* 40 (1992): 81–128, 85.

13. See, Kennefick (2000) and Peterson (2017). Also, Luis Reyes-Galindo, "Linking the Subcultures of Physics: Virtual Empiricism and the Bonding Role of Trust," *Social Studies of Science* 44, no. 5 (2014): 736–757.

14. See Shapin's (2012) discussion. The pragmatist Richard Rorty (1990) has similarly argued that science is a powerful form of solidarity.

15. Alvin Gouldner, *The Dialectic of Ideology and Technology* (London: MacMillan, 1976), 215.

16. Joan Fujimura, "Crafting Science: Standardized Packages, Boundary Objects, and 'Translation'." In *Science as Practice and Culture*, edited by Andrew Pickering, 168–211. (University of Chicago Press, 1992).

6. THE VERTIGO OF FREEDOM: SOCIAL PSYCHOLOGY AND THE DYNAMICS OF INTEREST

1. Charles S. Peirce, *Philosophical Writings of Peirce* (Mineola: Dover Publications, Inc., 1955), 375.

2. These are needed because subjects will sometimes quickly click through a study to finish quickly.

3. Joseph Simmons, Leif Nelson, and Uri Simonsohn, "False-Positive Psychology: Undisclosed Flexibility in Data Collection and Analysis Allows Presenting Anything as Significant," *Psychological Science* 22, no. 11 (2011): 1359–66.

4. Robert Rosenthal, "The File Drawer Problem and Tolerance for Null Results," *Psychological Bulletin* 86 (3): 638, 1979.

5. Kurt Danziger, "Does the History of Psychology Have a Future?" *Theory & Psychology* 4, no. 4 (1994): 467–484.

6. For instance, Collins (1998; 2001)

7. Murray Davis, "That's Interesting! Towards a Phenomenology of Sociology and a Sociology of Phenomenology," *Philosophy of the Social Sciences* 1, no. 4 (1971): 309–344.

8. Daryl Bem, "Writing the Empirical Journal Article," In *The Complete Academic: A Practical Guide for the Beginning Social Scientist*, edited by J. M. Darley, M. P. Zanna, and H. L. Roedigger III, 2nd ed., (Washington, DC: American Psychological Association, 1987), 171–201.

9. Kurt Gray & Daniel Wegner, "Six Guidelines for Interesting Research," *Perspectives on Psychological Science* 8, no. 5 (2013): 549–553, 551.

10. Bemm, "Writing the Empirical," 11.

11. Gray & Wegner, "Six Guidelines," 551.

12. Michael Buhrmester, Tracy Kwang, and Samuel Gosling, "Amazon's Mechanical Turk: A New Source of Inexpensive, Yet High-Quality, Data?" *Perspectives on Psychological Science* 6, no. 1 (2011): 3–5.

13. Joel Hektner, Jennifer Schmide, and Mihaly Csikszentmikalyi, *Experience Sampling Method: Measuring the Quality of Everyday Life* (London: Sage Publications, 2007).

7. CAN MERTON DISCIPLINE PSYCHOLOGY? METHODOLOGICAL REFORM IN PSYCHOLOGY

1. For instance, Paul Meehl, "Theory-Testing in Psychology and Physics: A Methodological Paradox," *Philosophy of Science* 34, no. 2 (1967): 103–115, and Paul Meehl, "Theoretical Risks and Tabular Asterisks: Sir Karl, Sir Ronald, and the Slow Progress of Soft Psychology," *Journal of Consulting and Clinical Psychology* 46, no. 4 (1978): 806–834.

2. Meehl, "Theory-Testing in Psychology and Physics," 14.

3. Adam Kramer, Jamie Guillory, and Jeffrey Hancock, "Experimental Evidence of Massive-Scale Emotional Contagion through Social Networks," *PNAS* 111, no. 24 (2014): 8788–8790.

4. Donald Baer, "Do We Really Want the Unification of Psychology? A Response to Krantz," *New Ideas in Psychology* 5, no. 3 (1987): 355–359.

5. See, Frickel & Gross (2005) and Peterson & Panofsky (2023).

6. David Peterson and Aaron Panofsky, "Self-Correction in Science: The Diagnostic and Integrative Motives for Replication," *Social Studies of Science* 51, no. 4 (2021): 583–605.

7. Matthew Makel, Jonathan Plucker, and Boyd Hegarty, "Replications in Psychology Research: How Often do They Really Occur?" *Perspectives on Psychological Science* 7, no. 6 (2012): 537–542.

8. Both Mitroff (1974) and Mulkay (1976) make important statements that Merton's norms make far more sense as rhetorical tools scientists wield rather than an accurate description of how scientists behave.

9. Steven Shapin, *A Social History of Truth: Civility and Science in Seventeenth-Century England* (Chicago: Chicago University Press, 1994), 413.

10. Pierre Bourdieu, *Science of Science and Reflexivity* (University of Chicago Press, 2004), 77.

11. For instance, Strang & Siler (2015).

12. Joseph Simmons, Leif Nelson, and Uri Simonsohn. "False-Positive Psychology: Undisclosed Flexibility in Data Collection and Analysis Allows Presenting Anything as Significant," *Psychological Science* 22, no. 11 (2011): 1359–66.

13. For instance, Grundmann (2013) and Mulkay (1976)

14. See, Yanchar & Slife (1997) for an overview.

15. Aaron Panofsky, *Misbehaving Science: Controversy and the Development of Behavior Genetics* (University of Chicago Press, 2014).

16. Naomi Oreskes and Erik Conway, *Merchants of Doubt: How a Handful of Scientists Obscured the Truth on Issues from Tobacco Smoke to Climate Change* (New York: Bloomsbury Publishing, 2010).

17. Pierre Bourdieu, *Homo Academicus* (Stanford University Press, 1988).

18. Neil Fligstein, "Markets as Politics: A Political-Cultural Approach to Market Institutions," *American Sociological Review* 61, no. 4 (1996): 656–673.

19. See, Owen-Smith (2001) and Peterson (2017)

20. Erving Goffman, *Relations in Public* (New York: Penguin, 1972).

21. Jeremy Freese & David Peterson, "The Emergence of Statistical Objectivity: Changing Ideas of Epistemic Vice and Virtue in Science." *Sociological Theory* 36, no. 3 (2018): 289–313.

22. Jeremy Freese & David Peterson, "Replication in Social Science." *Annual Review of Sociology* 43 (2017): 147–165.

23. Erving Goffman, "The Interaction Order: American Sociological Association, 1982 Presidential Address," *American Sociological Review* 48, no. 1 (1983): 1–17.

24. Kacey Beddoes, "Methodology Discourses as Boundary Work in the Construction of Engineering Education," *Social Studies of Science* 44, no. 2 (2014): 293–312.

25. Eli Finkel, Paul Eastwick, and Harry Reis, "Best Research Practices in Psychology: Illustrating Epistemological and Pragmatic Considerations With the Case of Relationship Science," *Journal of Personality and Social Psychology* 108, no. 2 (2015): 275–297.

26. Roy Baumeister, "Charting the Future of Social Psychology on Stormy Seas: Winners, Losers, and Recommendations," *Journal of Experimental Social Psychology* 66 (2016): 153–158, 1.

8. PROGRESS IN PSYCHOLOGY, REAL AND IMAGINED

1. Jeremy Shearmur, "Steve Fuller and Intelligent Design," *Philosophy of the Social Sciences* 40, no. 3 (2010).

2. See, Peterson & Panofsky (2021; 2023).

3. David Peterson and Aaron Panofsky. "Metascience as a Scientific Social Movement." *Minerva* 61 (2023): 147–174. https://doi.org/10.1007/s11024-023-09490-3.

4. E.g., Gilbert & Mulkay's (1984) distinction between the "empiricist repertoire" scientists use in their published work verses the "contingent repertoire" they use while in discussion with other scientists and Philip Kitcher, *The Advancement of Science: Science without Legend, Objectivity without Illusions* (New York: Oxford University Press, 1993).

5. The first aspect of scientific progress to Kitcher (1993) is conceptual progress. Conceptual progress changes the "reference potential" of a concept and is characterized by language that is increasingly specific and that more accurately refers to natural kinds. The second type of progress in Kitcher's schema is explanatory progress. This involves the improvement of schema through eliminating a schema that is incorrect or introducing one that is either correct, more complete, or an extended version of an existing schema. Although these represent accepted notions of scientific progress, it is important to note that both conceptual and explanatory progress are adjudicated by peers in the

core-set. Thus, theory-building occurs to the degree that members of the field agree that either conceptual or explanatory progress has occurred.

6. Harry Collins & Robert Evans, "The Third Wave of Science Studies: Studies of Expertise and Experience," *Social Studies of Science* 32, no. 2 (2002): 235–296.

7. For instance, Baars (1986), Gardner (1987).
   See, Ainsworth (1969), and Bowlby (1969).

8. Philip Kitcher, *Advancement of Science*.

9. See, Galison (1996) and Hacking (1996)

10. Thomas Kuhn, *The Essential Tension: Selected Studies in Scientific Tradition and Change* (University of Chicago Press, 1979).

11. Bruno Latour, *Science in Action: How to Follow Scientists and Engineers Through Society* (Cambridge, MA: Harvard University Press, 1987).

12. Nikolas Rose, "Engineering the Human Soul: Analyzing Psychological Expertise," *Science in Context* 5, no. 2 (1992): 351–369.

13. Loet Leydesdorff and Ismael Rafols, "A Global Map of Science Based on the ISI Subject Categories," *Journal of the American Society for Information Science and Technology* 60, no. 2 (2008): 348–362.

14. This can be a problem when these experts influence debates that occur outside their areas of expertise (see, Oreskes & Conway [2012]).

15. Nicole Nelson, "Modeling Mouse, Human, and Discipline: Epistemic Scaffolds in Animal Behavior Genetics," *Social Studies of Science* 43, no. 1 (2013): 3–29.

16. Harry Collins, *Gravity's Kiss: The Detection of Gravitational Waves*, (Cambridge: MIT Press, 2017).

17. See, Watson and Rayner (1920).

18. The sociologist Martin (2011:324) argues that "the social sciences have constructed a set of explanatory principles that might, just possibly, work if analysts were walking about a set of cages and injecting every other monkey with some strange solution." These highly controlled (and supremely unethical) environmental conditions might ("just possibly") provide the conditions for ongoing technological development. However, "the monkeys are out of the cages and are busily jabbing each other and themselves with whatever hypodermic needle comes readily to hand. We do not get far by increasing the sophistication of our mathematics for describing how the seeming chaos departs from the imposed order of the laboratory."

The implication of this passage is that prediction and control could perhaps be achieved under conditions of total environmental control. Lacking this, however, invites in a form of unwieldy complexity that cannot be met through mathematical force.

19. Gabriel Abend, "Thick Concepts and the Moral Brain," *European Journal of Sociology* 52, no. 1 (2011): 143–172.

20. Bruno Latour. "Give Me a Laboratory and I Will Raise the World," In *Science Observed,* edited by K. Knorr-Cetina and M. Mulkay (Sage, 1983), 141–170.

21. Cartwright (1999); Dupré (1995). As I wrote earlier, Hacking has argued that "when the laboratory sciences are practicable at all, they tend to produce a sort of self-vindicating structure that keeps them stable" (1992:30). Importantly, however, he did not suggest that such self-vindication was a virtue, only a fact that must be addressed. On a surface reading, this might imply a regression to the idealistic interpretation of science characteristic of a mid-20th century philosophy of science in which scientific theories and instruments achieve better and better findings that more closely approximate the true laws of nature. Subsequent work in this tradition makes it clear that what is being proposed here is, in some sense, both realist and relativist.

Cartwright (1999) has claimed that we should abandon the idea of universal laws altogether. Because supposed laws of nature can only be shown to be operative within restrictive "nomological machines" that shield interactions from potentially contaminating influences, all laws of nature should be understood to hold only ceteris paribus. That is, drop a ball within a vacuum and physicists may be able to accurately predict its trajectory and speed, but drop a dollar bill from the top of a building on a windy day, and they will have nothing to say. This leads her to the radical conclusion that she calls "metaphysical nomological pluralism" which is "the doctrine that nature is governed in different domains by different systems of laws not necessarily related to each other in any systematic or uniform way; by a patchwork of laws. Nomological pluralism opposes any kind of fundamentalism" (31).

Similarly, Dupré (1995) has advocated a "promiscuous realism" in which no ontology holds a privileged position. In place of essentialist or reductionist philosophies which order the sciences based upon their distance to the ontology they consider fundamental, he argues that the sciences may be guided by multiple values that could produce different ontologies.

Longino (2013) has pursued the question of scientific progress in the behavioral sciences, asking if genetic, neuroscientific, and social-environmental approaches to the study of violence and sexuality were moving toward integration or were producing evidence showing which was "best." Rather than integration or a reductionism which may reveal the fundamental pieces of these phenomenon, Longino argues that each field carves out the "causal space" in a unique way which requires that they hold some variables constant that are of interest in other fields. Thus, she explains that "research pursued under the aegis of any of these approaches pushes them in nonreconcilable directions. Refining and improving the methods of a given approach enables researchers to produce better knowledge within that particular framework but does not produce tools for cross-approach empirical evaluation" (126).

22. Isaiah Berlin, *The Proper Study of Mankind: An Anthology of Essays* (New York: Farrar, Straus, & Giroux, [1949] 2000), 5.

23. Ronald Giere, *Explaining Science: A Cognitive Approach* (University of Chicago Press, 1990), 80.

24. Philip Kitcher, "Unification as a Regulative Ideal," *Perspectives on Science* 7, no. 3 (1999): 337–48.

25. Giere, *Explaining Science*, 83.

26. Berlin, *Proper Study of Mankind*, 5.

27. John Dupré, *The Disorder of Things: Metaphysical Foundations for the Disunity of Science* (Cambridge, MA: Harvard University Press, 1995), 11–12.

28. Pierre Bourdieu, *Science of Science and Reflexivity* (University of Chicago Press, 2004), 73.

29. Fuchs and Turner (1986) similarly argue that sciences reach maturity when "a science is established as an autonomous and self-referential system of knowledge cumulation and administration" (145). However, Fuller (1991) notes that the social sciences have only become "partially autonomous from the societies that support them."

30. Berlin, *Proper Study of Mankind*, 13.

31. Hannah Arendt, *The Human Condition* (University of Chicago Press, 1958), 322.

32. Isaac Reed, "Justifying Sociological Knowledge: From Realism to Interpretation," *Sociological Theory* 26, no. 2 (2008): 101–129.

AFTERWORD: WHERE DOES ARCHIMEDES STAND?

1. Diederik Stapel, *Faking Science: A True Story of Academic Fraud* (Accessed 3/13/2014 from https://errorstatistics.files.wordpress.com/2014/12/fakingscience-20141214.pdf)

REFERENCES

Abbott, Andrew D. *The System of Professions*. University of Chicago Press, 1988.

Abend, Gabriel. "Thick Concepts and the Moral Brain." *European Journal of Sociology* 52, no. 1 (2011): 143–172.

Ainsworth, Mary D. "Object Relations, Dependency, and Attachment: A Theoretical Review of the Infant-Mother Relationship." *Child Development* 40 (1969): 969–1025.

Alac, Morena. "Working with Brain Scans: Digital Images and Gestural Interaction in fMRI Laboratory." *Social Studies of Science* 38, no. 4 (2008): 483–508.

Alder, Ken. *The Lie Detectors: The History of an American Obsession*. New York: Simon & Schuster, 2007.

Allport, G. W. "Human Nature and the Peace." *Psychological Bulletin* 42, no. 6 (1945): 376–378.

APAa. "APA Membership Statistics." APA.org. Last accessed June 19, 2018. http://www.apa.org/about/apa/archives/membership.aspx.

APAb. "About APA." APA.org. Last accessed June 19, 2018. http://www.apa.org/support/about-apa.aspx.

Arendt, Hannah. *The Human Condition*. University of Chicago Press, 1958.

Arribas-Ayllon, Michael, Andrew Bartlett, and Jamie Lewis. *Psychiatric Genetics: From Hereditary Madness to Big Biology*. Routledge, 2019.

Ashmore, Malcolm, Steven D. Brown, and Katie MacMillan. "Lost in the Mall with Mesmer and Wundt: Demonstrations and Demarcations in the Psychologies." *Science, Technology, & Human Values* 30, no. 1 (2005): 76–110.

Aspers, Patrik. "Performing Ontology." *Social Studies of Science* 45, no. 3 (2015): 449–53.

Baars, Bernard J. *The Cognitive Revolution in Psychology*. New York: Guilford Press, 1986.

Baer, Donald M. "Do We Really Want the Unification of Psychology? A Response to Krantz." *New Ideas in Psychology* 5, no. 3 (1987): 355–359.

Bailey, Michael. *The Boy Who Would be Queen: The Science of Gender-Bending and Transsexualism* (New York: Joseph Henry Press, 2003).

Bargh, John A. "Nothing in Their Heads." *Psychology Today*. Last accessed April 21, 2024 from https://replicationindex.com/wp-content/uploads/2020/07/bargh-nothingintheirheads.pdf.

Bargh, John A., Mark Chen, and Lara Burrows. "Automaticity of Social Behavior: Direct Effects of Trait Construct and Stereotype Activation on Action." *Journal of Personality and Social Psychology* 71, no. 2 (1996): 230–44.

Bauman, Zygmunt. *Liquid Modernity*. Cambridge: Polity, 2000.

Baumeister, Roy F. "Charting the Future of Social Psychology on Stormy Seas: Winners, Losers, and Recommendations." *Journal of Experimental Social Psychology* 66 (2016): 153–158.

Beck, Ulrich. *Risk Society: Towards a New Modernity*. New York: SAGE Publications, 1992.

Beddoes, Kacey. "Methodology Discourses as Boundary Work in the Construction of Engineering Education." *Social Studies of Science* 44, no. 2 (2014): 293–312.

Begley, C. Glenn, and Lee M. Ellis. "Drug Development: Raise Standards for Preclinical Cancer Research." *Nature* 483, no. 7391 (2012): 531–33.

Bell, D. *The Coming of Post-Industrial Society: A Venture in Social Forecasting*. New York: Basic Books, 1973.

Bem, Daryl J. "Writing the Empirical Journal Article." In *The Complete Academic: A Practical Guide for the Beginning Social Scientist*, edited by J. M. Darley, M. P. Zanna, and H. L. Roediger III, 2nd ed., 171–201. Washington, DC: American Psychological Association, 1987.

Ben-David, Joseph, and Randall Collins. "Social Factors in the Origins of a New Science: The Case of Psychology." *American Sociological Review* 31, no. 4 (1966): 451–465.

Berger, Peter. *The Sacred Canopy: Elements of a Sociological Theory of Religion*. New York: Anchor Books, 1990.

Berlin, Isaiah. *The Proper Study of Mankind: An Anthology of Essays*. New York: Farrar, Straus, & Giroux, [1949] 2000.

Bloor, David. *Knowledge and Social Imagery*, 2nd ed. University of Chicago Press, 1992.

Bourdieu, Pierre. *Homo Academicus*. Stanford University Press, 1988.

Bourdieu, Pierre. *Outline of a Theory of Practice*. Cambridge University Press, 1977.

Bourdieu, Pierre. *Science of Science and Reflexivity*. University of Chicago Press, 2004.

Bourdieu, Pierre. "The Specificity of the Scientific Field and the Social Conditions of the Progress of Reason." *Social Science Information* 14, no. 6 (1975): 19–47.

Bowlby, John. *Attachment and Loss, Volume 1: Attachment*. New York: Basic Books, 1969.

Brentano, Franz. *Psychology from an Empirical Standpoint*. Duncker & Humblot 1874, 2.

Brown, Phil, Stephen Zavestoski, Sabrina McCormick, Brian Mayer, Rachel Morello-Frosch, and Rebecca Gasior Altman. "Embodied Health Movements: New Approaches to Social Movements in Health." *Sociology of Health & Illness* 26, no. 1 (2004): 50–80.

Buchner, E. F. "Psychological Progress in 1906." *Psychological Bulletin* 4 (1907): 1–9.

Buchwalter, Ben. "Forget Your 'Junk'—The TSA Wants to Feel Up Your Mind." *Mother Jones*, February 2, 2011. Accessed June 18, 2018. http://www.motherjones.com/politics/2011/02/tsa-spot-scan-paul-ekman.

Bühler, K. *Die Krise der Psychologie*. Verlag Von Gustav Fischer, 1927.

Buhrmester, Michael, Tracy Kwang, and Samuel D. Gosling. "Amazon's Mechanical Turk: A New Source of Inexpensive, Yet High-Quality, Data?" *Perspectives on Psychological Science* 6, no. 1 (2011): 3–5.

Burman, Erica. *Deconstructing Developmental Psychology*. London: Routledge, 2007.

Burri, Regula V., and Joseph Dumit. "Social Studies of Scientific Imaging and Visualizations." In *The Handbook of Science and Technologies Studies*, 3rd ed., edited by E. J. Hackett, O. Amsterdamska, M. Lynch, and J. Wajcman, 297–317. Cambridge, MA: The MIT Press, 2008.

Caeiro, C.C., B.M. Waller, A.M. Burrows, E. Zimmermann, and M. Davila-Ross. "OrangFACS: A muscle-based coding system for orangutan facial movements." *International Journal of Primatology* 34, no. 1 (2013): 115–129.

Callon, Michel. "The Sociology of an Actor-Network: The Case of the Electric Vehicle." In *Mapping the Dynamics of Science and Technology: Sociology of Science in the Real World*, edited by M. Callon, J. Law, and A. Rip, 19–34. London: The Macmillian Press., 1986.

Callon, Michel. "Some Elements of a Sociology of Translation: Domestication of the Scallops and the Fishermen of St Brieuc Bay." *The Sociological Review* 32, no. 1 (1984): 196–233.

Camic, Charles, Neil Gross, and Michele Lamont. "The Study of Social Knowledge Making." In *Social Knowledge in the Making*, edited by C. Camic, N. Gross, and M. Lamont, 1–40. University of Chicago Press, 2011.

Canguilhem, Georges. *The Normal and the Pathological*. New York: Zone Books, [1966] 1991.

Capshew, James H. *Psychologists on the March: Science, Practice, and Professional Identity in America, 1929–1969.* Cambridge University Press, 1999.

Cattell, James M. "The Psychology Laboratory at Leipsic." *Mind* 13, no. 49 (1888): 37–51.

Cartwright, Nancy. *The Dappled World: A Study of the Boundaries of Science.* Cambridge University Press, 1999.

Cole, Stephen. "The Hierarchy of the Sciences?" *American Journal of Sociology* 89, no. 1 (1983): 111–139.

Cole, Stephen. *Making Science: Between Nature and Society.* Cambridge, MA: Harvard University Press, 1992.

Cole, Stephen. "Why Sociology Doesn't Make Progress Like the Natural Sciences." *Sociological Forum* 9, no. 2 (1994): 133–154.

Cole, Stephen. "Merton's Contribution to the Sociology of Science." *Social Studies of Science* 34, no. 6 (2004): 829–844.

Collins, Harry M. *Changing Order: Replication and Induction in Scientific Practice.* University of Chicago Press, 1985.

Collins, Harry M. *Gravity's Kiss: The Detection of Gravitational Waves.* Cambridge: MIT Press, 2017.

Collins, Harry M. "Lead into Gold: The Science of Finding Nothing." *Studies in History and Philosophy of Science Part A* 43, no. 4 (2003): 661–691.

Collins, Harry M. "Reproducibility of Experiments: Experimenters' Regress, Statistical Uncertainty Principle, and the Replication Imperative." In *Reproducibility: Principles, Problems, Practices and Prospects,* edited by H. Atmaspacher and S. Maasen, 65–82. Hoboken, NJ: John Wiley & Sons, Inc., 2016.

Collins, Harry M. *Tacit and Explicit Knowledge.* The University of Chicago Press, 2010.

Collins, Harry M. "The TEA Set: Tacit Knowledge and Scientific Networks." *Science Studies* 4, no. 2 (1974): 165–86.

Collins, Harry M., and Robert Evans. "The Third Wave of Science Studies: Studies of Expertise and Experience." *Social Studies of Science* 32, no. 2 (2002): 235–296.

Collins, Randall. *The Sociology of Philosophies: A Global Theory of Intellectual Change.* Harvard University Press, 1999.

Cronbach, Lee J. "The Two Disciplines of Scientific Psychology." *American Psychologist* 12, no. 11 (1957):673.

Danziger, Kurt. *Constructing the Subject: Historical Origins of Psychological Research.* Cambridge University Press, 1990.

Danziger, Kurt. "Does the History of Psychology Have a Future?" *Theory & Psychology* 4, no. 4 (1994): 467–484.

Danziger, Kurt. "Making Social Psychology Experimental: A Conceptual History, 1920–1970." *Journal of the History of the Behavioral Sciences* 36, no. 4 (2000): 329–347.

Danziger, Kurt. *Naming the Mind: How Psychology Found its Language*. London: Sage Publications, 1997.

Daston, Lorraine. "The Moral Economy of Science." *Osiris* 10 (1995): 2–24.

Daston, Lorraine, and Peter Galison. "The Image of Objectivity." *Representations* 40 (1992): 81–128.

Davis, Murray S. "That's Interesting! Towards a Phenomenology of Sociology and a Sociology of Phenomenology." *Philosophy of the Social Sciences* 1, no. 4 (1971): 309–344.

Dewey, John. *Experience and Nature*. New York: Dover Publications, Inc., 1958.

Dewey, John. *Logic: The Theory of Inquiry*. In *The Later Works of John Dewey, Volume 12, 1925–1953: 1938*. Carbondale, IL: Southern Illinois University Press, [1938] 2008.

Doing, Park. "Give Me a Laboratory and I Will Raise a Discipline: The Past, Present, and Future Politics of Laboratory Studies." In *The Handbook of Science and Technology Studies*, edited by E. J. Hackett, O. Amsterdamska, M. Lynch, and J. Wajcman, 279–295. MIT Press, 2008.

Doing, Park. "'Lab Hands' and the 'Scarlet O': Epistemic Politics and (Scientific) Labor." *Social Studies of Science* 34 (2004): 299–323.

Doyen, Stéphane, Olivier Klein, Cora-Lise Pichon, and Axel Cleeremans. "Behavior Priming: It's All in the Mind, but Whose Mind?" *PLoS One* 7, no. 1 (2012): e29081. doi:10.1371/journal.pone.0029081.

Driesch, H. *The Crisis in Psychology*. Princeton University Press, 1925.

Dupré, John. *The Disorder of Things: Metaphysical Foundations for the Disunity of Science*. Cambridge, MA: Harvard University Press, 1995.

The Economist. "The Roar of the Crowd: Crowdsourcing is Transforming the Science of Psychology." *The Economist*. Last accessed February 26, 2013. http://www.economist.com/node/21555876.

Ekman, Paul, and Wallace V. Friesen. *Facial Action Coding System*. California: Consulting Psychology Press, 1978.

Ekman, Paul, Wallace V. Friesen, and J.C. Hager. *Facial Action Coding System: The Manual*. Salt Lake City: Research Nexus, 2002.

Epstein, Steven. *Impure Science: AIDS, Activism, and the Politics of Knowledge*. Berkeley, CA: University of California Press, 1996.

Feyerabend, Paul. *Against Method: Outline of an Anarchist Theory of Knowledge*. New York: New Left Books, 1975.

Feynman, Richard. "Cargo Cult Science." Commencement speech, California Institute of Technology, Pasadena, CA, 1974. Retrieved April 18, 2024, from https://calteches.library.caltech.edu/51/2/CargoCult.htm

Finkel, Eli J., Paul W. Eastwick, and Harry T. Reis. "Best Research Practices in Psychology: Illustrating Epistemological and Pragmatic Considerations With the Case of Relationship Science." *Journal of Personality and Social Psychology* 108, no. 2 (2015): 275–297.

Fleck, Ludwik. *Genesis and Development of a Scientific Fact*. University of Chicago Press, [1935] 1979.

Fligstein, Neil. "Markets as Politics: A Political-Cultural Approach to Market Institutions." *American Sociological Review* 61, no. 4 (1996): 656–673.

Fodor, Jerry. "Look!" *London Review of Books* 20, no. 21 (1998): 3–6.

Foster, Jacob G, Andrey Rzhetsky, and James A Evans. "Tradition and Innovation in Scientists' Research Strategies." *American Sociological Review* 80, no. 5 (2015): 875–908.

Foucault, Michel. *The Essential Foucault*. New York: The New Press, 2003.

Foucault, Michel. *Technologies of the Self: A Seminar with Michel Foucault*. University of Massachusetts Press, 1988.

Fourcade, Marion, Etienne Ollion, and Yann Algan. "The Superiority of Economics." MaxPo Discussion Paper 14, no. 3 (2014): 1–26.

Freese, Jeremy, and David Peterson. "The Emergence of Statistical Objectivity: Changing Ideas of Epistemic Vice and Virtue in Science." *Sociological Theory* 36, no. 3 (2018): 289–313.

Freese, Jeremy, and David Peterson. "Replication in Social Science." *Annual Review of Sociology* 43 (2017): 147–165.

Frickel, Scott, and Neil Gross. "A General Theory of Scientific/Intellectual Movements." *American Sociological Review* 70, no. 2 (2005): 204–232.

Fuchs, Stephan, and Jonathan H. Turner. "What Makes a Science 'Mature'? Patterns of Organizational Control in Scientific Production." *Sociological Theory* 4, no. 2 (1986): 143–150.

Fujimura, Joan. "Crafting Science: Standardized Packages, Boundary Objects, and 'Translation'." In *Science as Practice and Culture*, edited by Andrew Pickering, 168–211. University of Chicago Press, 1992.

Fujimura, Joan. "The Molecular Biological Bandwagon in Cancer Research: Where Social Worlds Meet." *Social* Problem 35, no. 3 (1988): 261–83.

Fuller, Steve. "Disciplinary Boundaries and the Rhetoric of the Social Sciences." *Poetics Today* 12, no. 2 (1991): 301–325.

Galison, Peter. "Computer Simulations and the Trading Zone." In *The Disunity of Science: Boundaries, Contexts, and Power*, edited by Peter Galison and David J. Stump, 118–57. Palo Alto, CA: Stanford University Press, 1996.

Galison, Peter, and David J. Stump, eds. *The Disunity of Science: Boundaries, Contexts, and Power*. Palo Alto, CA: Stanford University Press, 1996.

GAO. "Aviation Security: TSA Should Limit Future Funding for Behavior Detection Activities." GAO-14-159, 2013.

Gardner, Howard. *The Mind's New Science: A History of the Cognitive Revolution*. New York: Basic Books, 1987.

Gardner, Howard. "Scientific Psychology: Should We Bury it or Praise It?" *New Ideas in Psychology* 10, no. 2 (1992): 179–190.

Geertz, Clifford. *The Interpretation of Cultures*. New York: Basic Books, 1973.

Gibson, David R. "Enduring Illusions: The Social Organization of Secrecy and Deception." *Sociological Theory* 32, no. 4 (2014): 283–306.

Giddens, Anthony. *The Consequences of Modernity*. Palo Alto, CA: Stanford University Press, 1991b.

Giddens, Anthony. *Modernity and Self-Identity*. Cambridge: Polity, 1991a.

Giere, Ronald N. *Explaining Science: A Cognitive Approach*. University of Chicago Press, 1990.

Gieryn, T. F. *Cultural Boundaries of Science: Credibility on the Line*. University of Chicago Press, 1999.

Gilbert, Daniel T., Gary King, Stephen Pettigrew, and Timothy D. Wilson. "Comment on 'Estimating the Reproducibility of Psychological Science'." *Science* 351, no. 6277 (2016): 1037–38.

Gilbert, G. Nigel, and Michael Mulkay. *Opening Pandora's Box: A Sociological Analysis of Scientists' Discourse*. Cambridge University Press, 1984.

Goffman, Erving. "The Interaction Order: American Sociological Association, 1982 Presidential Address." *American Sociological Review* 48, no. 1 (1983): 1–17.

Goffman, Erving. *Relations in Public*. New York: Penguin, 1972.

Gouldner, Alvin. *The Dialectic of Ideology and Technology*. London: MacMillan, 1976.

Gray, Kurt, and Daniel M. Wegner. "Six Guidelines for Interesting Research." *Perspectives on Psychological Science* 8, no. 5 (2013): 549–553.

Greenwood, John D. "Understanding the 'Cognitive Revolution' in Psychology." *Journal of the History of the Behavioral Sciences* 35, no. 1 (1999): 1–22.

Gross, Neil. "A Pragmatist Theory of Social Mechanisms." *American Sociological Review* 74, no. 3 (2009): 358–79.

Grundmann, R. "'Climategate' and the Scientific Ethos." *Science, Technology, & Human Values* 38, no. 1 (2013): 67–93.

Habermas, Jürgen. *On the Logic of the Social Sciences*. Cambridge, MA: The MIT Press, 1967.

Hackett, Edward J. "Essential Tensions: Identity, Control, and Risk in Research." *Social Studies of Science* 35, no. 5 (2005): 787–826.

Hacking, Ian. "The Disunity of the Sciences." In *The Disunity of Science: Boundaries, Contexts, and Power*, edited by P. Galison and D. J. Stump, 37–74. Palo Alto, CA: Stanford University Press, 1996.

Hacking, Ian. "Making Up People." *London Review of Books* 28, no. 16 (2006).

Hacking, Ian. *Representing and Intervening: Introductory Topics in the Philosophy of Natural Science*. Cambridge University Press, 1983.

Hacking, Ian. *Rewriting the Soul: Multiple Personality and the Sciences of Memory*. Princeton University Press, 1995.

Hacking, Ian. "The Self-Vindication of the Laboratory Sciences." In *Science as Practice and Culture*, edited by A. Pickering, 29–64. University of Chicago Press, 1992.

Hacking, Ian. *The Social Construction of What?* Cambridge: Harvard University Press, 1999.

Halfon, Saul. "The Disunity of Consensus: International Population Policy Coordination as Socio-Technical Practice." *Social Studies of Science* 36, no. 5 (2006): 783–807.

Haraway, Donna. *Simians, Cyborgs, and Women: The Reinvention of Nature*. New York: Routledge, 1991.

Hartley, James, Eric Sotto, and James Pennebaker. "Style and Substance in Psychology Articles." *Social Studies of Science* 32, no. 2 (2002): 321–334.

Hektner, Joel M., Jennifer A. Schmide, and Mihaly Csikszentmikalyi. *Experience Sampling Method: Measuring the Quality of Everyday Life*. London: SAGE Publications, 2007.

Henrich, Joseph, Steven J. Heine, and Ara Norenzayan. "The Weirdest People in the World." *Behavioral and Brain Sciences* 33, nos. 2–3 (2010): 61–83.

Henriques, G. R., and H. C. Cobb. "Introduction to the Special Issues on the Unified Theory." *Journal of Clinical Psychology* 60, no. 12 (2004): 1203–1205.

Herman, Ellen. *The Romance of American Psychology: Political Culture in the Age of Experts*. Berkeley, CA: University of California Press, 1995.

Hickman, Larry A. *John Dewey's Pragmatic Technology*. Bloomington, IN: Indiana University Press, 1990.

Hicks, Josh. "ACLU Sues for Details of TSA's Controversial 'Behavioral Detection' Program." *The Washington Post*, March 20, 2015. Accessed June 18, 2018. http://www.washingtonpost.com/blogs/federal-eye/wp/2015/03/20/aclu-sues -for-details-of-tsas-controversial-behavioral-detection-program/.

Hilgard, Ernest R. *American Psychology in Historical Perspective: Addresses of the Presidents of the American Psychological Association.* Washington, DC: APA Press, 1978.

Hilgartner, Stephen. "The Dominant View of Popularization: Conceptual Problems, Political Uses." *Social Studies of Science* 20, no. 3 (1990): 519–39.

Hobsbawm, Eric. *The Age of Extremes.* New York: Vintage Books, 1994.

Hook, Sidney. *The Metaphysics of Pragmatism.* Chicago: Open Court Publishing Company, 1927.

Husserl, E. *The Crisis of European Sciences and Transcendental Phenomenology.* Evanston, IL: Northwestern University Press, [1936] 1970.

Igo, Sarah. *The Averaged American: Surveys, Citizens, and the Making of a Mass Public.* Cambridge, MA: Harvard University Press, 2008.

James, William. *Psychology: The Briefer Course.* University of Notre Dame Press, 1892.

Jordan, D., and M. Lynch. "The Dissemination, Standardization, and Routinization of a Molecular Biological Technique." *Social Studies of Science* 28, nos. 5/6 (1998): 773–800.

Kahneman 2012

Kahneman Daniel. 2012. "A Proposal to Deal with Questions about Priming Effects." Open letter hosted on *Nature.com.* (http://www.nature.com/polopoly_fs/7.6716 .1349271308!/suppinfoFile/KahnemanLetter.pdf).

Kantor, Jacob R. "Can the Psychophysical Experiment Reconcile Introspectionists and Objectivists?" *American Journal of Psychology* 33 (1922): 481–510.

Kennefick, Daniel. "Star Crushing: Theoretical Practice and the Theoreticians' Regress." *Social Studies of Science* 30, no. 1 (2000): 5–40.

Kitcher, Philip. *The Advancement of Science: Science without Legend, Objectivity without Illusions.* New York: Oxford University Press, 1993.

Kitcher, Philip. "Unification as a Regulative Ideal." *Perspectives on Science* 7, no. 3 (1999): 337–48.

Knorr Cetina, Karin. *Epistemic Cultures: How the Sciences Make Knowledge.* Cambridge, MA: Harvard University Press, 1999.

Knorr Cetina, Karin. "The Ethnographic Study of Scientific Work: Toward a Constructivist Interpretation of Science." In *Science Observed: Perspectives on the Social Studies of Science,* edited by K. Knorr Cetina, 115–140. London: Sage, 1983.

Knorr Cetina, Karin. "Laboratory Studies: The Cultural Approach to the Study of Science." In *The Handbook of Science and Technology Studies*, edited by S. Jasanoff, G. E. Markle, J. C. Petersen, and T. Pinch, 140–167. Thousand Oaks, CA: Sage, 1995.

Knorr Cetina, Karin. "Social and Scientific Method or What Do We Make of the Distinction Between the Natural and the Social Sciences?" *Philosophy of Social Science* 11 (1981): 335–359.

Koch, Sigmund. "The Nature and Limits of Psychological Knowledge: Lessons of a Century qua 'Science'." *American Psychologist* 36, no. 3 (1981): 257–69.

Koch, Sigmund. "Psychological Science Versus the Science–Humanism Antinomy: Intimations of a Significant Science of Man." *American Psychologist* 16 (1961): 629–639.

Koch, Sigmund. "'Psychology' or 'the Psychological Studies'?" *American Psychologist* 48 (1993): 902–904.

Kohler, Robert E. *Lords of the Fly: Drosophila Genetics and the Experimental Life.* University of Chicago Press, 1994.

Kramer, Adam D.I., Jamie E. Guillory, and Jeffrey T. Hancock. "Experimental Evidence of Massive-Scale Emotional Contagion through Social Networks." *PNAS* 111, no. 24 (2014): 8788–8790.

Krantz, D. "Psychology's Search for Unity." *New Ideas in Psychology* 5, no. 3 (1987): 329–339.

Kuhn, Thomas. *The Essential Tension: Selected Studies in Scientific Tradition and Change.* University of Chicago Press, 1979.

Kuhn, Thomas. *The Structure of Scientific Revolutions.* University of Chicago Press, 1962.

Latour, Bruno. "Give Me a Laboratory and I Will Raise the World." In *Science Observed*, edited by K. Knorr-Cetina and M. Mulkay, 141–170. Sage, 1983.

Latour, Bruno. *Pandora's Hope.* Cambridge, MA: Harvard University Press, 1999.

Latour, Bruno. *Science in Action: How to Follow Scientists and Engineers Through Society.* Cambridge, MA: Harvard University Press, 1987.

Latour, Bruno. "Visualization and Cognition: Drawing Things Together." In *Knowledge and Society: Studies in the Sociology of Culture Past and Present*, edited by H. Kuklick, Greenwich, CT: Jai Press, 1986.

Latour, Bruno. *We Have Never Been Modern.* Cambridge, MA: Harvard University Press, 1993.

Latour, Bruno. "Why Has Critique Run Out of Steam? From Matters of Fact to Matters of Concern." *Critical Inquiry* 30, no. 2 (2004): 225–248.

Latour, Bruno, and Steve Woolgar. *Laboratory Life: The Construction of Scientific Facts*. Princeton University Press, 1979.

Law, John, and Marianne Elisabeth Lien. "Slippery: Field Notes in Empirical Ontology." *Social Studies of Science* 43, no. 3 (2013): 363–78.

Leahey, Erin. "Overseeing Research Practice: The Case of Data Editing." *Science, Technology, & Human Values* 33, no. 5 (2008): 605–630.

Lemov, Rebecca. "'Hypothetical Machines': The Science Fiction Dreams of Cold War Social Sciences." *Isis* 101, no. 2 (2010): 401–411.

Lemov, Rebecca. *World as Laboratory: Experiments with Mice, Mazes, and Men*. New York: Hill and Wang, 2005.

Leydesdorff, Loet, and Ismael Rafols. "A Global Map of Science Based on the ISI Subject Categories." *Journal of the American Society for Information Science and Technology* 60, no. 2 (2008): 348–362.

Longino, Helen E. *Studying Human Behavior: How Scientists Investigate Aggression and Sexuality*. University of Chicago Press, 2013.

Lynch, Michael E. "Ontography: Investigating the Production of Things, Deflating Ontology." *Social Studies of Science* 43, no. 3 (2013): 444–62.

Lynch, Michael E. *Scientific Practice and Ordinary Action: Ethnomethodology and Social Studies of Science*. Cambridge University Press, 1993.

MacIntyre, Alasdair. *After Virtue: A Study in Moral Theory*. London: Bloomsbury, 1981.

Makel, Matthew C., Jonathan A. Plucker, and Boyd Hegarty. "Replications in Psychology Research: How Often do They Really Occur?" *Perspectives on Psychological Science* 7, no. 6 (2012): 537–542.

Mandler, George. "Crisis and the Problems Seen from Experimental Psychology." *Journal of Theoretical and Philosophical Psychology* 31, no. 4 (2011): 240–46.

Marres, Noortje. "The Issues Deserve More Credit: Pragmatist Contributions to the Study of Public Involvement in Controversy." *Social Studies of Science* 37, no. 5 (2007): 759–780.

Martin, John Levi. *The Explanation of Social Action*. Oxford: Oxford University Press, 2011.

Mason, Winter, and Siddharth Suri. "Conducting Behavioral Research on Amazon's Mechanical Turk." *Behavior Research Methods* 44, no. 1 (2012): 1–23.

McCray, W. Patrick. "Large Telescopes and the Moral Economy of Recent Astronomy." *Social Studies of Science* 30, no. 5 (2000): 685–711.

Meehl, Paul E. "Theoretical Risks and Tabular Asterisks: Sir Karl, Sir Ronald, and the Slow Progress of Soft Psychology." *Journal of Consulting and Clinical Psychology* 46, no. 4 (1978): 806–834.

Meehl, Paul E. "Theory-Testing in Psychology and Physics: A Methodological Paradox." *Philosophy of Science* 34, no. 2 (1967): 103–115.

Mencken, H. L. "Psychologists in a Fog." In *A Mencken Chrestomathy*, edited by H. L. Mencken, 317–319. New York: Vintage Books, [1927] 1982.

Mercer, David. "Scientific Method Discourses in the Construction of 'EMF Science': Interests, Resources, and Rhetoric in Submissions to Public Inquiry." *Social Studies of Science* 32, no. 2 (2002): 205–233.

Merleau-Ponty, Maurice. *The Phenomenology of Perception*. Routledge, 1945.

Merton, Robert K. "Science and the Social Order." *Philosophy of Science* 5, no. 3 (1938): 321–37.

Mitroff, Ian I. "Norms and Counter-Norms in a Select Group of the Apollo Moon Scientists: A Case Study in the Ambivalence of Scientists." *American Sociological Review* 39, no. 4 (1974): 579–595.

Morris, Charles. "The Significance of the Unity of Science Movement." *Philosophy and Phenomenological Research* 6, no. 4 (1946): 508–15.

Mulkay, Michael J. "Norms and Ideology in Science." *Social Science Information* 15, nos. 4–5 (1976): 637–656.

Myers, Natasha. "Molecular Embodiments and the Body-work of Modeling in Protein Crystallography." *Social Studies of Science* 38, no. 2 (2008): 163–199.

Napoli, Donald S. *Architects of Adjustment: The History of the Psychological Profession in the United States*. Port Washington, NY: Kennikat Press, 1981.

Nelson, Nicole C. "The Methodologists: A Unique Category of Scientific Actors." *Engaging Science, Technology, and Society* 6 (2020): 20–33.

Nelson, Nicole C. *Model Behavior: Animal Experiments, Complexity, and the Genetics of Psychiatric Disorders*. University of Chicago Press, 2018.

Nelson, Nicole C. "Modeling Mouse, Human, and Discipline: Epistemic Scaffolds in Animal Behavior Genetics." *Social Studies of Science* 43, no. 1 (2013): 3–29.

Open Science Collaboration. "Estimating the Reproducibility of Psychological Science." *Science* 349, no. 6251 (2015).

Oppenheim, Paul, and Hilary Putnam. "Unity of Science as a Working Hypothesis." In *Minnesota Studies in the Philosophy of Science*, Vol. 2, edited by H. Feigl, M. Scriven, and G. Maxwell, 3–36. Minneapolis: University of Minnesota Press. 1958.

Oreskes, Naomi, and Eric Conway. *Merchants of Doubt: How a Handful of Scientists Obscured the Truth on Issues from Tobacco Smoke to Global Warming*. New York: Bloomsbury Publishing, 2010.

Owen-Smith, Jason. "Managing Laboratory Work through Skepticism: Processes of Evaluation and Control." *American Sociological Review* 66, no. 3 (2001): 427–452.

Paolacci, Gabriele, Jesse Chandler, and Panagiotis G. Ipeirotis. "Running Experiments on Amazon Mechanical Turk." *Judgment and Decision Making* 5, no. 5 (2010): 411–19.

Panofsky, Aaron. *Misbehaving Science: Controversy and the Development of Behavior Genetics.* University of Chicago Press, 2014.

Parr, L.A., B.M. Waller, A.M. Burrows, K.M. Gothard, and S.J. Vick. "MaqFACS: A muscle-based facial movement coding system for the macaque monkey." *American Journal of Physical Anthropology* 143 (2010): 625–630.

Pashler, Harold, and Eric-Jan Wagenmakers. "A Crisis of Confidence?" *Perspectives on Psychological Science* 7, no. 6 (2012): 528–530.

Peirce, Charles S. *Philosophical Writings of Peirce.* Mineola, NY: Dover Publications, Inc., 1955.

Peterson, David. "All that is Solid: Bench-Building at the Frontiers of Two Experimental Sciences." *American Sociological Review* 80, no. 6 (2015): 1201–1225.

Peterson, David. "The Baby Factory: Difficult Research Objects, Disciplinary Standards, and the Production of Statistical Significance." *Socius* 2 (2016): 1–10.

Peterson, David. "The Depth of Fields: Managing Focus in the Epistemic Subcultures of Mind and Brain Science." *Social Studies of Science* 47, no. 1 (2017): 53–74.

Peterson, David. "The Replication Crisis Won't be Solved with Broad Brushstrokes." *Nature* 594, no. 7862 (2021): 151.

Peterson, David, and Aaron Panofsky. "Metascience as a Scientific Social Movement." *Minerva* 61 (2023): 147–174. https://doi.org/10.1007/s11024-023-09490-3.

Peterson, David, and Aaron Panofsky. "Self-Correction in Science: The Diagnostic and Integrative Motives for Replication." *Social Studies of Science* 51, no. 4 (2021): 583–605.

Pickering, Andrew. *The Mangle of Practice: Time, Agency, and Science.* University of Chicago Press, 1995.

Pinch, Trevor J. "Normal Explanations of the Paranormal: The Demarcation Problem and Fraud in Parapsychology." *Social Studies of Science* 9, no. 3 (1979): 329–48.

Pinch, Trevor J. "Towards an Analysis of Scientific Observation: The Externality and Evidential Significance of Observational Reports in Physics." *Social Studies of Science* 15, no. 1 (1985): 3–36.

Polanyi, Michael. *Personal Knowledge: Towards a Post-Critical Philosophy.* University of Chicago Press, 1958.

Popper, Karl. *The Logic of Scientific Discovery.* New York: Routledge, [1934] 2005.

Popper, Karl. *The Poverty of Historicism.* New York: Routledge, 1957.

Porter, Theodore M. *The Rise of Statistical Thinking: 1820–1900.* Princeton University Press, 1986.

Porter, Theodore M. *Trust in Numbers: The Pursuit of Objectivity in Science and Public Life*. Princeton University Press, 1996.

Price, Derek J. de Solla. "The Science/Technology Relationship: The Craft of Experimental Science, and Policy for the Improvement of High Technology Innovation." *Research Policy* 13 (1984): 3–20.

Rasmussen, Nicholas. "The Moral Economy of the Drug Company-Medical Scientist Collaboration in Interwar America." *Social Studies of Science* 34, no. 2 (2004): 161–185.

Reed, Isaac. "Justifying Sociological Knowledge: From Realism to Interpretation." *Sociological Theory* 26, no. 2 (2008): 101–129.

Reyes-Galindo, Luis. "Linking the Subcultures of Physics: Virtual Empiricism and the Bonding Role of Trust." *Social Studies of Science* 44, no. 5 (2014): 736–757.

Rheinberger, Hans-Jörg. *Toward a History of Epistemic Things: Synthesizing Proteins in the Test Tube*. 1st edition. Stanford University Press, 1997.

Risen, James. "American Psychological Association Bolstered C.I.A. Torture Program, Report Says." *The New York Times*, April 30, 2015. Accessed October 16, 2018. https://www.nytimes.com/2015/05/01/us/report-says-american-psychological -association-collaborated-on-torture-justification.html.

Robinson, Daniel N. *An Intellectual History of Psychology*. Madison, WI: University of Wisconsin Press, 1995.

Rorty, Richard. *Objectivity, Relativism, and Truth: Philosophical Papers*. Cambridge; New York: Cambridge University Press, 1990.

Rose, Nikolas. "Engineering the Human Soul: Analyzing Psychological Expertise." *Science in Context* 5, no. 2 (1992): 351–369.

Rose, Nikolas. *Inventing Our Selves: Psychology, Power, and Personhood*. Cambridge University Press, 1998.

Rosenthal, Robert. "The File Drawer Problem and Tolerance for Null Results." *Psychological Bulletin* 86 (3): 638, 1979.

Ryle, Gilbert. *Collected Essays 1929–1968: Collected Papers Volume 2*. Routledge, 2009.

Salinas, Francisco J. "Bruno Latour's Pragmatic Realism: An Ontological Enquiry." *Global Discourse* 6, no. 1 (2016): 8–21.

Satel, Sally L. "Primed for Controversy." *The New York Times*, February 24, 2013, SR8. Accessed February 26, 2013. http://www.nytimes.com/2013/02/24/opinion /sunday/psychology-research-control.html?_r=1&.

Schatzki, Theodore R., Karin Knorr Cetina, and Eike von Savigny, eds. *The Practice Turn in Contemporary Theory*. London: Routledge, 2001.

Schutz, Alfred. *Collected Papers Vol. 1: The Problem of Social Reality*. The Hague: Martinus Nijhoff, 1973.

Scott, James C. *Seeing Like a State: How Certain Schemes to Improve the Human Condition Have Failed*. New Haven, CT: Yale University Press, 1999.

Shapin, Steven. "Here and Everywhere: Sociology of Scientific Knowledge." *Annual Review of Sociology* 21 (1995): 289–321.

Shapin, Steven. "The Invisible Technician." *American Scientist* 77, no. 6 (1989): 554–563.

Shapin, Steven. *Never Pure: Historical Studies of Science as if it was Produced by People with Bodies, Situated in Time, Space, Culture, and Society, and Struggling for Credibility and Authority*. Baltimore, MD: The Johns Hopkins University Press, 2010.

Shapin, Steven. "The Sciences of Subjectivity." *Social Studies of Science* 42, no. 2 (2012): 170–184.

Shapin, Steven. *A Social History of Truth: Civility and Science in Seventeenth-Century England*. University of Chicago Press, 1994.

Shapin, Steven, and Simon Schaffer. *Leviathan and the Air-Pump: Hobbes, Boyle, and the Experimental Life*. Revised ed. Princeton, NJ: Princeton University Press, 2017.

Shearmur, Jeremy. "Steve Fuller and Intelligent Design." *Philosophy of the Social Sciences* 40, no. 3 (2010).

Simmel, Georg. "The Metropolis of Modern Life." In *Simmel: On Individuality and Social Forms*, edited by Donald Levine, 324–339. University of Chicago Press, [1903] 1971.

Simmons, Joseph P., Leif D. Nelson, and Uri Simonsohn. "False-Positive Psychology: Undisclosed Flexibility in Data Collection and Analysis Allows Presenting Anything as Significant." *Psychological Science* 22, no. 11 (2011): 1359–66.

Sismondo, Sergio. "Ontological Turns, Turnoffs and Roundabouts." *Social Studies of Science* 45, no. 3 (2015): 441–48.

Sismondo, Sergio. "Some Social Constructions." *Social Studies of Science* 23, no. 3 (1993): 515–53.

Smith, Laurence D., Lisa A. Best, D. Alan Stubbs, John Johnson, and Andrea B. Archibald. "Scientific Graphs in the Hierarchy of the Sciences: A Latourian Survey of Inscription Practices." *Social Studies of Science* 30, no. 1 (2000): 73–94.

Smyth, Mary M. "Certainty and Uncertainty Sciences: Marking the Boundaries of Psychology in Introductory Textbooks." *Social Studies of Science* 31, no. 3 (2001): 389–416.

Soler, Léna, Sjoerd Zwart, Michael Lynch, and Vincent Israel-Jost. *Science after the Practice Turn in the Philosophy, History, and Social Studies of Science*. London: Routledge, 2014.

Solovey, Mark. *Shaky Foundations: The Politics-Patronage-Social Science Nexus*. New Brunswick, NJ: Rutgers University Press, 2013.

Stapel, Diederik. *Faking Science: A True Story of Academic Fraud.*

Strang, David, & Siler, Kyle. "Revising as Reframing: Original Submissions versus Published Papers in *Administrative Science Quarterly*, 2005-2009. *Sociological Theory* 33, no. 1 (2015): 71–96.

Strasser, Bruno J. "The Experimenter's Museum: GenBank, Natural History, and the Moral Economies of Biomedicine." *Isis* 102, no. 1 (2011): 60–96.

Sudnow, David. *Ways of the Hand: The Organization of Improvised Conduct.* Cambridge, MA: Harvard University Press, 1978.

Taylor, Charles. *Human Agency and Language: Philosophical Papers 1.* Cambridge University Press, 1985.

Taylor, Charles. *Philosophy and the Human Sciences: Philosophical Papers 2.* Cambridge University Press, 1985.

Timmermans, Stefan. "Matching Genotype and Phenotype: A Pragmatist Semiotic Analysis of Clinical Exome Sequencing." *American Journal of Sociology* 123, no. 1 (2017): 136–77.

Titchener, Edward B. *Experimental Psychology: A Manual of Laboratory Practice.* 4 vols. London: Macmillan and Co., LTD., 1915.

Titchener, Edward B. "A Psychological Laboratory." *Mind* 7, no. 27 (1898): 311–31.

Traweek, Sharon. *Beamtimes and Lifetimes: The World of High Energy Physicists.* Cambridge, MA: Harvard University Press, 1988.

Vertesi, Janet. "Seeing Like a Rover: Embodied Experience on the Mars Exploration Rover Mission." *Social Studies of Science* 42, no. 3 (2008): 393–414.

Vick, S.J., B.M. Waller, L.A. Parr, M.C. Smith Pasqualini, and K.A. Bard. "A cross-species comparison of facial morphology and movement in humans and chimpanzees using the facial action coding system (FACS)." *Journal of Nonverbal Behaviour* 31 (2007): 1–20.

Vygotsky, L.S. "The Historical Meaning of the Crisis in Psychology: A Methodological Investigation." In *The Collected Works of L.S. Vygotsky*, Vol. 3, edited by R.W. Rieber and J. Wollock, 233–344. New York: Plenum, [1927]1997.

Wacquant, Loïc. *Body and Soul: Notebooks of an Apprentice Boxer.* New York: Oxford University Press, 2004.

Waller, B.M., P. Kuchenbuch, M. Lembeck, A.M. Burrows, and K. Liebal. "GibbonFACS: A Muscle-Based Coding System for the Hylobatids." *International Journal of Primatology* 33, no. 4 (2012): 809–821.

Waller, B.M., K. Peirce, C.C. Caeiro, L. Scheider, A.M. Burrows, S. McCune, and J. Kaminski. "Paedomorphic Facial Expressions Give Dogs a Selective Advantage." *PLOS ONE* 8, no. 12 (2013): e82686.

Watson, John B. "Psychology as the Behaviorist Views It." *Psychological Review* 20 (1913): 158–177.

Watson, John B., and R. Rayner. "Conditioned Emotional Reactions." *Journal of Experimental Psychology* 3, no. 1 (1920): 1–14.

Weber, Max. *Economy and Society.* 2 vols. Berkeley, CA: University of California Press, 1968.

Weinberg, Robert. A. "The Molecules of Life." *Scientific American* 253, no. 4 (1985): 48–57.

Weinberger, Sharon. "Airport Security: Intent to Deceive." *Nature* 465 (2010): 412–415.

Whitley, Richard. *The Intellectual and Social Organization of the Sciences.* 2nd ed. New York: Oxford University Press, 2000.

Winch, Peter. *The Idea of a Social Science: And Its Relation to Philosophy.* London: Routledge, 1958.

Winter, Jana, and Cora Currier. "TSA's Secret Behavior Checklist to Spot Terrorists." *The Intercept*, March 27, 2015. Accessed April 18, 2024. https://firstlook .org/theintercept/2015/03/27/revealed-tsas-closely-held-behavior-checklist -spot-terrorists/.

Woodward, James. *Making Things Happen: A Theory of Causal Explanation.* Oxford University Press, 2003.

Woolgar, Steve, and Javier Lezaun. "Missing the (Question) Mark? What Is a Turn to Ontology?" *Social Studies of Science* 45, no. 3 (2015): 462–67.

Yanchar, Stephen C., & Slife, Brent D. "Pursuing Unity in a Fragmented Psychology: Problems and Prospects." *Review of General Psychology*, 1, no. 3 (1997): 235-255.

Young (2012a, 2012b).

Yong, Ed. 2012a. "Nobel Laureate Challenges Psychologists to Clean up Their Act." *Nature.com*. (http://www.nature.com/news/nobel-laureate-challenges -psychologists-to-clean-up-their-act-1.11535).

Yong, Ed. 2012b. "A Failed Replication Draws a Scathing Personal Attack from a Psychology Professor." Discovermagazine.*com*. (http://blogs.discovermagazine .com/notrocketscience/2012/03/10/failed-replication-bargh-psychology-study -doyen/#.UVMv9JMQZvl).

Zelizer, Viviana A. *Pricing the Priceless Child: The Changing Social Value of Children.* Princeton University Press, 1994.

Zuckerman, Harriet. "Norms and Deviant Behavior in Science." *Science, Technology, and Human Values* 9, no. 1 (1984): 7–13.

INDEX

269n6; social psychology contrasted with, 170; standardization of technique in, 268n39
molecular biology laboratories, 18, 49–50, 141–142
molecular neuroscience, 62
moral economy, drosophila geneticists developing, 72
mouse strains, new, 79–80
MTurk. *See* Mechanical Turk
Mulkay, Michael, 53, 262n3

narrative creation, data presentation and, 28
narrative structure, of psychological experiments, 136
National Science Foundation, 262n3
nativism, 157, 224, 239; within developmentalism, 123, 125; empiricism *versus*, 148, 151–155; experimental sciences of, 126; infant cognition in, 138; interpretation challenging, 127–128; Jones on, 154–155
nativists, social psychologists contrasted with, 195
natural sciences, social sciences contrasted with, 14, 20
natural selection, 231
Nelson, Nicole C., 268n33
neuroscience, molecular, 62
9/11 terrorist attacks, 1
nomological pluralism, 241, 280n21
nonscience, sciences contrasted with, 225–226
non-standardization, 79
normal sciences: developmental psychologists building, 19–20;

Gouldner on, 156; theoretical framework organizing, 151
norms, 20; anthropological, 14; ethical, 259n34; Mertonian, 212; scientific, 194; skepticism challenging, 218
novelty, 127, 168, 190

object of study, theoretical interest contrasted with, 125
one world hypothesis, 242–244
online experiments, 102, 175
ontological constraints, 116–120, 272n24
ontology, 118–120
Oreskes, Naomi, 217

Panofsky, Aaron, 12, 46, 147
paradigm, sciences without, 158–161
peer judgment, social psychologists constrained by, 181
peer review, 199, 209
Peirce, Charles S., 118, 172
p-hacking, 179, 208, 251
physical skills, 103–104, 109
physics: computational neuroscience contrasted with, 64; lack of scientific labor during first centuries of, 258n34; molecular biology contrasted with, 269n6
physiological data, 101
Pickering, Andrew, 38
planning, of experimentation, 26
pluralism, nomological, 241, 280n21
Polanyi, Michael, 40, 98
Popper, Karl, 8, 44, 121, 230, 268n37
popular press, psychology covered by, 234
post hoc theorizing, ethical limits to, 143
power manipulations, 238–239

Stapel, Diederik, 10, 251

statistical significance: analytic process impacting, 201; empirical flexibility ensuring, 180; p-hacking producing, 179; working backwards form, 141–144

statistical techniques, bench-building differentiated from, 56

stimulus-response schema (S-R schema), 7

STS. *See* science and technology studies

Study of the Status and Development of Psychology, by APA, 256n14

subfields, theoretical decisions impacting, 128

subject diversity, 148–151

tacit knowledge, 266n24; collection and somatic, 99; H. Collins clarifying, 98–99; in developmental psychology, 103–111, *106*, *107*; direct engagement teaching, 230; experimental sciences and, 63; in social psychology, 99–103

tacit skills: differences in, 110; psychology lacking in, 19; scientific development through, 72

technical developments, bench-building propelled by, 16, 79–80

technical skills, of social psychologists, 99–100

technique, 1–2; developmental psychologists lacking, 84; investment lacked in, 114–115; in psychology, 98–99; social psychologists lacking, 84;

standardization of, 268n39; statistical, 56; technology and research evolving with, 63

technological development: in data capture, 125; of psychology, 237; scientific progress equated with, 247–248

technologically evolving sciences, 20–21

technological psychology, social worlds withdrawn from by, 246

technologies of the self, 246

technology, x, 40, 66, 74, 83, 91; bench-building and, 24; developmental laboratories integrating, 96; developmental psychologists lacking, 84; DNA, 42–43; evolving, 41; expertise contrasted with, 3; floors and ceilings of, *87*, 92; history of, 42; interior design as, 111; investment and, 93–94, 114–115; laboratory practice and, 86; lack of standardization in, 80; lending to significant differentiation, 85; psychological, 89, *90*; psychology advanced by, xi; research and technique evolving with, 63; research driven by, 76; scientific development through, 72; Scientific Method and, 50; skills divided from, 270n2; social psychology laboratories not relying on, 92; sociology and, 268n41; specialized skills required to use, 97

technoscience, 16, 24

tension, harmony and, 235–236

"That's Interesting!" (Davis), 181

theories, surprise in interesting, 181–182

GPSR Authorized Representative: Easy Access System Europe, Mustamäe tee
50, 10621 Tallinn, Estonia, gpsr.requests@easproject.com